# TRANSFORMATIONS

PLATE I

Ram's head. Stone. Chinese, T'ang dynasty. Collection of Mr. Loo

# TRANSFORMATIONS

## CRITICAL AND SPECULATIVE ESSAYS ON ART

BY

## ROGER FRY

*Essay Index Reprint Series*

*Originally published by:*

## CHATTO & WINDUS

BOOKS FOR LIBRARIES PRESS, INC.
FREEPORT, NEW YORK

First Published 1927
Reprinted 1968

LIBRARY OF CONGRESS CATALOG CARD NUMBER:
68-14904


PRINTED IN THE UNITED STATES OF AMERICA

# PREFACE

THE title of this collection of essays needs perhaps a word of explanation. By the word "Transformations" I wish to suggest all those various transmutations which forms undergo in becoming parts of esthetic constructions. It is justified, I hope, by the fact that the discussion of these various transmutations occupies so large a part of the book.

In the following essays, though free use has been made of articles published from time to time in the monthly and weekly press, these have been so much remoulded and manipulated that in most cases it has hardly seemed worth while to refer the reader to the originals. In the few cases where articles have been left almost untouched, references have been made, but I take this opportunity to thank the editors of *The Burlington Magazine, The Dial, The Nation and Athenæum,* and *The New Statesman,* for allowing me to quote at such length from myself.

I am indebted also to *The Burlington Magazine* for allowing me to use some of their blocks, and to Mr. Colin Agnew for kind help in procuring photographs of certain pictures, and to Mr. R. R. Tatlock for kindly helping to see the book through the press.

I also take this opportunity to acknowledge gratefully the kind permission to make reproductions from their publications by the following : M. André Derain (" L'Enchanteur Pourrissant "), Mr. E. McKnight Kauffer (" Burton's Anatomy of Melancholy," illustrated), M. André Rouveyre (" Visages des Contemporains "), Dr. Julius Meier-Graefe (" Contemporary Art "), M. M. Bernheim Jeunes (" Cézanne "), M. Albert Morancé (" L'Art d'Aujourd'hui "), and Messrs. Yamanaka.

ROGER FRY.

*August,* 1926.

# CONTENTS

# ILLUSTRATIONS

vii

## ILLUSTRATIONS IN TEXT

# TRANSFORMATIONS

## SOME QUESTIONS IN ESTHETICS

IN approaching once again the general problem of Esthetics I wish to enforce two things : one, that such attempts at any general theory that I make are tentative efforts to make clear to myself the principles involved in exercising the critical faculty on works of art, and secondly that the problem is far too complicated, for me, at all events, to approach it by any other than an experimental method. The experiments have to be made by the inquirer and mainly on himself, by watching, with such honesty and detachment as he can command, his own reactions. That honesty is, of course, very difficult to come at, since in this matter we are all excessively auto-suggestible and apt to discover, with suspicious facility, whatever our predisposition of mind may have led us to desire and anticipate. The only guarantee that the inquirer can give under such circumstances is to lay his cards on the table and invite the reader to see whether his own reactions in any given case coincide. It is this that in the following pages I have tried to do.

The general notion which, in an essay in " Vision and Design," * I had tentatively put forward was to the effect that whenever we make a favourable esthetic judgment—whenever we say that a work of art is beautiful—we imply by that statement that it is of such a kind as to produce in us a certain positive response, and that if we compare in our minds responses experienced in turn in face of different works of art of the most diverse kinds—as, for instance, architectural, pictorial, musical or literary—we recognise that our state of mind in each case has been of a similar kind, we see in all these different experiences a general similarity in our attitude, in the pattern of our mental disposition, and further that the attitude common to all these experiences is peculiar to them and is clearly distinguishable from our mental

* " Vision and Design." Chatto & Windus. London, 1920.

attitude in other experiences. I therefore suggested that we might conveniently label this kind of mental disposition the specifically esthetic state of mind.

That position has been very vigorously and brilliantly attacked of late, notably by Mr. Richards in his " Principles of Criticism,"* and I shall have occasion to take some of his objections to the view outlined above as the basis for further investigations into the nature and ends of pictorial design.

And as this proceeding will lead me into a controversial attitude upon the points at issue, I take this opportunity to express my admiration of a great part of this work. Mr. Richards has arrived at a point of view which seems to me fertile and full of possibilities. He has opened up many striking new perspectives for the critic to explore, and I fully share his desire to do away with metaphysical entities and absolutes in esthetic discussion. Moreover, I take to heart, in so far as I may have offended in that direction, his wise protest against assuming any state of mind to be unanalysable. But all the same, as I shall have occasion to show, I cannot feel that he has solved certain questions as completely and decisively as he claims.

According to Mr. Richards our response to a work of art is of a similar nature to our response to other situations. He says : " When we look at a picture, or read a poem, or listen to music, we are not doing something quite unlike what we were doing on our way to the Gallery or when we dressed in the morning." †  That is to say, the responses to a work of art are the same responses as those of ordinary life and only differ in the manner in which the objects are presented to us, as, for example, the difference between our response to a real tree and what we recognise as a tree in a picture.‡  Now I hope to show certain reasons why we should regard our responses to works of art as distinct from our responses to other situations.

The question is, no doubt, made extremely difficult owing to the fact that many structures which profess to be works of art do not even aim at provoking the special kind of response which I hope to describe. And that many works which do provoke that special response also evoke at the same time many of the responses of ordinary life.

* Kegan Paul, 1924.          † P. 16.          ‡ P. 110.

It is necessary, therefore, for me to put up a preliminary hypothesis of the existence of pure and impure works of art—a distinction which Mr. Richards has the good fortune to be able to ignore.

It nowise invalidates this conception if such a thing as an absolutely pure work of art has never been created : the contention is that some works approximate much more nearly than others to this ideal construction. I cannot deny that the position I am trying to maintain is dangerously exposed. If it is to be held at all it must be held with regard to works of art of all kinds. And this is no easy matter. The idea of a special kind of experience, a special disposition of the mind, may seem plausible enough with regard to our experience of certain peculiarly abstract musical constructions or even of certain kinds of architecture. It becomes far less plausible the moment representation of actual forms comes in, as in painting or sculpture, still less when, as in poetry, the novel or the drama, the very stuff of which these are constructed, namely words, calls up images and memories of things and emotions of actual life.

And yet this must be faced if the idea of a special esthetic experience is to have any meaning. It would be fatal if in the case of any work of art on which we pass a favourable esthetic judgment we had to admit that the experience was of an altogether different kind from that which we had before others. We cannot hold our theory for music and architecture and drop it for poetry and drama.

Now the crucial fact which appears to me to arise from the comparison of a number of these experiences which are the subject of our inquiry is that in all cases our reaction to works of art is a reaction to a relation and not to sensations or objects or persons or events. This, if I am right, affords a distinguishing mark of what I call esthetic experiences, esthetic reactions, or esthetic states of mind.

Let us examine this in more detail. Our emotional reactions are not, I say, about sensations. This may at first sight appear paradoxical, because the arts seem to be peculiarly preoccupied with agreeable sensations, with relatively pure colours and pure sounds. But it is not difficult to see that, however valuable a predisposing and accompanying condition of esthetic apprehension such agreeably pure sensations may be, they are not essential, nor have we any difficulty in distinguishing between our response to sensations and our response to works of art. Those responses to sensation may be very rich and complex and tinged with emotion, but they are distinct. Thus a smell may, as Proust has admirably shown, produce a very profound response. By its associations in memory it may even excite a more poignant state of mind than many works of art, but we easily distinguish it from our feeling about a work of art. The evocations of smell are indeed so powerful that they would doubtless form the basis for an art similar to music in its deep emotional evocations, if only different perfumes could be perceived in relation one to another. It is this impossibility alone that deprives us of yet another art.

It is true that in nearly all works of art agreeable sensations form the very texture of the work. In music pleasurable quality of sound is the object of deliberate research, but it is by no means evident that this is essential. Some effects of modern music suggest that relations of more noises not in themselves agreeable can arouse esthetic pleasure, and many great composers have worked in sound textures which were generally proclaimed harsh and disagreeable. If it be said that though disagreeable to the audiences they had been found agreeable by the composer, we are none the less faced with the fact that his contemporaries did, after all, accept his work for its esthetic quality even whilst the sound-texture appeared unpleasing; although under stress of that esthetic satisfaction the unpleasure gradually changed to pleasure.

For vision, as for hearing, there are simple pleasant sensations and simple indifferent or even unpleasant sensations, notably with regard to colour. Pure, brightly luminous colours have a strong physiological effect of a pleasing kind. This is especially marked in children, but long after we have ceased to stop in front of the chemist's windows to gaze at lights seen through blue and red solutions we are still aware of the attraction. But when we come to arrangements of colour in a work of art all these sensational effects may be overridden by our emotions about colour relations. Some works of the greatest colourists are built up of elements each of which is devoid of any specially pleasurable quality, and they may even be, to particular observers, positively unpleasant, although that displeasure is immediately swamped by the pleasure which results from their interrelation.

In literature there is no immediate sensual pleasure whatever, though it may be a favourable predisposing condition for poetry to be spoken by a beautiful voice. There is, of course, the pleasure of rhythmic utterance, but this is already concerned with relations, and even this is, I believe, accessory to the emotion aroused by rhythmic changes of states of mind due to the meanings of the words.

In architecture materials are often chosen for the comparatively simple sensual pleasure which their surfaces arouse. But we distinguish at once between this pleasure and those emotions which are generated by our apprehension of architectural plasticity. Before too many buildings on which polished marble and gilt bronze are lavished our pleasure in these appearances is more than counterbalanced by the painful absence of esthetic purpose. The ensuing reflections on the waste of so much precious material cause them to become actually a source of mental pain.

The esthetic emotion, then, is not an emotion about sensations, however necessary a responsive sensualism may be for our apprehension of esthetic wholes. Nor is it an emotion about objects or persons or events. Here we touch the crux of the esthetic experience for the greater number of people who are accustomed to rely almost exclusively on their interest in, or emotion about, the persons or events called to mind by the imagery of the fine arts. Landscape, for such, is just reminiscence or revelation of pleasant natural scenes; portraiture interests by the beautiful or fascinating ladies and the celebrated gentlemen it presents; figure painting avails by its attractive or provocative nudes; literature by its exciting events or its imagined wish fulfilments. In fact, the vast mass of so-called works of art are designed primarily to arouse these interests and emotions even though in doing this some esthetic appeals may supply an accompaniment.

These observations appear to me to have made out a very fair *a priori* case for the existence in all esthetic experiences of a special orientation of the consciousness, and, above all, a special focussing of the attention, since the act of esthetic apprehension implies an attentive passivity to the effects of sensations apprehended in their relations. We have no need for our purposes to create the hypothesis of any mysterious or specific faculty.

There is no need to imagine that the state of mind here indicated is unanalysable, probably it may be resolved into different factors, none of which is peculiar to this state. The same mental faculties and aptitudes as enter into play in esthetic apprehension no doubt are employed elsewhere. What matters for us is that there should be a constant and recognisable pattern of the mental disposition in such situations. I believe that this is so, and that the pattern is distinct enough for us to say, in contradiction to Mr. Richards, that when we are in the picture gallery we are employing our faculties in a manner so distinct from that in which we employed them on the way there, that it is no exaggeration to say we are doing a quite different thing. On the way there our conscious attention must frequently have been directed to spotting and catching the right 'bus, or detecting the upright flag of a distant taxicab, or, at least, avoiding collisions on the pavement or recognising our friends. I exclude the case of those who being artists themselves may, in the course of their walk, have been preoccupied with distilling from their diverse visual sensations some vague sketches and adumbrations of possible harmonic combinations. Such, and such alone, might, I think, be said to have been similarly occupied on their way to and within the gallery.

If I am right, then it is not impossible to draw a fairly sharp dividing line between our mental disposition in the case of esthetic responses and that of the responses of ordinary life. A far more difficult question arises if we try to distinguish it from the responses made by us to certain abstract mental constructions such as those of pure mathematics. Here I conceive the emotional states due to the apprehension of relations may be extremely similar to those aroused by the esthetic apprehension. Perhaps the distinction lies in this, that in the case of works of art the whole end and purpose is found in the exact quality of the emotional state, whereas in the case of mathematics the purpose is the constatation of the universal validity of the relations without regard to the quality of the emotion accompanying apprehension. Still, it would be impossible to deny the close similarity of the orientation of faculties and attention in the two cases.

The special cases of literature and representative painting still call for further elucidation.

With regard to literature, much misunderstanding is likely to arise owing to the absence of any proper classification and nomenclature of the very various purposes which are covered by the term. We have no words to distinguish between writing used for exposition, speculation, criticism or exhortation, and writing used for the creation of a work of art. Moreover, the medium allows of sudden and often concealed shifts from its uses for one purpose to those for another. It is a medium which admits the mixture of esthetic and non-esthetic treatment to an almost unlimited extent. Even in the novel, which as a rule has pretensions to being a work of art, the structure may be so loose, the esthetic effects may be produced by so vast an accumulation of items that the temptation for the artist to turn aside from his purpose and interpolate criticisms of life, of manners or morals, is very strong. Comparatively few novelists have ever conceived of the novel as a single perfectly organic esthetic whole. An instance of the confusion to which this loose nomenclature may give rise, occurs in Mr. Richards' book,* where, in order to prove that literature may have ulterior ends which envisage morals, religion, etc., he says, " There seem to be kinds of poetry in which its value as poetry definitely and distinctly depends upon the ulterior ends involved. Consider the Psalms, Isaiah, the New Testament, Dante, the 'Pilgrim's Progress,' Rabelais, any really universal satire, Swift, Voltaire, Byron." Now only a few of the works alluded to here are works of art in any proper sense. In most, no doubt, some esthetic qualities are introduced. In the case of the " Pilgrim's Progress," for instance, the appearance of an esthetic structure is deliberately chosen as a bait to lure the reader for an ulterior non-esthetic end, but it is surely a common experience that a reader can fully relish the bait without so much as a scratch from Bunyan's hook. The fact that ulterior ends are pursued in many of these books does not show that those parts of them which appeal to the esthetic sensibility cannot be fully apprehended by those who reject the ends. It would need detailed investigation of the passages at issue to prove that these ulterior ends in any way contributed to the poetic effect, however much they may have been the pretext or the predisposing condition of their creation.

This suffices to show how unfortunate for our discussion is the want of a sufficient classification of kinds when we wish to inquire into the specific esthetic effects of literature when used as a form of art.

* *L.c.* p. 75.

In this passage Mr. Richards is attempting, I think unsuccessfully, to controvert a passage from Bradley's " Oxford Lectures on Poetry," * which appears to me the best account of the question which has yet been given.   He says :

"What then does the formula ' Poetry for Poetry's sake ' tell us about this experience ?  It says, as I understand it, these things. First, this experience is an end in itself, is worth having on its own account, has an intrinsic value.   Next, its poetic value is this intrinsic worth alone.   Poetry may have also an ulterior value as a means to culture or religion ;  because it conveys instruction or softens the passions, or furthers a good cause ;  because it brings the poet fame, or money, or a quiet conscience.   So much the better :  let it be valued for these reasons too.   But its ulterior worth neither is nor can directly determine its poetic worth as a satisfying imaginative experience ; and this is to be judged entirely from within. . . . The consideration of ulterior ends, whether by the poet in the act of composing or by the reader in the act of experiencing, tends to lower poetic value.   It does so because it tends to change the nature of poetry by taking it out of its own atmosphere.   For its nature is to be not a part, nor yet a copy, of the real world (as we commonly understand that phrase), but to be a world by itself, independent, complete, autonomous."

For poetry in this passage we may, I think, substitute the idea of any literature used as pure art.   This passage at least suggests to us that the purpose of literature is the creation of structures which have for us the feeling of reality, and that these structures are self-contained, self-sufficing, and not to be valued by their references to what lies outside.   All these points have been expounded by M. Charles Mauron in an essay † on the nature of literary beauty.   In that he tries to take us a step further by an ingenious analogy of literature with the plastic arts.   In them at least we can say with some confidence what they aim at, viz. the creation of volumes.   The idea of volumes here implies, of course, any kind of spatial construction which may further contain other volumes seen in plastic relief within it.   Volumes are for the plastic artist the material in which and through which he works.   M. Mauron suggests that we should, for literature, transpose

* A. C. Bradley, " Oxford Lectures on Poetry," p. 5.
† " The Nature of Beauty in Art and Literature."  Hogarth Essays, 1926.

the idea of volumes from the domain of space to the domain of spirit and conceive the literary artist as creating "psychological volumes." This analogy proves, in his hands, full of fruitful suggestions, for the details of which I must refer the reader to his work. It may be no more than an analogy, but it enables us for the first time dimly to grasp what it is of which the relations are felt by us when we apprehend esthetically a work of literature. Up to now, owing to the extreme complexity and rich variety of evocation in literature, we have not been able to isolate its special and peculiar substance. I believe M. Mauron has at least pointed in the right direction, and he is able to show in some detail how the different types of literary structure correspond to different aspects of "psychological volumes."

But, apart from M. Mauron's brilliant suggestion, on which it would perhaps be premature to lay too much stress, I believe that the cinema has provided us with a new angle of perspective which helps us to a clearer idea of what our experience really is before at least one type of literary structure, the tragic drama. I must cite in this context what was for me a crucial experiment and one which every one is sure to have opportunities to repeat. I was present at a film which recorded the work of rescue from a ship wrecked off the coast of Portugal. One saw at a considerable distance the hull of the vessel stranded on a flat shore and in between crest after crest of huge waves. In the foreground men were working desperately pulling at a rope which ever so slowly drew away from the distant ship a small black object which swayed and swung from the guide rope. Again and again the waves washed over it in its slow progress shorewards. It was not till it was near shore that one realised that this was a basket with a human being in it. When it was finally landed the men rushed to it and took out—a man or a corpse, according to the luck of the passage or the resistance of the individual. The fact that one was watching a film cut off all those activities which, in the real situation, might have been a vent and mitigation of one's emotions. One was a pure, helplessly detached spectator, and yet a spectator of a real event with the real, not merely the simulated, issue of life and death.

For this reason no situation on the stage could be half so poignant, could grip the emotions of pity and terror half so tensely. If to do this were the end and purpose of drama, according to Aristotle's purgation theory, and not a means to some other and different end, then the cinema had surpassed the greatest tragedians. But, in point of fact, the experience, though it was far more acute and poignant, was recognisably distinct and was judged at once as of far less value and significance than the experience of a great tragic drama. And it became evident to me that the essential of great tragedy was not the emotional intensity of the events portrayed, but the vivid sense of the inevitability of their unfolding, the significance of the curve of crescendo and diminuendo which their sequence describes, together with all the myriad subsidiary evocations which, at each point, poetic language can bring in to give fullness and density to the whole organic unity.

We come now to what is, for our present inquiry, the most important and difficult question of all the meaning and purpose of representation in graphic art. This has always been a crux of such a puzzling nature that I need have little shame in confessing that I have at various times put forward very different attempts at a possible solution. I have certainly varied from a position where I underlined what we may call the dramatic possibilities of painting to one where I have insisted on the pre-eminence of purely plastic aspects, and almost hinted that no others were to be taken into account. I have some hopes that in the present essay I may be able to push the inquiry a little further ; to bring it to a point which may conciliate, or at least explain, these two apparently contradictory attitudes.

Before entering upon the question itself I must clear up a possible misapprehension of the foregoing phrases. I have contrasted the plastic purpose of painting with representation, since it is only by representation of persons or events that any dramatic element can enter into a picture. But though all drama in pictures is due to representation, all representation is not dramatic. Since the painter realises his vision on a flat surface he is bound to have recourse to representation in order to create any three-dimensional volume, and a great deal of very precise and detailed representation may yet envisage purely plastic and spatial expression.

However pre-eminent in graphic art plastic expression may be, one use of it alone must prevent us from saying that that is its sole purpose—I mean the art of caricature. Here clearly we are dealing primarily with " psychological volumes." Provided that surprising, vivid and consistent suggestions of a peculiar psychological entity are given to us we need not clamour for significant plasticity. One can imagine a case where a few disjointed dots and dashes suggesting the glance of an eye or the curve of a mouth would produce the effect without even the suggestion of a plastic volume. And even if, as is more usual, plasticity is given it will be used generally to support or underline the psychological impression.

Caricature, in fact, is the most central and typical example of graphic art used for psychological expression. We are, as it happens, accustomed to regard it as a somewhat trivial and insignificant art, as a mere diversion, as " comic," not even as comedic. And yet this has been by no means universal. Certain early Chinese paintings may be regarded as religious caricature with the most serious and elevated pretensions. The same is true of some of Jerome Bosch's mystic caricatures. Daumier used it frequently to express a deadly earnestness of moral indignation. But certainly one of the most interesting of serious caricaturists is M. André Rouveyre, who is not nearly as well known in this country as he deserves to be. I reproduce two of his drawings, " Professor Jules Soury " and the " Duchesse d'Uzès douairière." ★ It will give an idea of the spirit in which these drawings are conceived when we know that M. Rouveyre attended Professor Soury's lectures for a whole term in order to arrive at this concentrated expression of the psychological unity of his subject. I may add that Professor Soury was sufficiently enlightened and detached to be able to appreciate with grateful admiration the insight here shown into his character and the beauty, psychologically speaking, of the result. Now it would be absurd to deny that M. Rouveyre has here made use of plastic expression. He even relies on it very much, for our realisation of the volumes of head and body, of arms and hands, and the relation of these to one another counts for much in the result. But everywhere it is the *moral* significance of which these are indications that inevitably preoccupies us. Though these plastic volumes are marvellously indicated I doubt whether they are in themselves of sufficient interest to hold

* From " Visages des Contemporains," *Mercure de France*, 1913, with grateful acknowledgments to the author.

PROF. JULES SOURY. ANDRÉ ROUVEYRE.

LA DUCHESSE D'UZÈS DOUAIRÈIRE.          ANDRÉ ROUVEYRE.

us for long, and in any case their further implications are so powerful and so immediately arresting that the focus of attention is surely on the psychological structure. Perhaps our second example is even more striking in the brilliant indications of plastic volumes. But how instantly we are absorbed in contemplating the kind of character that holds itself in this way, the sublime self-confidence and indifference to opinion of the descendant of a great aristocratic race with all that these conditions of life have engraved on the pale and faded countenance. It puts us at once in the position that we might be in had we read a brilliant short biography of such a person, and had had time for all the facts to fade from our memory and leave only the quintessence, the psychological experience, as it were, which gives significance to the facts.

The art of caricature, then, forces us to admit that drawing can envisage directly and by a specific mode psychological phenomena—it can, that is to say, from its own angle, with its own specific aptitudes and limitations, handle the same stuff as literature : it can, to use M. Mauron's simile, model psychological volumes.

This constatation might seem to prepare the way for our accepting that view of the painter's art which declares that its main purpose is to arouse emotions by its representation of moving or interesting events or persons, and that what we derive from its specific formal character, its creation of plastic complexes, is accessory to that, and is used to heighten or reinforce the emotion aroused by representation. This appears to be the view indicated by Mr. Richards. He says : " There are great pictures . . . in which the contribution to the whole response made through representation is trivial and may be disregarded. It is equally certain that there are great pictures in which the contribution to the whole response made through representation is not less than that made more directly through form and colour. To those who can accept the general psychological standpoint already outlined, or indeed any modern account of the working of the mind, the assertion that there is no reason why representative and formal factors in an experience should conflict, but much reason why they should co-operate, will need no discussion. The psychology of ' unique esthetic emotions ' and ' pure art values ' upon which the contrary view relies is merely a caprice of the fancy."

PLATE II

Christ Carrying the Cross.   Pieter Brueghel the Elder

Vienna Gallery

Let us take this passage as the text for a further inquiry into this interesting and intricate problem. It is a problem also that is of too vital importance to the critic of pictorial art for me to be altogether satisfied by such a summary and theoretical conclusion as Mr. Richards' last two sentences supply. I prefer in this, as in other matters, a more experimental method. Instead of deciding on *a priori* grounds that these two elements should always co-operate, let us take various instances and see what happens.

Let us take first a picture in which the representational element is obviously of great importance, for instance, Pieter Brueghel's " Carrying of the Cross " in the museum at Vienna (Pl. II.). Here we look out upon a large stretch of country filled with crowds of figures which are inevitably so small in scale that they can hardly be related plastically with the picture space. Nor is any attempt made to do this. Rather we are invited by the whole method of treatment to come close and peer at each figure in turn, and read from it those details which express its particular state of mind so that we may gradually, almost as we might in a novel, bring them together to build up a highly complex psychological structure. We are able thus to distinguish the figure of Christ bearing the Cross, and, with the knowledge of the Gospel story which is presupposed, we get the central motive of the dramatic theme which is pursued throughout the picture with that leisurely accumulation of separate psychological elements which is characteristic of some dramatic literature. In the distance we recognise the hill of Calvary and on it what looks like a black ring, too small indeed to have any significance in a plastic sense, but when we look close and realise that it represents the crowds who have long been struggling for a favourable point of view for the forthcoming spectacle of the Crucifixion, we get a peculiar thrill of dramatic terror and pity. We recognise at once that this is a great psychological invention, setting up profound vibrations of feeling within us by its poignant condensation of expression. It is such an invention as Shakespeare will at times throw in in a couple of lines of description. But it is, I repeat, purely literary, and throughout this picture it is clear that Brueghel has subordinated plastic to psychological considerations. It is indeed to my mind entirely trivial and inexpressive when judged as a plastic and spatial creation. In short, it is almost pure illustration, for we may as well use that as a convenient term for the visual arts employed on psychological material. And we must regard illustration as more closely akin in its essence to literature than it is to plastic art, although in its merely external and material aspect it belongs to the latter. It is indeed this, from a fundamental point of view, accidental association which has been the source of so much difficulty and confusion about the nature and purpose of pictorial and glyptic art.

The next case I propose to examine is Daumier's " Gare St. Lazare " (Pl. III.). Speaking for myself, the first impression derived from this is of the imposing effect of the square supports of the arcade, the striking and complicated silhouette of the man to the right, the salience of the centre figure so firmly planted on his feet, and the contrast of all this with the gloomy space which retires to the left, and finally the suggestion of wide aerial spaces given by the houses glimpsed to the right. The first effect, then, is mainly of feelings aroused by plastic relations. But I am almost immediately seized by curiosity about the striking silhouette to the right. Not only the strong contrast of light and shade, but the intricate and accented contours and the agitated movement help to attract attention. The interpretation of these forms as representing an extremely fussy, egoistic, well-to-do, middle-aged, professional gentleman of the '50's sets my imagination going down quite other paths, and so vivid is the notation and appropriateness of every detail that vague adumbrations of his whole domestic life with his pretty, timid, conventional wife, flit across the consciousness. In a similar but less acute way we almost instantly " place " the stout, self-possessed, retired colonel or country gentleman with the muffler. In between these we note the two poor people waiting patiently and uncomplainingly against the column, and share for an instant Daumier's slightly sentimental attitude about the poor which helps to excite, by its adroit contrast, our critical feelings towards the professional gentleman, and we come back to note the avaricious grasp with which he clutches his umbrella.

Then the incident of the sportsman turning round to whistle his dog gives another suggestion of human life and a hint at quite another type of character. We note the extreme aptness to the type of the florid features and the alert gesture, not without a thrill of admiration

PLATE III

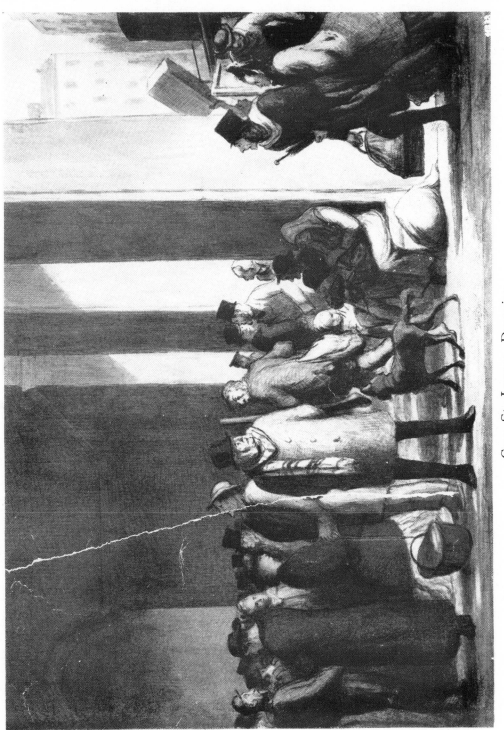

Gare St. Lazare, Daumier

at the economy with which all this is given, since the imagination is always most satisfied when it is forced into activity by having to complete the suggestions given to it. Then we turn to the groups to the left—less emphatic because enveloped in the penumbra of the arcade—to the soldier and the priest who merely contribute vague suggestions of the variety of human types without adding anything very pointed ; and then to the rather too noble old man invoking the protection of heaven on his daughter leaving him for service in a distant place, and here, speaking personally, I feel that for the first time in this picture a slightly false note is struck, a note that mars though ever so slightly the perfection of the psychological structure.

So all this time we have been entirely forgetting plastic and spatial values we have, through vision, plunged into that spaceless, moral world which belongs characteristically to the novel, and we can hardly help noting, by the way, how distinct this state of mind is from that with which we began. If, however, having for the moment exhausted the rich illustrational matter we return to the contemplation of plastic relations we shall find, I think, that it is not possible to push them much further. We find, no doubt, a generally coherent and intelligible disposition of the volumes in the space. The ample block made by the colonel's figure creates the chief salience and divides the space left to right satisfactorily—or nearly so, for I find myself always wondering whether it should not be a little further to the left for perfect balance ; nor is it after all quite big enough as volume to fulfil the function it has to perform. For this it should be fused more closely with some other mass to the left instead of being, as it is, rather sharply cut off from the light on the pious father, whose forms, thus cut into, are rather meagre and insignificant. And this failure in plastic completeness seems actually due to Daumier's desire to bring out more clearly this particular dramatic incident. Nor can we be much interested in the solid rectangle of figures to the left from which four, too equally spaced, upright volumes detach themselves ; no interesting plastic sequences here invite us to further contemplation. We see at once that one of the hardest plastic problems of such a scene is due to the fact that human beings are all of about the same height and that a crowd produces a rectangular mass which it is very difficult to relate significantly with the architectural setting. Daumier was clearly conscious of this, for it would be absurd to suppose that his illustrational preoccupations blinded him to plastic considerations, and the seated peasants are an excellent device to break this monotony, as is also the space left between them and the colonel which invites the eye to break into the too monotonous mass by a diagonal receding movement. This may have suggested the excellent pose of the sportsman which is all-effective in enforcing this movement, though its value is somewhat lessened by an uncertainty as to his position in the space. If we regard his head and shoulders he appears to be, like the child beside him, some way back ; the light appears to fall on him through the second opening in the arcade ; but when we see, none too clearly, his feet, we find that he is far nearer to us and is, in fact, lit by the first arcade. In addition to this the dog is so placed that, although his pose is rightly conceived for assisting the diagonal movement, he blocks the space and hinders the spatial organisation. Had the man been definitely situated in the second opening and the dog had been moving towards him through the shadow we should have been more able to articulate this part of the composition intelligibly. The group to the right is the most plastically satisfactory of all, and the device of the box being lowered from the cab roof and carrying on the diagonal of the man's top-hat breaks for the first time the monotony of the horizontal line of heads.

We have to admit, then, that impressive as the general setting is, the design is not so organised plastically as to unfold to our contemplative gaze new interrelations and correspondences. Nor do I think we have ever been able, except perhaps in the case of the sportsman, definitely to relate plastic with psychological considerations, or find any marked co-operation between the two experiences.

A third case shall be Poussin's " Ulysses discovering Achilles among the daughters of Lycomedon," in the Louvre (Pl. IV.). I do not consider this as by any means one of Poussin's masterpieces. I have chosen it because it bears a sufficient likeness to the Daumier, so far as the problem of a group of people related to architecture is concerned. Proceeding in the same manner as before, let us note our impressions as nearly as possible in the order in which they arise. First the curious impression of the receding rectangular hollow of the hall seen in perspective and the lateral spread, in contrast to

PLATE IV

Achilles discovered by Ulysses among the daughters of Lycomedon.
Nicholas Poussin, Louvre

that, of the chamber in which the scene takes place. This we see to be almost continuously occupied by the volumes of the figures disposed around the circular table, and these volumes are all ample and clearly distinguished but bound together by contrasted movements of the whole body and also by the flowing rhythm set up by the arms, a rhythm which, as it were, plays over and across the main volumes. Next, I find, the four dark rectangular openings at the end of the hall impose themselves and are instantly and agreeably related to the two dark masses of the chamber wall to right and left, as well as to various darker masses in the dresses. We note, too, almost at once, that the excessive symmetry of these four openings is broken by the figure of one of the girls, and that this also somehow fits in with the slight asymmetry of the dark masses of the chamber walls. So far all our interests have been purely plastic. What the picture is about has not even suggested itself. Perhaps in taking my own experience I am not quite typical: others may at an earlier stage have felt the need of inquiring a little more curiously into this. But at whatever stage we do turn to this we are not likely to get much for our pains. The delight of the daughters in the trinkets which they are examining is expressed in gestures of such dull conventional elegance that they remind me of the desolating effect of some early Victorian children's stories, nor is Ulysses a more convincing psychological entity, and the eager pose of his assistant is too palpably made up because the artist wanted to break the rectangle behind and introduce a diagonal leading away from the upright of Ulysses. Finally, Achilles acts very ill the part of a man suddenly betrayed by an overwhelming instinct into an unintentional gesture. Decidedly the psychological complex is of the meagrest, least satisfactory, kind, and the imagination turns from it, if not with disgust, at least with relief at having done with so boring a performance. We return to the contemplation of the plasticity with the conviction that our temporary excursion into the realm of psychology has led us nowhere. But on the other hand our contemplation of plastic and spatial relations is continually rewarded. We can dwell with delight on every interval, we accept the exact situation of every single thing with a thrilling sense of surprise that it should so exactly satisfy the demands which the rest of the composition sets up. How unexpectedly, how deliciously right! is our inner ejaculation as we

turn from one detail to another or as we contemplate the mutual
relations of the main volumes to the whole space. And this contemplation arouses in us a very definite mood, a mood which, if I
speak for myself, has nothing whatever to do with psychological
entities, which is as remote from any emotions suggested by the
subject, as it would be if I listened to one of Bach's fugues. Nor
does the story of Ulysses enter into this mood any more than it would
into the music if I were told that Bach had composed the fugue after
reading that story. As far as I can discover, whatever Poussin may
have thought of the matter—and I suspect he would have been speech-
less with indignation at my analysis—the story of Achilles was merely
a pretext for a purely plastic construction. Nor can I, in this case at
least, discover any trace of co-operation between the psychological and
the plastic experiences which we derive from this work of art, though
we have seen, in the pose of Ulysses' attendant, at least one instance
of plastic needs making the psychological complex even more insignificant than it would have been otherwise.

Are we not almost forced by these considerations to conclude
that our experiments fail to confirm those theoretical and *a priori*
conclusions laid down by Mr. Richards? I think in these matters it
is safer to base ourselves on exact observation of our own reactions
than on results predicted from a theoretical consideration of how our
sensibilities ought to function. There are, indeed, in the long sequence
of European art a good many cases which must make us pause before
accepting as a fact the co-operation between the illustrational and
plastic elements in a picture so confidently predicted by Mr. Richards.
We may omit the innumerable cases where, as in Poussin, the illustrational element may be entirely neglected and look at one or two where
it is undoubtedly effective. In the case of Raphael, we find a psychological realisation which, whatever we may think of it ourselves, has
proved its crudely popular but effective appeal on each succeeding
generation for centuries; and, in astonishing divergence from that, a
plastic realisation of so rare and subtle a perfection that those who are
capable of responding to its appeal can generally disregard, more or less
completely, the distracting impertinences of Raphael's psychology.

El Greco affords another interesting case. I suspect that for his
own generation his psychological appeal was strong. His contem-

poraries knew intimately, or at least admired profoundly, those moods of extravagant pietistic ecstasy which he depicts. Those abandoned poses, those upturned eyes brimming with penitential tears, were the familiar indications of such states of mind. To us they seem strangely forced and hint a suspicion of insincerity which forbids our acquiescence, and we almost instinctively turn aside to invitations to a quite different mood which his intense and peculiar plasticity holds out. No less does the colour, with its entrancing sublimation of Venetian opulence, draw us in a direction which, to us at all events, is utterly distinct from that given by his illustration which, to tell the truth, clamours for a quite other method, for something more akin to the penitential gloom of Ribera.

Co-operation, then, between the two experiences derived from the psychological and plastic aspects of a picture does not appear to be inevitable. I have not sought to prove that it is impossible or that it never occurs.

Indeed, one case at once suggests itself of possibly finding that fortunate correspondence, namely Rembrandt. Rembrandt is certainly rare, if not unique, among artists in having possessed two separate gifts in the highest degree. His psychological imagination was so sublime that, had he expressed himself in words, he would, one cannot help believing, have been one of the greatest dramatists or novelists that has ever been, whilst his plastic constructions are equally supreme. To what extent he could control these two methods of expression, when using illustration instead of words for his psychological constructions, so that they should always reinforce one another would require a detailed examination of his whole work. I suspect that there was often a tension between the two. In the early work illustration tends to predominate, often to the evident diminution of plastic completeness. Of this one may take the " Philosopher " in the National Gallery, and the " Last Supper " of the Jacquemart-André collection as examples. Throughout his life there was a gradual shift of emphasis from psychological to plastic expression, as though, after all, the medium of paint was more nicely suited to that than to the other. In short, I do not know whether the world would not have gained had Rembrandt frankly divided his immoderate genius into a writer's and a painter's portion and kept them separate.

I find it hard in looking through his work to find examples where either one or the other element does not clearly predominate or where the mutual accommodation of the two does not entail some sacrifice. Perhaps one of the best examples will be that of the " Christ before Pilate," in the National Gallery (Pl. V.). This is surely a masterpiece of illustration. As Rembrandt has seen it, Christ Himself falls into the background. This in itself is a striking indication of how fresh and original Rembrandt's dramatic imagination was. As he reconstructed from the Gospel text the whole scene before his inner vision he saw that such a moment as he has chosen must have arisen. It is the moment of greatest dramatic tension, where the protagonists are no longer Pilate and Christ, but Pilate and the Rabbis. And he has given this moment with astonishing perception of exactly the kind of characters involved and the inevitable effect of their clash. Pilate is an elderly, cultured, civil servant, a diplomat who has always moved in polite society and has found how to shelter his essentially feeble character behind an entrenchment of decorum and precedent. The shock to his feelings produced by this sudden onrush of elderly churchmen maddened with theological prejudice and hatred is admirably given in the fussy indignation of his gesture. No less perfect are the various types of the Rabbis, one, hardly moved from his self-satisfied, self-important grossness, one so abandoned to the passion of hate that he shakes the prætorial wand of office in his frenzy, one screaming out his vindictive fury, one turning back to restrain for a moment the crowd that they have hypnotised into madness. Behind, and hardly more than indicated, since at this moment it falls dramatically into the second place, the group of soldiers who out of sheer indifference and habit continue to buffet and maltreat the tortured figure of Christ, which too is given with that unmitigated psychological truth that Rembrandt was bound to follow. Certainly as drama this seems to me a supreme example of what the art of illustration can accomplish. And as a plastic construction it is also full of interest and strange unexpected inventions. The main group piles up into a richly varied but closely knit plastic whole which leads on by the long upward curve of Pilate's robe and turban to the less clearly modelled volume of the soldiers around Christ. Around these Rembrandt has created first of all the concavity of shade beneath

PLATE V

Christ before Pilate.  Rembrandt National Gallery

the overhanging baldachin of the judge's seat, and this opens out into the vaster concavity of the public place through which a diagonal movement, hinted at by the inpouring crowds, leads us away under the arched entrance.

Personally I feel that the great, uprising pillar surmounted by the bust of Cæsar, admirable as it is in its dramatic suggestiveness, is a little detrimental to the spatial harmony. Still, one cannot deny the plastic beauty of the whole conception, although it is somewhat too crowded and overlaid with detail to be considered one of Rembrandt's great discoveries. This may, perhaps, be placed to the psychological account, since the general agitation and bustle of every detail increases the idea of the whole mad turbulence of the scene.

Here, then, is perhaps as good an instance as one can get of that co-operation of the dramatic and plastic experiences in a single picture. But I think that we cannot help noticing that even here we are compelled to focus the two elements separately. Indeed, I cannot see how one is to avoid this. How can we keep the attention equally fixed on the spaceless world of psychological entities and re-lations and upon the apprehension of spatial relations ? What, in fact, happens is that we constantly shift our attention backwards and forwards from one to the other. Does the exaltation which gratifica-tion in one domain gives increase our vigilance and receptiveness when we turn to the other, as would be implied by true co-operation ? In this case I incline to think it does, although I doubt whether this more than compensates for a certain discomfort which the perpetual shifting of focus inevitably involves.

We may get a little further light on our question by examining another example of Rembrandt's art, and this time we will take one of those innumerable drawings in which the point of departure was a dramatic event or situation.

In the " Parable of the Hidden Talent " (Pl. VI.) the psychological complex formed by the clash of these two characters seems to me to be vividly realised. The types which give this its significance are chosen with Rembrandt's unfailing psychological insight. The dignified, grave and austere man of business one guesses to be a man of conscious rectitude, just but inflexible, and the other exactly such a type of slovenly incapacity as would not be able to restrain his ready, pot-house eloquence even at the risk of still further outraging his master by his self-justification. It will be noticed that the full value of the representational element almost always depends on a reference to something outside the actual work of art, to what is brought in by the title and such knowledge as the title implies to the spectator, whereas plastic values inhere in the work itself.

Now in this drawing the plastic and spatial elements are also such as to give us a keen satisfaction. The volumes of the two figures are made vivid to the imagination by the amazing evocative power of Rembrandt's few hasty indications; we accept with delight the interplay of their movements. No less clear and significant is the relation of these volumes to the enclosing space, though this too is given rather by a few vivid suggestions than with any full realisation. So that here, far more definitely, I think, than in any picture, that co-operation which we have been seeking for seems realised. This may, perhaps, give us a hint as to the nature of such combinations of two arts, namely, that co-operation is most possible where neither of them are pushed to the fullest possibilities of expression, where in both a certain freedom is left to the imagination, where we are moved rather by suggestion than statement.

It may be interesting to examine in the light of these considerations some cases of contemporary artists. There can be no doubt that the tendency of European art, as centred in Paris, has for a long time been towards a more deliberate and conscious concentration on plastic expression than heretofore, but there are, perhaps, more exceptions to this than appear at first sight. The case of Rouault at once rises to the mind as that of an artist who is clearly inspired in the main by conceptions of a moral order. It is quite evident, for instance, that his distortions of actual appearances arise from a different feeling and envisage a different end from those of his fellow-pupil Matisse. It is clear that his imagination is haunted by strange psychological beings to which he gives visible embodiment. It is true that in doing this he can rely also on a powerful and original plastic feeling. It may be noticed from the example here given (Pl. VII. B) that his method comes curiously near at times to that of Rouveyre. But whereas in Rouveyre's case the plastic complex is only indicated, Rouault realises it more fully, it appears of sufficient richness and plenitude to interest

PLATE VI

The Hidden Talent.  Pen drawing.  Rembrandt
(Copy of the drawing in the Louvre)

Albertina, Vienna

PLATE VII

B

St. John the Baptist.    Tempera.        Rouault

A

Le Ménage des pauvres.              Etching.   Picasso

us in and for itself. But we cannot ever quite forget the psychological evocations which accompany it and often emanate from it. The psychological material is of the strangest, most disquieting kind, as of the projection of the psychological beings of real life on to an imaginary plane where their qualities and characteristics become portentous and menacing. Here he is to some extent the follower of Odilon Redon, though not in his method of expression. With Rouault, then, both the plastic and psychological material has great imaginative intensity, and yet it is hard to say upon which of the two our focus is most fixed. Does he, then, provide us with the case of perfect fusion into a single expression of the double experience? Or is there not, after all, a certain tension set up? Different people will answer this in different ways, according to their ruling preoccupation. Perhaps, as in the case of El Greco, in process of time the psychological elements will, as it were, fade into the second place, and his plastic quality will appear almost alone. I do not profess to give an answer. I may note, however, in passing this phenomenon of evaporation. I believe that in nearly every one, wherever a psychological appeal is possible this is more immediately effective, more poignant than the plastic, but that with prolonged familiarity it tends to evaporate and leave plasticity as a more permanent, less rapidly exhausted, motive force. So that where pictures survive for a long period their plastic appeal tends to count more and more on each succeeding generation.

Bonnard is another case of an artist who admits some illustrational element. But his case and that of Picasso are further discussed in the article on Modern Drawings. With regard to the latter, however, we note that his cubist art is essentially plastic in purpose; but it is noteworthy that the cubist idea has been seized on elsewhere and turned to illustrational purposes. Futurism is essentially a literary and psychological adaptation of this new plastic conception, and in England Mr. Nevinson at one time made use of it for frankly illustrational and dramatic appeals. It is probable that new means of expression are always discovered by the plastic researchers, but that they are subsequently pressed into the service of illustration. Thus Marie Laurencin has used the general formula of modern plastic designers like Matisse, but used it almost entirely for decorative-psychological fantasies.

This brings us to yet another question, namely, the relation of the decorative treatment of the picture surface to illustration. This again is a question of the co-operation of two arts. It is doubtful whether a purely flat surface, without suggestions of significant volume, can arouse any profound emotion, so that we should expect that it would easily co-operate with some illustrational matter, and here Raoul Dufy supplies an interesting confirmation. It is obvious that if the decorative accompaniment is to be properly felt the psychological appeal must also be slight. It would be a hopeless task to use Daumier's bitter satires or even Rouveyre's profound interpretations of character as elements in a decorative design. Dufy shows perfect tact in this respect. In some of his brocades he includes witty and charming allusions to contemporary life, to Longchamps, to tennis, or any of the amusements of fashionable society, and these allusions, which only brush the surface of life, avoiding any serious appeal, perceptibly heighten the pleasant effect of his harmonious decorative dispositions. On this plane of playful and amused responses co-operation seems to be entirely successful (Pl. XXI. B).

A curious incidental confirmation of the view here put forward is afforded by the history of painting in England. It is notorious that as a nation our aptitudes for literature are developed out of all proportion to our aptitude for the other arts. And so we find that the English have cultivated almost exclusively the illustrational aspects of painting in defiance of the great plastic tradition of European art. In this branch we might have attained to pre-eminence had we not been always so anxious to arrive at dramatic effect that our draughtsmen could not wait to master the medium of draughtsmanship adequately for its expression in pictorial form. As it is, Hogarth is but a sorry champion to pit against a Daumier.

In view of this characteristic of so large a proportion of English painting it is possible that I may sometimes have criticised some of our more celebrated popular painters from a wrong standpoint. It is, perhaps, unfair to ask the painters of the Royal Academy to give us significant plastic expression, since they have all the time been envisaging only psychological entities. But I fear the change of terrain will not make much difference, since nothing could well be more cheaply sentimental or vulgarly trivial than most of the psychological constructions which annually obtain their ephemeral success. Even if we abandon all questions of plasticity and confine ourselves to psychology, Luke Fildes's " The Doctor," to take a typical and celebrated instance, is on the level of only our fifth-rate writers. Why is it that our *litterateurs* of the brush are so palpably inferior to their *confrères* of the pen ? I may cite as an exception the case of Mr. Stanley Spencer, who is also a pure illustrator, indifferent to plastic significance, but whose psychological creations are at least original, curious and vividly apprehended. They at least never sink to the deplorable level of stereotyped sentimentality which rules in the Royal Academy.

Our experiments and inquiries have then, I hope, given us one result on which we may rely with some confidence : the notion that pictures in which representation subserves poetical or dramatic ends are not simple works of art, but are in fact cases of the mixture of two distinct and separate arts ; that such pictures imply the mixture of the art of illustration and the art of plastic volumes—the art of Art, our horribly incorrect vocabulary almost forces us to say.

The conception of pictures, in which illustration counts, as being cases of a mixture of two distinct arts, changes for us the whole question of content and form in a picture. The old view, still put forward by Mr. Richards, was that the representational element corresponds to the subject, and the plastic element to the form.* This view has led to innumerable difficulties in attempting to explain plastic relations by fancied analogies with the dramatic or poetic idea. It is a great simplification to be rid of the whole business and to look upon both illustration and plastic as having each their proper form, the one psychological, the other spatial.

Such representational pictures, then, as we have been discussing must be considered as cases of mixed arts and closely similar in structure to song in which the psychological unity of the words is accompanied by a musical unity.

What the exact possibilities and limiting conditions of such

* It is, by the by, a little surprising that he should not have seen what an awkward predicament this lands him in when he admits that there are great pictures with no representation at all or only of trivial and negligible import. Some pictures, then, according to him, have only form without content, in others content is of supreme importance.

mixtures of two or more arts may be has, I think, never been properly inquired into. I offer the following suggestions, which occurred to me in connection with the performance of Handel's " Semele " at Cambridge nearly two years ago, as giving hints of possible lines of inquiry.

These reflections on " Semele " are not, of course, reflections on the lady herself, though she does seem to have been rather a climbing minx, needing all the antipathy which Juno evokes to set her in a favourable light ; nor reflections on the lady who took the part at Cambridge. Indeed, I wonder how Opera ever is criticised. Who can know enough of music, the optic and scenic arts, choreography and poetry ever to criticise an opera, and who ever heard of four critics co-operating ? But " Semele " suggests certain esthetic speculations on the possibility and nature of Opera as a form of art which interests me, and that is my excuse for rushing in.

As a young man I spent so many years trying to avoid the odium which my inveterate dislike of nearly all Wagner's operas, except the " Meister Singers," naturally brought upon me from my contemporaries that I began to question whether the Opera is a possible genuine form of art, or only a jumbling together of different arts, leaving now one and now another sticking out in either pleasurable or painful prominence. In those old Wagner operas, for instance, the visual sense was outraged at every turn by the monstrous and pretentious bad taste of form and colour. It was evident that one must, to begin with, get over that. Then, again, it was almost certain that one could hardly expect to find many figurants who could sing such difficult music well, and who possessed, over and above that, the art of beautiful or significant gesture. So that gradually one whittled it down, not without the painful effort of a willed insensibility to sight, to words and music arranged in dramatic sequence. But even then difficulty beset me. In the high pitch of dramatic tension which Wagner's themes implied, the *tempo* of passionate speech seemed to me to be altogether at variance with any possible *tempo* of the analogous musical development. In so far as one was really interested in the drama one began to be impatient at the slowness of the music, which, of course, was absurd, seeing that the only really important esthetic event was, so evidently, the music itself.

In fact, these operas put to me with almost painful insistence this question of the mixture of the arts. Is there really such a thing as a true song? That is to say, such a setting of words, in themselves esthetically moving, to music, also in itself esthetically significant, that both are apprehended at once, not only in their full significance, but mutually exalted by the co-operation of the other. It is fairly clear that anything at all like great poetry must be lessened by any other way of pronouncing the words than that of beautiful speech. In that direction, there must be loss of poetical beauty, however the words are set, since the intonation of music must always distort in some way the rhythmic quality of verse and the speech emphasis of words. A probable explanation of the song, then, may be that the words are to some extent sacrificed to the music. Their function is accessory; namely, to suggest to the mind a channel along which the much vaguer and more general emotions of music may flow. It may be doubted if people who have a full appreciation of music ever feel dissatisfied at the vagueness, the want of outline or clearly marked direction, of the emotions aroused by musical form, but probably many people who are put by music into an emotional state do feel a kind of comfort and relief at having some intelligible idea or known object around which to weave them, or let us say a channel into which to conduct this wide-spreading welter of emotion. Words will supply this, but in supplying it they have to sacrifice their essential poetical significance.

I can, of course, imagine, what I understand the Greeks practised, the other alternative mixture, in which the words of the poem are regarded as the fundamental esthetic substance and music could be used as an accompanying stimulant. Such a " melodrama " may be quite conceivable. In that case the whole attention would be fixed on the poetic sequence, but there would be a kind of physiological exaltation of feeling-tone brought about by a vague musical accompaniment which does not ever lay claim to our conscious attention.

So that the mixture must apparently be of such a kind that there is really only one esthetic substance, the rest being merely ancillary, either, so to speak, a mechanical support for the musical emotions or a physiological stimulant, a drug to heighten the sensibility.

But in all these cases we have been considering emotion at a high pitch of tension, and, indeed, the Wagner operas made one suspect that this might be an important element in the problem, since it appeared, to me at least, that it was precisely at the moments of greatest dramatic intensity that the mixture became least manageable. In them the poignancy of both words and music set up a painful conflict of attention. On the other hand, it was quite clear that that conflict was far less in the " Meister Singers " and disappeared altogether in great parts of Mozart's operas, where the tension was lower, and most of all where the treatment was most playful and least intense.

And now that I have seen " Semele " I am converted to the idea of Opera being a possible art-form. I was told by people of taste that Congreve's words were absurdly bad. I found them perfectly suited to their purpose. Congreve was so great a literary artist, had so clear a sense of stage presentment, and, I must suppose, so good an understanding of this problem of song, that he knew exactly where to keep his emotional pitch. He knew that any intense poetical quality of words must either be lost in song or must intrude impertinently on the musical effect, so he gave to his words just as much generality and colourlessness as was consistent with clear sense and good writing. No doubt this was particularly easy to a seventeenth-century writer, since his generation had reacted from the sharp poetical accent of the Elizabethans, and in their desire for greater elegance and lucidity in the general structure had seen fit to flatten and smooth out the texture of their verse. Emotionally, too, they liked to keep at a distance from life, to present everything in those more generalised terms which enabled them to be fitted easily into a single well-knit pattern. Sharpness of character and poignancy of emotion—the very essence of Shakespearian drama—had had their day, and were sedulously avoided.

So Congreve found no difficulty in taking up an attitude towards the story of Semele which is admirably exhibited in the opening sentence of his argument : " After Jupiter's amour with Europa, the daughter of Agenor, King of Phœnicia, he again incenses Juno by a new affair in the same family, viz. with Semele, niece to Europa and daughter to Cadmus, King of Thebes."

We need have no fear, after that, that Juno's jealousy, Jupiter's omnipotence, Semele's passion or her sad combustion at an early age will be taken very seriously. It is certain that we are not going to be harrowed or even deeply moved, except by the pure delight of finding music and words happily blended and just enough dramatic movement set agoing as will allow of the pleasing contrast of many diverse musical effects, and yet not even these so absorbing but that a fair spectacle of ritual processions, pastoral dances, and divine apparitions can be held at the same moment by the unjaded attention.

And so Congreve's words start the game in exactly the right key. They always express the most obvious, least recondite, least characterful emotions clothed in language which is perfectly clear and as unemphatic as possible. The libretto seems to me a literary masterpiece, not indeed taken by itself, as poetry, but becoming, when read with an idea of the music, a masterpiece of literary self-obliteration. So we have such admirable song words as " Where'er you walk "; one little tiny, transparent conceit is expanded at sufficient length and exposed with sufficient obviousness to allow the music time for all its unhasting effects. It is precisely because as poetry it is so tenuous and flimsy in texture that it is so suitable to give Handel his chance.

Or take again—

> But hark ! the heav'nly sphere turns round,
> And silence now is drown'd
> In ecstasy of sound.
> How on a sudden the still air is charm'd.
> As if all harmony were just alarm'd !
> And every soul with transport fill'd,
> Alternately is thaw'd and chill'd.

The poetry, by no means despicably written, makes so little claim on the attention that music has it all its own way, and yet takes its clue from the words and derives from them a certain clearly felt direction.

Or this for a four-part song :

> CADMUS : Why dost thou thus untimely grieve
> And all our solemn rites profane ?
> Can he, or she, thy woes relieve ?
> Or I ? Of whom dost thou complain ?
> INO : Of all ; but all, I fear, in vain.
> ATHAMAS : Can I thy woes relieve ?
> SEMELE : Can I assuage thy pain ?

etc., etc., for the musician can make his mimes repeat these vaguely pathetic questions and answers for as long as ever he sees fit without our dramatic feelings growing the least bit impatient, even if we were not sustained by the pleasing anticipation of hearing, sooner or later, that " all is vain."

The great secret of " Semele " is that every one keeps his distance from the others and all from the too poignant emotions of real life. We are always suspended in a delightfully unreal world with just enough vague references to sublimated and almost conventional emotions to give variety, movement, and rhythmical accumulation to the esthetic effects of music and colour and moving human forms.

Then Handel came along and took all that Congreve offered, and, though he had clearly been left free to fill the grand *rôle*, to be the essential esthetic creator, even he did not presume. He kept his music well in hand, and, though he had much the largest liberty of any one, he knew he might not do quite what he would if he were all alone. If the poetry must be almost ridiculously simple the musical composer must not, after all, be too profound. Though we have far more attention free for music than for anything else, we have not quite our whole attention; sense and sight still occupy a corner of it. And so Handel's music is all through of a lucidity and acceptability, of a melodious ease of flow, that makes it at once intelligible even to the only half-musical ear. And Handel, too, keeps, I think, the same humorous aloofness from dramatic intensity that Congreve did. They don't, together, exactly make fun of the story, but they treat it with that kind of indulgent, amused condescension which we give to the world of pleasant make-believe.

Alas ! as it was done at Cambridge, one cannot say that the opportunities for the visual arts were as fully exploited. Not, of course, that one's esthetic sense was violently outraged as in the old Wagner operas. It was all too make-shift and unpretentious for that. But the real chance was missed. Why, one wondered, why on earth dig up these archaic Greek figures in all their grotesque austerity when we wanted to be in a more playful mood ? Surely the thing to do was to take the worst, the most florid and decadent Græco-Roman style and give it a strong flavour of Baroque fantasy and extravagance. Veronese's architecture, surely, not pre-historic, and soldiers like Tiepolo's Roman soldiers, not even Mantegna's, still less the black-figured vases. What fun they might have had !

But there all the same (and how grateful I am for it!) was enough to make one see what Opera may safely be and what, I rather guess, human limitations being what they are, it can scarcely transcend. But why not be contented with three or four hours' pure enjoyment, even if we are left with no tremendous or overwhelming spiritual experience? Anyway, the attempt to get that and miss it is a far greater waste of time.

A confirmation of my surmises comes to hand as I write in an interesting article by Mr. Cecil Gray in the *Nation and Athenæum* for July 10, 1926. In discussing Stravinsky's music for " Les Noces," he says : " I think it can be admitted without hesitation that ' Les Noces ' of Stravinsky, which has been the most interesting of the new productions of the Russian Ballet this season, is an exceedingly attractive spectacle, and from this point of view of ensemble, is remarkably successful. On the other hand, one has even less hesitation in coming to the conclusion that Stravinsky's score, considered by itself, is pretty poor stuff. Indeed, in my opinion, this applies to practically all his work. However apt and appropriate it may be as a single element in the ensemble, it never, or very rarely, succeeds in holding our attention in the concert-room. For example, the symphonies for wind instruments and the more recent piano sonata are admitted, even by his warmest admirers, to be complete failures. It is quite possible, however, that if they had first been presented in conjunction with an elaborate *mise-en-scène* and all the exquisite artistry of the Russian dancers they would have been hailed as masterpieces. The same applies, to a certain extent, to ' Les Noces.' The music of Stravinsky's earlier ballets first became known to most of us in association with these other elements ; this was the secret of their great and immediate success. The music of ' Les Noces,' on the contrary, had been published for some years before its presentation in ballet form, and there has consequently been ample time and opportunity for forming a fair estimate of its intrinsic qualities. One's conclusion is that, like nearly all Stravinsky's other works, it is little more than an effective musical *décor* which has no independent existence apart from the whole. . . . In the first place, the work reveals a complete lack of melodic invention. The thematic material consists entirely of monotonous little pentatonic wisps of tune which

D

are never developed or combined, but only repeated. Now, it may be true that a seeming triviality may assume significance through development, but certainly not through mere reiteration and restatement. It is not an exaggeration to say that at least half the score could have been written out with . . . the musical equivalent of etc. Secondly, the rhythmical poverty which must inevitably result from the necessity of co-relating the music with the movement and gestures of a number of dancers is too obvious and flagrant to need labouring. Indeed, this metronomic, machine-like inflexibility of rhythm is characteristic of all ballets without exception, of all concerted dance music whatsoever, and constitutes the fundamental objection to its claim to be considered as one of the higher forms of musical art."

Here, at last, we have the independent evidence of the trained musician upon the subject and its coincidence with conclusions derived from the study of the mixture of plastic and illustrative elements in a picture is highly significant. It leaves open to Stravinsky the reply that he was only fulfilling the needs of collaboration, and that his very restraint from profound musical expression was, in its way, a proof of his artistic tact.

My own reflections on Opera were made without any exact idea of what bearing they might have upon the representational picture. To some extent they appear to support, however, the results of our comparison of Rembrandt's drawings and pictures. They confirm the suspicion that perfect co-operation between two arts becomes difficult in proportion as they reach a high pitch of intensity or completeness of expression. Of course, if either art definitely preponderates in intensity or completeness the attention is kept focussed on that one, and receives only vague suggestions from the other, in which case we approach the situation of the Greek melodrama as described above, and we are spared the disquiet of the shift of focus.

To return once again to the pictorial problem, we have seen that representation in a picture may be of two kinds : one in which, by the choice of objects and the manner of their presentment they invite us to apprehend " psychological volumes," the other in which they serve to the construction of spatial and plastic wholes. These two kinds of representation are, likely enough, governed by different principles, and imply certain differences of emphasis which explains in part the great difficulty of conciliating them. For instance, where drama is in question minute changes of tone in the face will be likely to have a far greater significance than they would have on plastic grounds, and it is almost inevitable that the dramatic painter should give them ultra-plastic values.

The approach from this angle may, I think, give us a new perspective of the old hard-fought question of realism. It can now be discussed from the point of view of its success in helping to create either a psychological or a spatial volume. I shall leave on one side the former aspect and examine a little more clearly the *rôle* of realistic representations in spatial constructions.

The issue of realism *versus* idealism in graphic art has been, as I say, the occasion of many a hard-fought battle and with no decisive result. It will be one advantage of the view here suggested that we can now see why so little came of the fight. It was because the battle was waged by both parties at cross purposes. Too little analysis of the nature of a work of art had been attempted for the question to be put in any really intelligible form, with the result that both sides took their stand in defence of those obvious and hasty assumptions which " common sense " invariably supplies in any complex situation. A vague notion, natural enough, no doubt, to a superficial glance, was current, that realistic representation held the spirit in contact with the banality of everyday life, whilst more abstract fictitious entities, personifications of abstract ideas, fauns, satyrs, angels—beings of which we can have no actual experience—liberated the spirit and allowed it to rise free from the trivialities of common life. In a vague way imagination was associated with idealism, whilst dull and literal matter-of-factness was the lot of the realist.

Against this position of the idealists there was opened about the middle of last century a vigorous attack led, as far as the plastic arts were concerned, most conspicuously by Courbet. The realists, relying on a supposed analogy between esthetic and scientific truth, based themselves on the need for objective validity in representation, claiming that their work was good because it was true. In literature, Zola, in his " L'Œuvre," backed this up by a vague pantheistic mysticism which gave to the crude fact a kind of divine authority. Courbet, who was profoundly and innately an artist, was impelled by a sure instinct to the method he adopted in his painting, but the theoretical grounds on which he supported it appear now to be a gratuitous and cumbersome justification. He was right in practice, because for him personally, as for many other great artists, the fullest liberation, the most effective functioning of his plastic imagination occurred when his whole sensibility, was intent upon the thing seen. It was then and then only that the full significance of plastic relations could be apprehended. His aptitudes were such that images called up before his " inner vision " either lacked coherent relations or held together by some other principle than plastic necessity. When he had not some object clearly before his eyes he either substituted a theatrical convention or became a realist in the photographic sense, that is to say, he sacrificed plastic significance for a crude and meaningless verisimilitude to actual objects. This accounts, I think, for the existence in his œuvre of such purely descriptive works as the " Bonjour M. Courbet " and " Les Vanneurs." Even in the same picture the contrast between Courbet's rich plastic imagination before the thing seen and the shifts which his uncertain " inner vision " pushed him into may be seen in many of his pictures. His innate plastic instinct led him irresistibly to the nude as a pretext, and he painted it as few have done since Rembrandt, and with much of that master's frankness and abandonment to the impression of the thing seen. Unfortunately Courbet was not strong enough, for all his boasted realism, to resist altogether the poetising conventions of romanticism, and, as often as not, having painted his nude with all sincerity from the model posed before him in the studio, he faked it into a " poesy " by the addition of rocks and overhanging boughs and cascades. One such work, a " Baigneuse endormie," was seen lately at the French Gallery. In my notes made at the time I remarked : " How nearly Courbet comes to the total transmutation of the theme into plastic values, and by what a curious misunderstanding of the problem he misses complete purity ! Here he touches the imagination almost in exact proportion to his absorption in the thing seen. He painted his ' Baigneuse ' with a passionate intensity of feeling which carries one entirely away from the actual world, but when he sought the adventitious aid of a poetical *mise-en-scène* and borrowed from literature and the theatre the stereo-

PLATE VIII

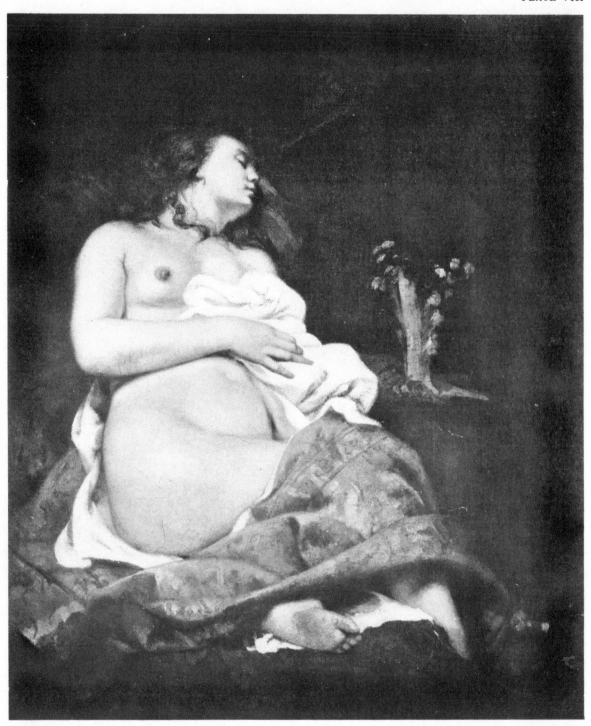

La Blonde Endormie.          Collection of M. Henri Matisse, by courtesy of the owner

types of rocks and overhanging foliage and water, he went near to destroying all sense of illusion. Their want of plastic consistency refers us back, for all their poetical intention, to the actual world."

In the " Blonde endormie," belonging to M. Matisse (Pl. VIII.), Courbet for once was true to his principles and has accepted the thing seen in its true setting, and here we are in the world of pure imagination. However "realistic" this is we are not tempted ever to refer to what lies outside the picture. This plastic unity holds us entirely within its own limits because at every point it gives us an exhilarated and surprised satisfaction. Everything here is so transmuted into plastic terms and finds therein so clear a justification that we are not impelled to go beyond them or to fill them out, as it were, by thinking of the model who posed more than half a century ago to M. Courbet in Paris, or of any other woman whatever.

Corot is an extreme and pathetic case of the ravages of what painters might well label the " poetic fallacy." Here was a man who was so constituted that almost any *coup d'œil* upon nature liberated within him the rarest, strangest, subtlest harmonies of tone and colour. These he " found " at once and with unexpected freshness and unfailing certainty in the thing seen. In face of that it was impossible to him to be commonplace, matter-of-fact, or insignificant. In his youth he was asked to paint the portrait—one can call it nothing else—of a huge, bleak, ugly, factory-like building, and being the most obliging of men and without any notion of the dignity of the artist, he complied. He did the portrait so as to give complete satisfaction to the owner, leaving out no detail of all the dull square windows ; he gave fully every architectural commonplace ; he did the iron railing of the entrance full justice ; but, without interfering with his patron's satisfaction in all this, he found an entirely unexpected and exquisite harmony of colour between the sunlit surface of the ugly building and the luminous sky behind, he disposed the cast shadow in the foreground and chose the proportions of everything relatively to his canvas so adroitly that he created a moving spiritual reality out of an incredibly boring suburban scene. Later on, in Italy, the same thing happened, only that now he had freedom of choice and did not set himself quite such hard problems of transmutation. Whether it was that his transmutations were too subtle to be understood or what, the time came when he was entrapped by the common-places of idealism, by the strange notion that only the make-believe could liberate the spirit from the bonds of actuality. Even from early days he had supposed that his Salon picture at least must always soar into this region, and he would laboriously justify a fairly realistic landscape—though even this was weakened by poetical adjustments—by introducing Homer among the Shepherds or Hagar or some such poetical matter in which he had only the most tepid interest. He survives now in those little spontaneous notes of the thing seen which he thought entirely unworthy of exhibiting, and which he supposed no one would ever care to buy. But little by little poetry gained on him, nymphs began to crowd into his landscapes and destroyed in time its whole quality. Little by little trees, sky and water adapted themselves to these intruders and became the vapid, vaporous poetical machines which delighted for long, and perhaps still delight, the magnates of the Middle West.

In the exhibition at the French Gallery to which I alluded above, there were two pictures by Corot which exemplified this. One was a view of Honfleur. It might be called almost a topographical picture, so literally had the artist accepted the banal facts—the straight row of houses along a bare empty quay, and the view out beyond them to distances of sea and sky. By no accent whatever was there an attempt to give to this any picturesque or dramatic suggestiveness. The plain matter-of-fact reality was accepted without protest, rather, indeed, with a certain avidity, for to Corot's eye these simple appearances yielded one of those mysteriously perfect chords of colour in which every note gets a new meaning and resonance, and at the same time helps to create the plastic unity of the space with all its content of air and light. And that harmony is found by such subtle, infinitesimal and unconscious adjustments of the ordinarily accepted facts of appearance that to one who missed Corot's real meaning it would have the non-esthetic meaning, such as it is, of an exact reproduction of the scene. What concerns us here is that the realism, complete as it is, is so entirely transmuted into plastic values that to say before it, " How like Honfleur ! " would be felt to be totally irrelevant to the mood it evokes—a mood as detached from any actual experience as that of the purest music. In short, Corot creates here an entirely spiritual reality.

PLATE IX

Chez le docteur.  Corot

The Louvre

But in his " Venus au Bain," where he envisaged more directly an exalted lyrical mood, there is no such liberation of the spirit. The deliberate poetical make-believe of this figure is fatal to any conviction. The figure itself was, perhaps, studied from a model. But then Corot set to work to " idealise " it from the first. That is to say, he rubbed out whatever in his model did not conform to some vague memory of Græco-Roman types of beauty. In doing so he lost hold of any consistent plastic rhythm. For fear that the forms should be mutually incompatible the artist is forced to make them vague and accentless. No less fatal here is the want of any consistence in the landscape. It, too, is bathed in " poetical " vagueness and plastic indecision. One may, perhaps, suppose that in these later works Corot had subordinated plastic to psychological values, that his Venus was the illustrative equivalent of some lyric to Aphrodite. Certainly the plastic values have disappeared, but there is nothing to set against that loss but the evident intention of the artist to move us through this other appeal. It meets with no response, because in that domain he lacked both personal conviction and expressive power.

Still, every now and again in those long years devoted to " poetical " fabrication, some vision in his studio would arrest his gaze and wake up in him once more his slumbering but unimpaired plastic sensibility, and he would do masterpieces such as the figure of a woman known as " La Perle " in the Louvre. I give here an earlier work, " Le Torse " (Pl. IX.), in which Corot's unique delicacy of perception, his impeccable interpretation of values of colour and tone are fully apparent. For directness and intimacy of feeling, for an almost reckless indifference to all else but the artist's own fascinated response, this has rarely been surpassed. The fabricator of so many vague, insipid dreams was, after all, the sincerest of plastic artists. Such a nude has not, of course, the fullness and rich complexity of plastic evocations of Courbet's, but, in its more elementary and limited harmonic structure, it surprises one even more by its intimacy, directness and absolute purity.

In this matter of realism we must once more consult Rembrandt, for, after all, he may be said to be the first great realist. The first, that is, to find complete spiritual freedom in the contemplation of no matter what actual vision. Wherever light played upon a solid object before his eyes, Rembrandt had the elements for creating a harmonious plastic unity. And no one ever could accept quite so many of the data of vision and bind them all at once into so compelling, so richly evocative a rhythm.

This power of deciphering and interpreting the data of actual vision grew upon Rembrandt immensely in his later years. It went naturally enough with that gradual transference of his interest from psychological to plastic values alluded to above. I take as an example of his realism, therefore, the very late picture of " A Schoolboy at his Desk," in Lord Crawford's collection (Pl. X.). The boy was at his lessons. Puzzled and bored by them, he looked up from his task; his thoughts wandered, and he sat there day-dreaming, with his cheek propped on his thumb. Rembrandt painted this scene with complete realism, without a thought of anything but the vision before him. He realised the modelling in all its solidity and density, but also with all that is infinite, intangible and elusive in the play of light on its surface. In painting such a work, in accepting so much of the whole complexity of appearance, Rembrandt was taking on tremendous odds. To get that density and mass as he felt it he had to paint with a full brush and model in a rich paste, but he had to get everywhere transitions of tone and colour of impalpable subtlety: at every point the drawing had to have the utmost sensitiveness and elasticity. If one looks carefully in the original at the passage where the thumb indents the cheek one can see why such works occur at very rare intervals. If for a moment Rembrandt had thought about his picture he was undone; nothing but complete absorption in his vision could sustain the unconscious certainty and freedom of the gesture. Each touch, then, had to be an inspiration or the rhythm would have broken down.

But what is of even more interest for our present inquiry is the painting of the desk. This is a plain flat board of wood, but one that has been scratched, battered and rubbed by schoolboys' rough usage. Realism, in a sense, could go no further than this, but it is handled with such a vivid sense of its density and resistance, it is situated so absolutely in the picture space and plays so emphatically its part in the whole plastic scheme, it reveals so intimately the mysterious play of light upon matter that it becomes the vehicle of a strangely exalted spiritual state, the medium through which we share Rembrandt's deep

PLATE X

Boy at Lessons. Rembrandt
Collection of Lord Crawford of Balcarres. By courtesy of the owner

contemplative mood. It is miraculous that matter can take so exactly the impress of spirit as this pigment does. And that being so, the fact that it is extraordinarily like a schoolboy's desk falls into utter insignificance beside what it is in and for itself. Perhaps it is a mere accident, but it is a fortunate and symbolic accident that this particular piece of matter would be paid for to-day not at the price of the original wood but at many times the value of so much gold. Compare Rembrandt's wood with Alma Tadema's marble. The whole point of Alma Tadema's celebrated performances lay in his having given one a rather weak illusion of marble itself. To say " How like marble ! " was precisely all that could be said. It had no other purpose, no further meaning than that, being, in fact, totally inexpressive of anything else. Whereas nothing appears more impertinent before this Rembrandt than to call attention to this likeness, exact though it may be.

Here, then, we get a possible resolution of this ever-recurrent trouble about realism. If I am right, the constant criticism of Courbet to the effect that though he was manifestly a great painter his art was purely material, that it revealed nothing of the spirit, and was therefore inferior, falls to the ground. It was based on a false assumption that spiritual values could only be attained through psychological structures, that spatial and plastic ones had no such function.

This habit of putting psychological above spatial values in graphic art comes, of course, only too naturally to men of letters who occupy themselves with plastic art. Diderot's celebrated critiques of the Salons of his day are almost entirely devoted to the psychological aspects of illustration. No wonder that for him Greuze was the greatest of painters. But the same habit persists through most of the criticism of the nineteenth century, and has undoubtedly exercised a powerful effect on the practice of art. This has been especially the case in this country, and not unnaturally, since we attach a superstitious reverence to certain ethical values, a reverence which by no means always serves the cause of the mutual adjustments of individuals in a society and which leads us to estimate them out of all proportion to other moral values (using that word in its widest sense). Now, as psychological values hold out more possibilities of being related to these sacrosanct ethical ones than spatial values do, they appear *ipso facto* to have a superior value and a potential effect upon conduct.* Hence the strange pretensions claimed for Watts's symbolical lucubrations.

This prejudice has, as I say, obscured critical judgment, and has also turned many artists aside from their proper functions. It causes them frequently to overlook certain ethical considerations more pertinent to their activity, namely, that they are doing a more difficult † and a more useful task for the world at large in creating those harmonies for which they have a special aptitude than in doing very ineffectively what can be done better by other means.

We get, then, from the point of view to which our inquiries have led us, a method of distinguishing between good and bad realism—a method by which we can more or less judge whether realistic representation is esthetically justified or no. We can say, supposing the picture to envisage plastic expression, that the moment anything in it ceases to serve towards the edification of the whole plastic volume, the moment it depends on reference to something outside the picture, it becomes descriptive of some other reality, and becomes part of an actual, and not a spiritual, reality. That process of incorporating any given visual datum in a spiritual whole is what I endeavour to describe by the words interpretation or transmutation. That transmutation of the visual values of natural objects into plastic and spatial values is the great problem of most modern artists, since the majority of them take some actual *coup d'œil* as their point of departure for plastic construction.

I have left on one side the question of realism in relation to psychological expression. We may take Rouveyre's heads as excellent instances of a complete transposition of certain very carefully selected visual appearances into forms mainly evocative of psychological entities. We may note in passing that violent distortion and alteration of the proportions of natural appearances are much more easily tolerated by most people where a psychological end is envisaged than where the end is plastic. The irritation which the public of his day felt before Ingres' figures, the accusations of defacing the human form divine, and the similar outcry in our own day against Cézanne show how much

---

* *Cf.* on this point, Mr. Richards' admirable criticisms, *l.c.*, Chap. XXXI.

† More difficult because the pretence to subserve moral values always gets a good hearing. The financial prospect of the "expressionist" is, other things being equal, brighter than that of the plastic artist.

more difficult it is for people to recognise plastic than psychological purpose. The moment the utility of any such distortion to the ultimate expression is recognised all disquiet at its unfamiliarity is subdued.

I have some hopes that in the present essay I have got a little nearer to an explanation of the ends envisaged unconsciously by painters in the practice of their art, and also found some hints of the causes that have led to failure. I scarcely can venture to hope that a recognition of these principles may assist artists to avoid the pursuit of impossible or contradictory ends and enable them to concentrate on the development of their specific response to the spectacle of nature.

# ART AND THE STATE *

THE recently appointed Commission of Fine Arts, which is the new name for the Committee of Taste for the nation, will doubtless adopt as a motto *de gustibus non disputandum*. They will be well advised to do so. Any discussion of their fitness for the task would be so likely to have unpleasant results for them. It is much better, they will doubtless consider, that they should simply lay down the law as to what the nation is to admire and approve. Some of the members of this august body have given us already proofs of what we must expect. We may yet live to see a monument similar to the Nurse Cavell in every square in London, and every public building tricked out with the borrowed, and rather ill-borrowed, finery of the Victoria and Albert Museum, even if we should be spared the full splendours of Birmingham University, where reminiscences of half a dozen celebrated buildings of antiquity jostle one another in a bewildering confusion of periods and styles. It would be absurd to labour the point ; to every one whose opinion has been formed by any serious attention to matters of art the Committee of Taste would be merely a bad joke were it not such a serious menace.

It is a serious menace only because we, as a nation, do not really think that art matters. There are doubtless many excuses for this point of view. The mere existence of the Nurse Cavell monument is just the kind of excuse which people make for sparing themselves the trouble of making an effort to avoid its repetition. But for whatever reason, it is impossible to doubt that the nation is indifferent. We shall be told that it is only the highbrows that are indignant. Well, so be it. The dramatic critic of the *Times*, who dispenses such admirable sense while dexterously pretending that he is only talking the same kind of nonsense as a reputable journalist, has shown us recently the true meaning of " highbrow " by treating it as the opposite of " commercial." One may be thankful that it is not an English word. Only a people for whom the love of money is the root

* *Nation*, Feb. 23, March 1 and 22, 1924.

of all romance could have coined it as a term of abuse wherewith to overwhelm all who refuse to bow down and worship the golden image The highbrows then are in revolt, and precisely because they recognise in the Committee of Taste the supreme symbol of the tyranny of the commercial artists and their great Trade Union, the Royal Academy.

So unqualified a demonstration of the power of this group to impose themselves as representing the artistic effort of the nation may, after all, do good. It may bring to a head the whole question of the relation of the State to Art. The State has gradually drifted into its present position in relation to art without at any one moment having occasion to pause and consider what it was about. It originally considered art as a private matter lying outside its sphere of action. Gradually it found itself saddled with some of the Royal collections of pictures, until little by little, and without being brought to the point of formulating a policy, it finds itself spending annually very large sums of money on the upkeep of museums, on the teaching of art, and the employment of artists in public works.

However troublesome it is for the ordinary man, and perhaps even more so for the average politician, to have dealings with those odd and incalculable beings who call themselves artists, it has become by now a matter of sheer common sense and good economy to consider first whether we need spend all this money on art, and, if so, whether we are spending it wisely and getting full value for it.

What is wanted is some clear understanding of what the policy of the State with regard to art should be. It is a most difficult and intricate question, and has never been properly threshed out. I am far from being able to give an answer as to what that policy should be, nor do I believe any one is capable of doing so until all the relevant facts are elicited by inquiry into the workings of the existing administrative customs. I say customs since no definite and coherent policy exists. What I may be able to do in this essay is to indicate the kind of questions which it would appear desirable to have considered.

There are, I should say, three main branches of public expenditure upon art, and it is possible that each of these would require a separate inquiry. They are (1) the teaching of art in primary and secondary schools and in the Universities, and the more specialised teaching of the Royal College of Art. (2) The employment of artists by the State in the construction and ornamentation of public buildings and public monuments of all kinds. (3) The acquisition, care, and preservation of the artistic treasures of the country. This would include the preservation of ancient monuments throughout the country and the museums and picture galleries belonging to the State.

The teaching of art is by itself a vast and complicated subject, and one of extreme difficulty. I do not know what sums are spent on it by the State and local public bodies acting under State supervision, but in the aggregate they must be very large, and yet there are not a few people who have grave doubts whether any result is produced comparable to this expenditure. It is certain that the positive results are neither brilliant nor encouraging. It is even uncertain whether artistic progress might not be more rapid were the whole of this teaching abandoned. It is fairly certain, for instance, that in the arts of applied design we find ourselves in a backward position as compared, say, with France, and perhaps with other countries, and yet there is reason to think that the people of England have greater aptitudes for art than have ever been realised.

The fact is that the whole question of whether art can be directly taught or not has yet to be answered. Since it is a question of the full development of a sensibility which is peculiar to each individual, and depends for its whole value upon that unique individual quality, it is at least reasonable to suppose that the idea of teaching as doctrine the results attained by other sensibilities is mistaken. It does seem rather futile to teach a child how to draw, when one considers that what it has to discover is how it alone of all created beings can draw. The thing to be taught is a thing that does not exist, but has to be discovered. There can be no doubt in any case that the average child has extraordinary inventiveness in design and the average adult none whatever, and that in between these two states there occurs the process known as art teaching. Is this a causal relation or not? That question anyhow must be answered before we undertake so vast an expenditure of public money.

We must remember, too, that drawing in the sense of the more or less accurate representation of objects may have other uses than esthetic ones. It may be that drawing as a training in accurate observation has educational value quite apart from art, and that such drawing should be taught, excluding, perhaps, from such teaching any child who showed special artistic aptitude.

Leaving the question of art teaching in primary and secondary schools, we come to the question of more specialised art teaching for those whose aptitudes mark them out for some kind of artistic career. This is really another branch of State expenditure on art, and is one that needs very careful consideration if we are ever to make full use of native talent. The idea that it might be a work for the State to foster the talent for design originated, I believe, as far as England is concerned, with the Prince Consort—at all events, it was a leading motive in the establishment of the Victoria and Albert Museum, and it is still conceived of as one of its functions. But the results, after all these years, are by no means reassuring. The notion has been too much that by merely recommending good models of ancient craftsmanship and encouraging pupils to study and imitate these, good modern work would result. At various times the work of different styles and epochs has each had its vogue among our cultured classes, and each in turn has been recommended as the model for this process of pastiche, with the result that no notion of anything but " styles " has penetrated to the student's mind. He has at the end great facility in designing in any given " style," but he has no notion of the underlying principles of all good work, no basis on which to create when once he cannot clutch at the authority which he follows. In fact, he possesses the " styles " but not " style." Such notions are fatal to the development of good design. Here, at least, is a question of immense economic importance to any modern State which depends on its manufactures, and which has to meet competition in design as well as other things in the world market.

In a country like ours, which depends largely on exported manufactures of all kinds, any scheme which really succeeded in fostering native talent in applied design would be a source of immense wealth to the country, and might, indeed, justify a far larger expenditure of money than is at present devoted to all the various artistic enterprises of the State.

Is it possible to suggest the lines along which this highly desirable end might be attained ? They would, I think, need a radical change in our attitude towards design. For hitherto our attitude of mind has been wrong from the beginning. It has been coloured by too romantic and uncritical an admiration for the artistic products of past ages and the belief that the work of some period—the periods vary nearly as fast as fashions in dress—had a divine authority. There has resulted from this a fatal idea of orthodoxy and authority. If an authority could be found in the particular period in fashion at the moment for any single element in a design, then it was good ; if not, it was bad, unorthodox, and unscholarly. The method is curiously like that of producing Latin verses in the Public Schools, and the result bears the same relation to real design that a prize scholar's Latin verses do to poetry. The whole history of the Gothic revival in architecture in this country is a glaring instance and an all too eternal monument of the hopelessness of such ideas.

Design can never be copied ; it has always got to be discovered. That is the fundamental fact. It has to be discovered as much as a new chemical compound has to be discovered by following certain laws, though in the case of design those laws must be apprehended instinctively. That instinctive sense of the laws of design can no doubt be acquired by the intelligent and appreciative contemplation of past examples of design, but not by direct imitation.

If we are to develope, then, the unguessed and unexplained possibilities of native talent for design, both the manufacturer who wishes to employ the designer and the educational authority that desires to train him must adopt an attitude far more like that which they have gradually been forced to accept—not without much reluctance—about the position of the scientific researcher in regard to industry.

What I believe is wanted for those young men who have shown special aptitude in this direction, and who desire to adopt design as a profession, is a Laboratory of Design rather than a School of Design. I imagine an institution where all the necessary apparatus, which is by no means complicated or expensive, for making designs would be supplied, where also there would be a certain small staff fully equipped with the purely technical knowledge of the exact requirements of various industries—men to whom the pupil could always apply to answer such questions as, how a design must be made so as to repeat on a textile fabric, what are the conditions for a woven as opposed to a printed design, and so forth.

Further—and this is of the utmost importance—there should be facilities for the production of trial pieces of a certain number of designs. One of the great difficulties of developing applied design in industry is the fact that a manufacturer is very unwilling to incur the expense of trying designs which do not conform more or less exactly to those already on the market. He dare not risk money in experiment. The result is that he is tempted to go on making minute and often entirely meaningless changes in existing patterns. He is naturally conservative in such matters. Even in France, I believe, M. Dufy had a very hard fight to get the Lyons silk weavers to give his designs a trial, although the moment these got on to the market their success was indisputable, and the very men who obstructed him have reaped enormous benefit from his success. Here in England the opposition of such a purely negative attitude is far stronger, and is alone enough to prevent the growth of a vital tradition of applied design.

I do not doubt that in process of time this attitude of the manufacturer would be overcome, as it has been in the case of scientific research, but at first it would be essential that the burden of executing trial pieces and getting them tested on the market should be borne by the Laboratory of Design itself. Such a scheme as this could be tried on a small scale and in a single institution. I believe the results would prove the fact that it is not inventiveness and talent that are lacking in our countrymen so much as opportunity to develop them. In that case it would have to be extended, and perhaps different laboratories of design would have to be established in different industrial centres, where they would be specialised to meet the requirements of the local industry.

Here, then, is a subject of great national importance which has never been even inquired into of late years. It is one that I feel certain would at least repay investigation. One may even venture to hope that our manufacturers, at last shaken out of their accustomed self-complacency by our scandalous failure in the Paris Exhibition of decorative design of 1925, are in a position to consider the results of such an inquiry with an open mind.

With regard now to the second of my main groups of State expenditure on art, namely, the employment of artists by the State on public buildings and monuments. Here I feel at a loss to suggest

E

any method by which we might be extricated from the position in which we find ourselves. That position is, in fact, almost ridiculous. It would seem that the tradition of employing artists who do not command the respect or admiration of the profession in general—and still less of people of trained critical judgment—was too deeply rooted in our public policy to be changed. We have only to look at our one-pound and ten-shilling notes, at our postage stamps, at our public statues, at the Admiralty Arch, and, alas! too many sad and familiar sights, in order to realise how desperate the situation is. I need not labour again the argument that to appoint as an advisory committee in such matters the very type of artist that is responsible for such a grotesque state of affairs is not the way out. The artistic profession has no organisation. It lacks any representative body. It may even be doubted whether under modern conditions it could ever attain such organisation, and it is perhaps absurd to blame the State for turning to the one well-established and well-organised Trade Union of artists which exists, namely, the Royal Academy. It is notorious, of course, that that body does not represent the more vital or scholarly artistic effort of the country, that every artistic movement of consequence has arisen outside it, and meets with its determined opposition until such time as it too has attained popular recognition and in turn become obsolete. All this is well known, and yet there is no obvious way of replacing that body by a more representative one.

In discussing the position of museums, I see in one direction a possible way out of this *impasse*, but it is an indirect one, and would depend on the gradual formation, along quite different lines, of a new professional tradition. In the meantime, I suppose we must be content to allow our official national art to be a gross misrepresentation of national artistic talent and to be an object of ridicule to the peoples of some other nations which, bad as their official art is, have yet the right to laugh at ours.

The third division of the suggested inquiry into the nature of artistic effort by the State concerns the acquisition and care of the artistic treasures of the nation. The first and most obvious function in this respect is the care and preservation of historical monuments. There may, no doubt, be difficult questions of detail in this connection, but, on the whole, the general policy is fairly established, and commands general acquiescence. We may hope that the age of ruthless restoration of old buildings is past, and that preservation and not restoration is now accepted as the guiding principle. In this respect, at all events, our activity or want of activity compares favourably with French practice, which has created a vested interest in the continually repeated and devastating interference with the great cathedrals. The question there is not " How little can we safely do ? " but " How much can we find an excuse to do ? "

Far more complicated and more difficult are the problems connected with national museums and picture galleries. The passion for collecting and hoarding treasures begins in the individual in a rather indiscriminate and haphazard fashion, and is often pursued in many different directions without any clear understanding of the object to be attained, and something of this random character still attaches to a good deal of national collecting. In some institutions different and often divergent ends are pursued at the same time. No one can doubt that there is much confusion and overlapping in different and sometimes competing institutions. To take a few instances. The nation's pictures are supposed to be gathered together at the National Galleries, but a large number have found themselves in the Victoria and Albert Museum, isolated there among objects collected with a view to illustrating the applied arts of design. In the same building we have fortunately some of our best examples of pure sculpture, but the remainder of the works of this class are in the British Museum. The British Museum itself is a compound institution. In certain departments everything is apparently selected for its bearing on historical and ethnological problems, and yet here too, inevitably, the esthetic importance of objects cannot altogether be lost sight of. But no consistent policy seems to be pursued in either direction. In some departments history seems to predominate, in others esthetic claims are more recognised. Thus, in the Egyptian department, it is to be presumed that the claims of Egyptology are met, since scarcely any objects worthy of esthetic consideration have found their way there, with the result that despite our special position with regard to Egypt, Berlin has acquired most of the masterpieces of Egyptian art and left us the mere journeyman's handiwork. On the other hand, the department of Oriental Art clearly keeps esthetic value well in view. Even in the National Gallery the conflict between the two ideas makes itself evident. At one time the nation saves up its resources in order to acquire a small number of supreme masterpieces, at another, many small and insignificant pictures are bought on the plea of filling gaps in a historical series. Even more striking is the conflict which we meet with in the National Portrait Gallery. Here one would suppose, from the general appearance of the collection, that history reigned supreme and art was a mere accidental interloper, and yet the obvious conclusion we should draw from this would be that above all the collection should contain the best possible photographs of the great men of the Victorian epoch, since these are incomparably better as historical documents than the painted effigies. But here the theory breaks down, and history is suddenly abandoned, though whether art is attained remains doubtful.

Clearly, then, it would be highly desirable that some method should be introduced into the national collections. It is evident that to some extent the claims of historical and ethnological science on the one hand and art on the other should be met. It is not so evident that both should be met by the same institution.

Let me throw out here a suggestion. Why should not the main body of the collections be formed on historical lines, while a special gallery, or galleries, are set apart for displaying chosen objects grouped together and exhibited on purely esthetic lines? Such a method would be clearly applicable to an institution like the British Museum. There, we may take it, the main idea is historical and ethnological. In collections so formed, works of the greatest esthetic value rub shoulders with others that are without any esthetic quality, but may have the utmost importance on historical grounds. Take, for instance, the splendid collection illustrating Negro and Polynesian cultures. In the overcrowded cases of this gallery there are single specimens of sculpture of the greatest beauty, but their beauty is hidden from all but the acutest eyes. One has to peep behind half a dozen quite ordinary pieces to get a glimpse of the masterpiece in a dark corner of a shelf. Now here, clearly, the esthetic importance of these cultures could be brought to light if there existed one or more galleries devoted to purely exhibition purposes. In these, from time to time, different collections of objects could be arranged so as to allow of altogether new confrontations of masterpieces from different cultural centres. Here, from time to time, historical and geographical boundaries might be overridden, and we could compare analogous specimens of Egyptian, Sumerian, Greek, Chinese, and Negro sculpture.

Similarly in the National Gallery we might come to the idea of a historical storehouse of painting, on the one hand, kept for the use of students, and, on the other, of galleries in which the finest work of different schools and periods should be displayed to the utmost advantage.

No doubt, any complete scheme of organisation of the nation's collections on these lines might be judged Utopian, but it would not seem altogether impossible to lay down a definite policy in these respects for particular institutions, or for one institution to pursue both ends but in separate departments. What is undesirable is an uncertain and hesitating policy and the zigzag course it entails.

The question of the amount the nation spends on museums and galleries would naturally come up for inquiry, and here I can hardly doubt that some of the money which perhaps ought to be saved in other branches of expenditure would be well spent upon this—for in no other direction of its artistic enterprise are results of such value for the general education of the people, produced at so small an outlay as in this. It will, I suspect, be found that as compared with similar institutions in some other countries our museums are starved. The salaries of the staffs are, moreover, not of a kind to attract the best talent, or would not be, but that in this respect the State is probably served better than it deserves, owing to the tradition of disinterested and devoted service which has sprung up in some of these institutions. But devotion is not by itself enough, and there can be no doubt that want of funds often prevents these men from exercising the functions demanded of them in the best possible manner. To take a simple instance of the kind of question that should be considered. The nation possesses a considerable collection of Chinese and Japanese paintings, but it has never been thought necessary to allow the officials in charge the opportunity of spending a year or so in the Far East, without which a thorough knowledge of the subject is impossible. If the question were once fairly faced, it would surely be seen that if it was worth while to spend considerable sums in acquiring such objects, it would be a matter of merely ordinary good economy to obtain the fullest possible training for those who have to advise on its expenditure.

What I believe is of the utmost importance is a clearer recognition of the profession of the—and here the tell-tale fact obtrudes itself that we have no English word for it—the recognition of the—one has finally to fall back in desperation on the German—the *Kunstforscher*. It should be realised that the intelligent understanding of the artistic products of mankind is a quite serious profession, and one which requires a very thorough and somewhat special training from comparatively early years. It is a humane study, and one that requires as a basis a knowledge of the humanities, and therefore it could take its place in a liberal education more readily than many subjects which have none the less acquired a status in our Universities. A degree given on such a subject would indeed imply a more liberal education than, let us say, a degree in Brewing. Whilst a great deal of archæological knowledge would inevitably be acquired in such a course of study, its aim should not be purely archæological. It should be rather a course of comparative applied esthetics. The idea would be that the student should acquire such a wide knowledge of artistic form as exemplified in all the various known cultures of the world that, when in presence of any new form, he would recognise its kinship and analogies with other forms belonging to different ages and countries.

We have only to turn to Germany to see that there the possibility of some such training has been partially realised. The result has been a quite extraordinary emancipation from the narrow-minded partialities of traditional orthodoxies. The Germans have been pioneers not only in the matter of archæological research and erudition. Far more remarkable has been their open-mindedness with regard to the products of cultures which had been previously regarded as somehow outside the pale. Probably certain artists were the first to see the esthetic significance of Negro and Polynesian sculpture, but the German *Kunstforschers* were quick to accept the hint from them and to begin the serious study and the careful collection of such works. With no less enthusiasm have they, more than any other people, given to Peruvian and Maya remains the kind of attention which was once regarded as only applicable to European art. This, then, is the point I wish to make. If the study of art-history be carried on as a comparative study of all cultures alike, we get an antidote to the kind of orthodoxies and *a priori* judgments which result from a narrow concentration. The *Kunstforscher* under such conditions attains by another route to something of the freedom of the artist, to whom the object in itself is everything, its historical references of no interest. Now the advantage for art of there being such a body of men with this special but somewhat detached interest in esthetic values is very great. Not only does it mean that the museums would be likely to acquire the most significant objects of any given culture, but these men would exert an influence on public opinion which no one else could. The pure archæologist is too insensitive to esthetic values, the artist is too closely interested in his own particular type of creative effort. To such a body, if it existed, the State could turn for direction and guidance with at least more prospect of a well-pondered and judicial opinion than to any body of men at present constituted in this country. I am far from saying that the German *Kunstforscher* is the ideal of the type ; he is often, of course, narrow-minded and bigoted or minutely specialised, like many learned persons in all countries, but in Germany there has been an approach to such an ideal of detached and scientific evaluation of esthetic objects, and no one can deny that the museums of Germany have benefited largely by the freedom from prejudice and convention which they have often displayed. If one could but find an English word for *Kunstforscher* the battle would be half won.

# CULTURE AND SNOBBISM *

IT is a nice point, and one on which I have never yet been able to make up my mind, whether culture is more inimical to art than barbarism, or *vice versâ*. Culture, no doubt, tends to keep a tradition in existence, but just when the tradition thus carefully tended through some winter of neglect begins to show signs of life by putting out new shoots and blossoms, culture must needs do its best to destroy them. As the guardian and worshipper of the dead trunk, it tries to wipe off such impertinent excrescences, unable as it is to recognise in them the signs of life.

The late Sir Claude Phillips, for instance, pays tribute throughout his book, "Emotion in Art," to the greatest achievements of the art of the past; he exalted and kept alive the memory of Titian and Giorgione, but when he comes to talk of his contemporaries he makes us wonder what he found to admire in the old masters by speaking in almost the same glowing terms of Böcklin and Fritz von Uhde; he alludes to Monet, but he is silent about Seurat and Sisley and Cézanne, not to mention those more modern artists whom also he had every opportunity to appraise.

For this book of reprinted articles makes it quite clear that Sir Claude was a very distinguished High Priest of Culture. The unction of his style was as oil to feed the undying flame in the Temple, and the savour of his epithets rose like incense before its altars. Like many great ecclesiastics, he was also an accomplished man of the world, neither an ascetic nor a prude; like them he enjoyed polished society, good wine, good food, and good stories. He was a charming and witty companion, whose good things were drawn from the vast store of learning and experience which his wonderful memory retained. But like other ecclesiastics, when he entered the Temple indued with his priestly garments, his whole manner changed. His language took on the peculiar unction of almost all devotional writing, and he bowed perpetually before the great gods of his Temple and rarely alluded to

---

* *Vide* "Emotion in Art," by Sir Claude Phillips. Heinemann, 1925.

one of them without some time-honoured and sanctifying epithet.
The very quality of his phrases changed; they took on the liturgical
resonance which relegates sense to a subsidiary position. Perhaps
Ruskin had showed the way, but it was Phillips more than any one
else who framed and consolidated the ritual and liturgical use of the
great Temple of Culture. He borrowed, no doubt, from other
religions, but he adapted with extraordinary tact and skill. Thus it
was that he came week after week to intone in the columns of the
*Daily Telegraph* those reverential, decorous, and richly adorned ser-
vices, some of which are reprinted here. Throughout these pages
we hear " the blessed mutter of the Mass "—a Mass in which the
names of all the deities and saints and all their great works are brought
up in succession. It hardly matters whether Sir Claude Phillips says
anything about their works or not; the main purpose is served if
one after another their glorious names are brought to the worshipper's
mind, in order to arouse his reverent awe and conduce to his edification.
As we read these pages we are conscious of the presence of the Thrones,
Dominations, Principalities, and Powers of the realm of art; we
share humbly and at a distance in that new communion of the Saints.
Almost infallibly Sir Claude strikes the right devotional attitude and
finds the edifying epithet.

One of the well-known signs of this attitude is the reference to
holy beings by some allusive translocution. A well-trained ecclesiastic
having once named Elijah could hardly fail afterwards to refer to him
as the " indomitable Tishbite." The effect of this is admirable, it
assumes that reverent familiarity on the worshipper's part which is
so desirable. Thus, Sir Claude has his repertory of allusions, " the
gentle Urbinate," " the bee of Urbino," " the divine Sanzio," " the
faultless Andrea," " the Frate," " the poet-painter of Valenciennes,"
" the great Cadorine," by which we are, as it were, made free of the
mysteries. Still more significant is the fact that not even the objects
that have to do with the cult may be left without their appropriate
adjective. I quote a passage in which he speaks of dancing in art :
" Akin to these, but perhaps more vigorous still, and with less of
cosmic suavity, are the child-angels who in joyous procession pass
dancing along the front and sides of Donatello's ' Cantoria,' once in
the Cathedral of Santa Maria del Fiori at Florence, but now in the

little museum at the back of that mighty church." Here the information given in the last phrase is, of course, quite irrelevant to the argument, but it seems to bring up vague memories of holy things, and, what reveals the attitude, even this little scrap of topography helps to elevate us by reason of the insertion of the word " mighty." The true emotional touch is shown by this almost unconscious gesture. But let me quote another passage where the fervour of Sir Claude's Apostolate has more scope :

" And Mantegna, harsh and tender, severe with a more than Roman severity, and yet of a mysticism in devotion as intense as that of any contemporary master, maintains the beholder in realms where the spirit droops and can hardly follow. The sublimity of Michelangelo himself is equalled in a ' Sybil and Prophet ' of very moderate dimensions, formerly in the collection of the Duke of Buccleugh ; the ' Infant Christ, as Ruler of the World,' of the Mond collection, stands apart in the quiet intensity with which it expresses worship on the one hand, and, on the other, the irradiation of the Universe by Divine Love. The ' Madonnas ' of the Poldi-Pezzoli at Milan and the Gallery at Bergamo, express, as by hardly any other master they have been expressed, the sublime devotion, the tragic apprehension, of maternal love that is all human and yet in its immensity Divine. Face to face with his ' Adoration of the Magi ' (formerly in the Ashburton collection), we experience the feeling of religious awe, almost of terror, that possessed the Wise Men of the East when, though royal still in splendour and in gravity, they knelt subdued and prostrate in worship at the feet of the Divine Babe."

There surely is the full organ roll of the Anglican liturgy at its best ; see how the very names of Italian towns and of ducal collectors help to swell the diapason, and urge the worshipper to fresh ecstasies of acquiescence.

Decidedly Sir Claude Phillips was a great High Priest in that religion of culture which is so well adapted to the emotional needs of polite societies, and let me add that he had to the full the sense of his sacerdoce. He was the first to denounce any act of vandalism, he was the most scrupulous in avoiding any hint of simony, the most punctilious in the assertion of the claims of his religion, and the most conscientious in their observance.

There remains, of course, the question with which I started, what relation, if any, has this religion of culture to art? Some connection it surely has. It would be impossible for any one to have written these glowing pages unless he had looked long and with some genuine emotion at the innumerable masterpieces whose images he recalls and whose glories he recounts. But so far as I can find, there is no single piece of strictly esthetic appreciation in the whole of this book. Not once does Sir Claude come into contact with the actual vision of the artist. So far, indeed, does his habit of day-dreaming about pictures instead of looking at them go, that in an essay on " What the Brush cannot Paint," he actually says that, " The word-painting of the poet gives as definite a vision as that which arises from the brush-work of the painters." The word " definite " here is, of course, the exact opposite of the truth—the essence, and to a great extent the value, of the poet's image lying precisely in its indefiniteness.

But Sir Claude did not accept definite images from pictures. He allowed the vision to set up in his mind an emotional state in which the vision itself was lost in the vague overtones of associated ideas and feelings. He shows his method when he says : " Not Millais in his ' Chill October,' not even Theodore Rousseau or Diaz, painting the festering herbage on some dark pool of the forest, walled in by the trees from which the last sere leaves drop in the silence, one by one." It matters little how poor the quality of the painting is (and how poor are these he cites !), when this agreeable day-dream with its soothing verbal accompaniment replaces so rapidly the painter's vision.

It is to this that we must look for the explanation of the strange paradox of this fervent hierodule of Raphael, Titian, and Poussin giving his priestly blessing to Böcklin and Fritz von Uhde, and turning aside from the more sincere efforts of modern art to write long rhapsodies over sentimental war-pictures which have already passed into Time's rubbish heap.

No doubt, then, Sir Claude derived a very genuine enjoyment from works of art, but I think that enjoyment was obtained without any direct communion with the artists' sensibility ; what he saw and felt was the dramatic interpretation of the scene and its decorative setting, but most of all he felt the status of the work in question in the hierarchy of art, its cultural value, the exact degree of reverence which it might rightly claim from the devout. Reverence is, indeed, the key to all such religious attitudes, and reverence is, of course, as inimical to true esthetic experience as it is to the apprehension of truth. Reverence, and that goodwill which belongs to edification, may be, perhaps, of use to help the beginner to overcome the first difficulties of approach to what is finest in art, but if he is to get any real esthetic experience, he must learn to eschew reverence and to distrust his goodwill.

This is, indeed, the greatest difficulty of criticism, for past esthetic experiences always tend to stereotype themselves in our minds and set up within us the religious attitude. Sir Claude Phillips not only did not understand this, but would have looked upon such an attempt to react purely and freely in each case as a blasphemy against the whole religion of culture.

I still find I must leave the question open. Picture galleries and museums are Temples of Culture, not of Art. The artist and the esthete use them, no doubt : indeed, they depend on them ; they would, none the less, never have had the social prestige, nor, perhaps, the energy, to have created them. The artist's debt to culture in that respect is immense, but he pays it in full when he discovers that the same social prestige of culture will turn upon him the moment he tries to create along the lines of the tradition which culture has preserved. To the cultured man the unpardonable sin is the creation of just those works which will become the ark of the covenant to some succeeding generation of cultured men.

This question of the part played by culture in a civilisation prompts the similar question of the *rôle* of snobbism. This useful word, the interest which we have received on lending the word "snob" to the French, describes a well-known class of experiences. Snobbery, from which it comes, describes the uncritical and enthusiastic acceptance of certain social values or pretensions, and snobbism should, I think, be kept for the distinct phenomenon of the equally blind acceptance of certain spiritual values or pretensions, whether intellectual or esthetic.

Can we distinguish between culture and snobbism ? In both a certain religious attitude of worship is evident, and they are concerned largely with the same values. In both, too, communion with fellow worshippers is a matter of supreme importance, so that it is not always an easy matter to say of a particular act of devotion or article of faith to which Church it belongs. It may, indeed, partake of both, since these are not mutually exclusive doctrines.

There is, however, I think, a difference of mental attitude which the words enable us to distinguish. The snobbist, by his pilgrimage to the " right " picture gallery at the " right " moment, and his display there of the " right " enthusiasm before the " right " works of art is really upheld by the consciousness that those acts bring him into close communion with a certain group of people, and it is not altogether remote from his consciousness, although, perhaps, kept below its surface, that those people are socially influential. His acts tend to make certain that he will be " in the swim." It is this subtle connection between a certain esthetic creed and its social adherents that is, perhaps, too frankly revealed by the word " snobbism." The man of culture, on the other hand, lives in a world more detached from these considerations. His communion is not only with the living. By his acts of devotion he unites himself to a long line of historical precedents. He upholds the tradition which sensitive and contemplative spirits have handed on from generation to generation. And, since the verdicts of esthetic sensibility have a tendency to violent fluctuations, this traditional esthetic doctrine has called to its aid the steadying influence of learning and scholarship. So that the devotees of culture often acquire more merit by what they know about the history of a work of art than by what they feel in front of it. To them an artist does not become a serious artist until a learned monograph has been consecrated to his life work. Thus the cultured, linked to the past by a long line of predecessors and filled with a sense of responsibility for the future, tend to adopt a conservative attitude to contemporary art. Their imprimatur must not be lightly given. They yield in the end, and become the guardians of what they resisted, judging, perhaps rightly, that only its irresistibility justifies this consecration. The snobbist, on the other hand, whilst always respectful of learning, is too anxious to know the latest word to await its judgment. He tends, therefore, to march in step with the vanguard of any esthetic movement as soon as its victory is no longer in doubt. Until victory is fairly in view the movements of the true snobbist afford a fascinating spectacle, he—or perhaps she, for, thanks to the quicker social sense of women, they form the greatest and most devout part of the communion—shows the greatest anxiety and trepidation. A too overt adherence to the new doctrine at such a moment would precipitate him along a social blind alley and leave him in a position from which recovery is difficult and sometimes slightly ridiculous. On the other hand, to be left behind on the right track, though a fault more easily repaired, is to miss a supreme opportunity.

In thus describing some of the familiar experiences of modern life which affect the production of works of art, I have, I confess, a little over simplified for the sake of clearness. The situation is never so definite as I have suggested. To represent the true facts we must allow for the admixture in infinitely varying doses according to temperament and character of genuine esthetic feeling. Since social facts are of supreme importance to people's lives the social sense is likely to be more alert and potent than the esthetic, but it not unfrequently happens, especially with the young, that, impelled at first merely by a vague, and in itself respectable, instinct to share in the most vivid life of the day, not to be too much " out of it," they do acquire a genuine appreciation of works of art and pass through snobbism into the ranks of that small group of amateurs—in the proper sense of the word—whose influence is most profound in the creation and survival of works of art.

What is most to be admired in culture is its love of the contemplative attitude and its passion for exact scholarship. Its besetting sin is an over-cautious timidity, its desire for security above everything, its fear of life. Snobbism, at least, has the merit of trusting to the life of the moment with a certain recklessness. The roads of culture have been long laid down and are well patrolled, the snobbist follows into newly opened territory, and however anxiously he watches events, is bound to miss a genius or back a dud now and again.

Primarily, however, we are not concerned here with the psychology of the cultured or snobbist, but with the effect on art of their varying influence. And this can hardly be exaggerated, since the emergence and survival of any particular work of art are, I believe, as strictly conditioned by its ambience as is the emergence and survival of a type of animal or plant.

The artist, in whose breast the divine flame is kindled, finds himself confronted, then, with these two religions of culture and snobbism. But he is also aware of the presence of a vast inert mass, the great body of Philistines. These are the esthetic atheists who own no obedience to any doctrine, whose only allegiance is to their untutored and wayward satisfaction. These he regards from the first as enemies; but they are his frank and loyal enemies. Mr. Podsnap's view of the arts he knows. It is clear, concise and perfectly intelligible. Dickens has explained it once for all in the following terms :

" Mr. Podsnap's notions of the Arts in their integrity might have been stated thus. Literature ; large print, respectively descriptive of getting up at eight, shaving close at a quarter-past, breakfasting at nine, going to the City at ten, coming home at half-past four, and dining at seven. Painting and sculpture ; models and portraits representing Professors of getting up at eight, etc. Music ; a respectable performance (without variations) on stringed and wind instruments, sedately expressive of getting up at 8, etc. Nothing else to be permitted to those same vagrants the Arts, on pain of excommunication. Nothing else To Be—anywhere ! "—(" Our Mutual Friend.")

The artist knows, then, exactly where he stands with the Philistine. With culture, too, his position is ascertainable. He finds himself, indeed, inspired and consoled by the great tradition which culture guards and proclaims. Through culture he is made free of the great art of the past and is encouraged to emulate its glories. It is only when he proceeds to do so that culture turns on him a sterner aspect. In imitating the attitude of the great masters he cannot possibly repeat their results, and thereupon the Grand Inquisitors of Culture scent heresy and make ready the *Auto da Fé*.

In this quandary snobbism alone appears to hold out a succouring hand. To express anything at all is a crime with the Philistine, to express anything vital is a crime with culture, among the snobbists alone novelty may, under certain circumstances, be a positive virtue. It must be a novelty that is not altogether unprepared for, it must go further along a track to which snobbism has recently become habituated. Then, and then only, the snobbist will help with unstinting generosity.

The artist, then, is likely to find in snobbism his most potent ally, but, as happens in other alliances, he is likely at times to feel more kindly towards his open antagonist the Philistine than he does towards an ally whose activities are capricious and uncertain. He will find snobbism always pressing forward to catch the last word, far too eager to see any point in subtle or unobtrusive work. He will find it continually the victim of charlatanism and advertisement, or even where, as may well happen, it has accepted genuine talent, doing so with so undiscriminating an enthusiasm that only the strongest and purest natures can resist its dangerous seduction. His indignation will be the greater in that in its light-hearted way snobbism distorts the values and confuses the issues in just those things that he most cherishes, until he may come to regard it as the abomination of desolation desecrating his holiest places.

What I have elsewhere defined as the " Opificer " * is backed by considerable funds, both from the patronage of the State and other public bodies, and from the private patronage of the Philistine. But the pure artist finds that, apart from the support of those few individuals who not only have cultivated by careful study a natural love of art but possess the means to gratify their passion, almost the only fund on which he can rely depends on the favour of snobbism. At rather rare intervals in modern life this favour has been actively exercised, and when such a situation arises, as it has notoriously of late years in Paris, the enthusiasm of the snobbist has stirred to activity a crowd of speculative buyers who hope by spotting the winner in the field of aspiring talent to reap fabulous profits.

The artist, too, in so complex a world must be upheld by a religious conviction, an unwavering faith by which to steer his course among the devious currents of modern civilisation. Since he is in a small minority his creed will always tend to have a protestant tinge. He is a protestant against the materialism of Mr. Podsnap, against the pontifical authority of the high priests of Culture, and against the capricious interferences of Snobbism. His religion, too, is a very intimate personal affair, it compels him to the assertion, often with fanatical vehemence, of his private values. He is a member of no wide communion—may, indeed, shun all communion whatever, though more probably he links himself in a close alliance with the few who share his convictions.

* *Vide* " Art and Commerce." Hogarth Press, 1926.

It is to Paris of the mid-nineteenth century, from 1830 to 1870, that we must turn to study the heroic period of this religion, the epoch of its great saints and martyrs. There we see to what a pitch of ecstasy and devotion this faith could raise its votaries. It was the age when Daumier produced almost day by day, for some infinitesimal sum, masterpieces of tragic irony which made ministers tremble with rage and hate, and landed him in prison : it was the age when the Odéon was run by a director madly in love with poetry, who, backed by a troupe of famished but heroic actors, produced romantic plays one after another in the face of the outraged bourgeoisie and the frenzied enthusiasm of the Bohemians : it was the age when the fervour touched even the cafetiers and restaurant keepers, and a Mère Cadet would extend credit year after year, without a hint or a frown, to her penniless clients : it was the age when through the thousand accidents of open-air life in the streets and gardens of Paris the faithful, whether poets, actors, painters or musicians, discovered one another by almost invisible signs, and cemented life-long friendships on the strength of a chance word.*

It was an age when snobbism scarcely existed or had not as yet tendered its munificence to the genuine artist. He, indeed, had to rely entirely on the far slenderer aid which disinterested but passionate amateurs could afford him—and these, it must be remembered, are always the decisive factor in the highest kinds of artistic creation—and on the unstinting generosity with which the faithful helped one another out of their own poverty.

And here we touch on a curious economic accident the importance of which as a determining condition of art production has never been properly emphasised. In modern life great works of art have generally been, and, I suspect, almost must be, produced in defiance of the tastes and predilections of society at large. The artist, therefore, except in those cases where he possesses inherited means, must be able to live and function on an extremely small sum. He must exist almost as sparrows do, by picking up the crumbs that fall from the rich man's table. That is to say, that Bohemian life, a life deprived of all superfluous and unnecessary elements, must not be too degrading, and must leave those who follow it some amenities, especially the possibility

* *Vide* the story of Emile Deray in Theodore de Banville's " Mes Souvenirs."

F

of meeting and exchanging their impressions and convictions. These conditions are fulfilled only where the standard of life in general is not too exacting. At first sight it may appear to make no difference whether the rule of life is, as in the United States, that salaries are high and prices and profits are also high, or, as in France, that salaries and prices are both low. But, in point of fact, one condition, the American, is fatal to the existence of a true Bohemia, and the other is propitious. In the case of America the sum necessary to support life is a large one, and though it can be earned with proportionate ease it can only be earned by some work the value of which society can recognise at once. In the case of France it is, or certainly was in the nineteenth century, so small that it might be picked up by part-time work at any one of the smaller crafts of industrial design for which France is conspicuous.

The highly organised production on a grand scale of America, with its large wages and high profits, leaves far fewer of those interstices in the social system into which the artist can insert himself, than does a society based on a multiplicity of small and individual producers. Here, indeed, we touch on one of those small accidental factors in social life which may exercise a decisive influence on artistic production. What wonder, then, that periods of artistic creation and impotence are as hard to predict or account for as the weather itself! Hitherto we have not made anything like as strenuous an effort at estimating and calculating these forces and conditions, doubtless because societies always tend to regard their spiritual products as superfluities. And yet there is a certain irony in the fact that every civilisation is ultimately judged by what of spiritual value it has contributed to the human patrimony. It is only at each present moment that this appears to be of so little consequence as to be negligible by the governing class.

# SOME ASPECTS OF CHINESE ART

ALMOST every work of art comes to us with some letter of introduction or other. There is almost inevitably some intermediary who or which modifies the state of mind with which we approach the interview. If it is a modern work it may be by an artist whom we know and like personally, and at once we are prepared to give it the benefit of every doubt. It may be by an artist whose work has previously bored or irritated us, and the chances are a thousand to one against our giving it a patient hearing. It may come to us with the romantic thrill of intense antiquity, and we feel inclined to make every allowance for a man who took the trouble to live so very long ago and yet to be a quite recognisable human being not altogether unlike ourselves.

It may belong to some exotic civilisation which has already in quite unrelated and accidental ways stirred our imagination, and we are in a hurry to find confirmation of all our past emotions. Or it may be just the contrary, the strangeness, the foreignness of the conceptions may repel us by hinting from the first at what a lot of trouble we should have to take to get sufficiently familiar with the religious or philosophical ideas which we dimly guess at behind the artist's iconography.

There is no doubt that some of these accessary feelings which cluster round a work of art, like the patina on an ancient bronze, may have a genuine value for our imaginative life, but it is also certain that we cannot make full contact with a work of art, cannot really come to terms of intimacy with its creator, until we have recognised and made allowance for this intervening medium.

When we are considering works of Chinese art this intervening medium tends to distort our vision in various and sometimes contrary directions. There are still, I believe, many people well acquainted with some aspects of European art who yet feel that the Art of China is strange to them. They lack a clue to direct them in so unfamiliar a world. They may know but little of Christian hagiology, but at least the names of the Christian Pantheon are familiar to their ears, whereas they have no feelings at all about Avalokatesvaras, Amidhas and Arhats. Again, the whole Chinese symbolism will be unintelligible to them. They know, perhaps, that the dragon is symbolical of the heavens, but they do not feel any point in the symbol, being familiar with dragons only in quite other settings. It may well be that this remoteness of subject-matter in Chinese art makes them feel it is a closed book to them. They may feel happy enough in the presence of the trifling bibelots, the Chinoiseries of later periods, which have become acclimatised in our drawing-rooms, but the great art, above all the early religious art, will repel them by its strangeness.

Now, I believe this is a mistaken fear. Chinese art is in reality extremely accessible to the European sensibility, if one approaches it in the same mood of attentive passivity which we cultivate before an Italian masterpiece of the Renaissance, or a Gothic or Romanesque sculpture. A man need not be a Sinologist to understand the esthetic appeal of a Chinese statue. It may represent some outlandish divinity, but it is expressed according to certain principles of design and by means of a definite rhythm. And it so happens that both the principles of Chinese design and the nature of their rhythms are not half so unfamiliar to the European eye as Chinese musical rhythms are to our ears. On the contrary, they are so similar that I could point to certain much-loved European artists who are nearer in this respect to the Chinese than they are to certain other great European artists. Chinese art is nothing like so difficult of access as Hindu art. It has, to begin with, colour schemes that are pre-eminently harmonious to the European eye ; it has the same general notions of logical and clear co-ordination of the parts within the whole ; it aims at a similar equilibrium, and it does not allow the elaboration of detail to destroy the general structure ; whereas in much Hindu art and in some of the art of the Near East, we must, I think, abandon some of these demands and content ourselves with other and, to our feelings, less important qualities, with mere diversity, multiplicity and intricacy.

The distorting influence which I have described will affect us chiefly, then, with regard to those works of sculpture in which the human figure is treated from a religious point of view, to the great period of Buddhist art of the Wei, Sui and early T'ang periods.

When, on the other hand, we are confronted with that large series of early objects of ritual use of which the Chou bronzes are the central type, our attitude is likely to be distorted in other ways. Here, I think, the exotic quality of all very early art, together with the exotic quality more or less present in all Chinese objects, make a favourable appeal. These rich and elaborate bronzes are exotic certainly, but not too exotic. One thinks instinctively of the makers and owners of these bronzes as " quaint," no doubt, but as having an Epicureanism not altogether unlike our own. These Chinese objects have an air of belonging to people who were polite, traditional and sophisticated, and that brings them near to our own ways of living and feeling, more so, I think, than is the case with those odd athletic beings who drank out of the black and red Greek vases. With them we hardly know when Epicurean habits might not suddenly give way to explosive irruptions of passion. But with the Chinese, I feel sure that even if one had been put to death at the end of a feast with a dignitary of the Chou Empire all would have been conducted with reassuring decorum to the very last, for the Chinese have something very safe and comfortable about them which even the grinning monsters' faces on their bronzes do little to dispel. It is this, surely, that makes their objects, even those of the remotest antiquity, fit so comfortably into our own homes.

There is a great delight in enjoying the exotic thrill without stirring from one's own armchair, and this being so, we have the added thrill of antiquity. The imagination of our times is, it would seem, more easily and instantly stirred by great antiquity than by any other appeal. The historical sentiment must be universal for Tutankhamen to become a music-hall favourite. So here, too, we are put into an indulgent frame of mind before these works of art, which makes a severely exact appreciation of them difficult. And the Chinese, I think, complicate the matter themselves by their excessive love of ritual, and I mean by this, esthetic rather than religious ritual.

One feels that one must be a little on one's guard with people who invented the " tea ceremony," people who deliberately hypnotised themselves into an attitude of expectant esthetic adoration. They would say, no doubt, that this hypnotic business of walking along the garden path in silence to the tea-house only served to produce a due receptivity, only put one into a favourable attitude. But that is just it; they are always getting one into too favourable an attitude, hypnotising away one's critical common sense. They have a way of making things seem precious even before they are cunningly mounted and tastefully displayed.

I know that all these remarks apply still more to the Japanese, but I feel that even with these bronze workers of 500 B.C. you can never quite catch the artist unprepared for you, never see him so completely absorbed in his idea that he does not know you are looking over his shoulder.

Perhaps I am making too much of my suspicions and scruples, but there is no doubt that the impression of almost barbaric clumsiness and crudity which we feel at first before these antique bronzes very quickly yields to a sense of their conscious preciosity. That very roughness seems to be the expression of a highly trained sensibility to the quality of the material. Not but what that is an artistic merit, only it seems most expressive when it comes by accident, as it were, out of the artist's vehemence of statement rather than as the result of deliberate research. At any rate, however far back we go we still find that extraordinary feeling for style which permeates Chinese art. From the first we feel that the Chinese, so refractory to other religions, had adopted as no other race ever has the religion of culture. To culture, indeed, rather than to Philistine indifference, we must attribute, I suspect, that strange atrophy of the creative spirit which has affected Chinese art during the last few centuries.

This excessive reverence for the tradition is so strong that at this day artists in Pekin execute water-colours which repeat almost unaltered the forms of certain Sung paintings. No new aspect of vision compels them to break the accepted scheme. However delicate or intense their feeling towards appearance may be it never bursts the limits of the inherited formula.

The fate of modern Chinese art is, indeed, a warning against the *rigor* which culture may induce. One feels its force to be present from the first, but with these early artists it restrains but does not stiffen their movements. Here, indeed, its influence is felt mainly in a singular poise and moderation. Where there is so much under-lying vigour as these bronze workers of the Chou dynasty evince, it

PLATE XII

Bronze vessel Chou Dynasty, from Imperial Palace of Mukden
By courtesy of Messrs. Yamanaka

only imposes a singular tact and reticence which impresses us as the most distinguished good manners. Look, for instance, at the neck of the jar (Pl. XI.) and note the absence of any emphasis in the two slight ridges which mark it, the clear salience of the lip, which is exactly enough, and only just enough, to satisfy the eye and give a perfect close to the curves of the galb which lead up to it. And in those curves themselves, for all their apparent bareness and simplicity, what variety and flexibility there is ! Look at the firmness and weight of the base, the audacious transition to the belly, and then the gradual and ever so subtle softening of these blunt assertions as one rises to the almost elegant neck. Or again, how subtly the artist has felt the exact relief necessary to make the monster's head (the T'ao-t'ieh) and the two horns stand out from the flat patterning of the jar ! How bluntly and firmly they are stated, and yet with only the least possible relief to enable them to dominate and give life to the whole surface ! This particular specimen of Chou craftsmanship shows an impeccable feeling for proportion. It suggests the happiest equilibrium in the artist's spirit between the vehemence with which he has grasped his idea, the blunt frankness with which he has stated it, and that controlling influence which has made him shun any undue emphasis, any flourish of the virtuoso as a piece of vulgar self-assertion. Such a complete plastic idea expressed with such perfect assurance and ease as we have here is by no means universal in these early bronzes. Not only their decoration, but the forms of the vessels themselves appear to have been often dictated by the exigencies of symbolic statement. Thus, in a vessel in Mr. Eumorfopoulos's collection the body is formed by the fore parts of two rams joined back to back. Sometimes the artist can scarcely reduce all these data to a clearly felt plastic system, and the chief beauty then resides in the richness and perfection of the surface adornment. But the vase shown in Pl. XII., which was formerly in the Imperial Palace at Mukden, is another example of the finest plastic feeling. It is elliptical in section and the contours are everywhere exquisitely rhythmic and free-flowing. The mouldings of base and neck show again the delicate taste and plastic sensibility of the craftsman. No less striking is the treatment here of the T'ao-t'ieh, which is no longer a linear decoration but treated as a fundamental part of the plastic volume, giving it at once greater amplitude and a more vigorous sense of relief. And then, as though all those gentle modulations of surface curvature might leave an impression of weakness, the artist has marked the sides by the almost harsh salience of two serrated ribs and by the positiveness of the knob at the top of the lid. The same idea dictates the knobby modelling of the rhinoceros heads which terminate the massive but gently curved handle. Such play of contrasting effects of rhythm as are here shown indicate a highly developed and perfectly conscious esthetic feeling. Here, if anywhere, in these Chou bronzes we may be allowed to find the indigenous and essential spirit of Chinese art, since, from Han times on, foreign influence of one kind or another has frequently impinged.

It is a curious result of our newly recovered memory of all those thousands of forgotten years that we should have to regard as essentially Chinese objects like these bronzes, so very different from the peculiarly agitated flamboyant silhouettes which the eighteenth century grafted readily enough on to its own rococo. Then the Chinese flavour was as clearly marked and distinct as the smell of a Chinese cabinet. Now we are hard put to it to recognise, and still more to define, any common fundamental and persistent characteristics.

It would, indeed, be surprising if one could generalise readily about the art of so vast a territory, extending through such long periods of human history, so that if I do now attempt to make certain generalisations, it is rather with a view to pointing out lines along which our attention may be profitably directed than in the hope of establishing any important general principle.

The first thing, I think, that strikes one is the immense part played in Chinese art by linear rhythm. The contour is always the most important part of the form.

To take their painting, to begin with. No doubt European painting started on a linear basis, and no doubt it frequently returns to it, but from very early times the linear rhythm began to be influenced by other considerations, and as our knowledge of external appearance progressed, or rather as we absorbed more of it into the material of the painter's expression, the linear rhythm became more and more subordinate to other considerations. When we come to Rembrandt it is hard to say that any linear basis survives. Now, a Chinese picture,

PLATE XI

Bronze sacrificial vessel.  Chou Dynasty.        Collection of Mr. Takeuchi (Tōkyō)

even of the later and more highly sophisticated periods—and, by the way, Chinese art seems to have been sophisticated from the remotest antiquity—never loses the evidence of the linear rhythm as the main method of expression. And this is only natural, the medium used being always some kind of water-colour, and the art of painting being always regarded as a part of the art of calligraphy. A painting was always conceived as the visible record of a rhythmic gesture. It was the graph of a dance executed by the hand.

This predominance of linear rhythm is felt in all Chinese decorations and even in sculpture. In sculpture it makes itself felt in the emphatic continuity and flow of the contour and in the treatment of drapery, which is often rather inscribed on the form than modelled as a plastic element. And wherever such drapery is inscribed or however it is indicated, the direction of the folds takes on the character of a linear rhythm.

Secondly, the linear rhythm of Chinese art is peculiarly continuous and flowing. It is never so flaccid as Hindu rhythms, nor is it ever so harshly staccato, jerky and broken as certain rhythms with which Europe is familiar. There is nothing in Chinese art as ungracious and literally shocking as the rhythms of fifteenth-century sculpture in Germanic lands and of contemporary painting of the Netherlands. It hardly ever attains quite the refinement and nervous subtlety of the rhythms of certain early Persian draughtsmen, but it is more closely akin to that than any other. Certainly to our eyes the linear rhythms of the Chinese artists present no difficulty. We are familiar with very similar ones in much Italian art. The contour drawing of certain pictures by Ambrogio Lorenzetti comes very close indeed to what we can divine of the painting of the great periods. Botticelli is another case of an essentially Chinese artist. He, too, relies almost entirely on linear rhythms for the organisation of his design, and his rhythm has just that flowing continuity, that melodious ease which we find in the finer examples of Chinese painting. Even Ingres has been claimed, or denounced, as the case may be, as a " Chinese " painter ; and with some reason, for he, too, holds intensely to his linear scheme, and, however plastic the result, even the plasticity is effected more by the exact planning of the linear contour than by any other means which the European can rely on.

It would be a mistake to suppose that because the Chinese rely on their linear rhythms, their paintings are flat, like the works of some modern pre-Raphaelites. On the contrary, they show a keen feeling for the volumes which their contours evoke, and avoid anything in the nature of the rhythm or in the manner of drawing it, which will check the idea of plasticity, will bring us up, as it were, with a jerk on the surface of the picture.

None the less, the eye is held by the contour by reason of the fact that the artist concentrated his attention on that, relied on that to reveal the plasticity of the whole volume. Chinese painters were never tempted to explore in natural appearances those hints of a continuous plastic weft to which the study of light and shade and atmospheric colour have given so great a *rôle* among the later Western masters.

Chinese rhythm, then, tends to be continuous to avoid very sudden transitions of movement. Its basic idea, especially in early art, is that of the square with rounded angles. See, for instance, the horns of the T'ao-t'ieh (Pl. XI.) and the handle of the jar (Pl. XII.), or the spiral lines which define the shoulders of the beast in Pl. XV. B. The Chinese artists avoid a rigidly straight line as being incompatible with continuity of flow, but they do not like to forget it altogether. They therefore also avoid curves which are segments of a true circle as being too positive and incompatible with the more complex intermediate curves. The galb of the vase in Pl. XI. is eminently characteristic of this feeling. We pass from nearly straight lines at the base to a nearly spherical shoulder, but both are so far modified that the eye can accept it as an unbroken rhythmic phrase.

This peculiarly subtle sense of rhythmic continuity is made evident in a curious way in some objects of the T'ang dynasty in which certain Alexandrine or Roman models have been followed so closely that in the case of certain silver vases one would be inclined at first sight to say that they had come from excavations at Pompeii. But when we look closer we find that everywhere the Chinese feeling has subtly modified the original. It is characteristic of a great deal of later Greek design that it accepts willingly circular curvature. It is this fact that gives to these objects that peculiarly tight, mechanical elegance which was so dear to our ancestors a hundred years ago. An elegance

PLATE XIII

The art of Weaving.   Relief on Campanile, Florence.          Italian sculptor influenced by Giotto

which now appears to us to be distressingly devoid of vitality and elasticity. And so, though perhaps all unconsciously, the T'ang silversmiths must have felt, for, by innumerable minute readjustments of proportion and modifications of the galb they have given to their vases just those qualities which the Greek craftsman lacked. Again, in those T'ang dishes, which so strangely anticipate our rococo, the complex bracketed curves are always slightly flattened out as though the finer sensibilities of the artist had shunned the effect of rollicking self-confidence which, centuries later, European craftsmen gave to almost identical designs.

Next with regard to the Chinese feeling for plasticity. Here, I think, there is a general tendency which distinguishes it from that of European sculpture. Plastic forms in the round are, I think, always referred, however unconsciously, to some basic mental schema. It seems to me that the Chinese keep as their basic schema and point of departure the egg, whereas the European bases himself upon the cube, or some simple polyhedron.

This becomes clear by the compartation of two examples (Pl. XIII. and Pl. XIV.). I have chosen these from what may be considered great periods of the respective arts. The Buddhist figure of the T'ang epoch is certainly one of the grand conceptions of Chinese plastic art, and the figures from Giotto's " Campanile," in which that artist's influence is generally admitted, are among the greatest of all European sculpture.

Now, both of these are essentially plastic. I mean that in both, the artist is free of the third dimension. This, I need hardly add, is by no means universal in European sculpture, for it is always very difficult for an artist really to create in the round. The imagination grasps easily relations on a flat surface ; it rapidly loses its way in trying to seize relations in three dimensions, since the number of possible movements is so immensely greater. It seems, therefore that the artist is forced to cling to some kind of simple abstract solid form and to conceive his sculpture in terms of a deviation from that.

Now, it is clear that the Italian felt solid form as being constituted of facets. It derives from the cube. Look at the torso of the seated woman, and see how the plane of the breast is felt, and how clearly the sculptor has noted where this plane, with its almost uniform direction, changes into a plane nearly at right angles to it—edge of a cube—where the breast descends to the belly. And compare this with the shoulders and breast of the Chinese figure. It scarcely departs from the abstract egg-shape which permeates almost every part of this design, even to the flower-like base on which the figure stands. Allied to this is the cylinder, another easily apprehended solid form. And, sure enough, the arms are cylindrical, while in Giotto's standing figure we can see the flat plane of the top forearm continued into the back of the hand.

When we Europeans refer to plasticity we talk, naturally, in terms of planes, but I doubt if the Chinese artist has ever conceived of this method of handling plastic form. I do not know what language he uses, but I suspect he would, even in speaking, refer shapes to cylinders, spheres and ellipsoids.

Again, notice the drapery. In the Chinese statue the folds scarcely have any plastic existence. They are inscribed on the surface of the figure and are used to envelope it in an exquisitely lovely system of simple linear rhythms which harmonise with and illustrate the linear scheme of the whole contour.

If I am right, we touch here on some profound difference in the creative methods and in the imaginative habits of European and Chinese artists, but though they affect the creative artist profoundly, these differences hardly ever form a barrier to our appreciation and understanding of the other method.

In this connection it is interesting that among the many instances of Chinese influence on modern Western art we may note a tendency among contemporary sculptors to accept this ovoid schema. Brancusi is, of course, the most striking example. In his work such forms predominate almost exclusively, but even Maillol, in spite of his strong predilection for, and deep study of, Greek sculpture, seems to have admitted ovoid and cylindrical elements into his plastic themes. Maillol's widespread influence on the younger sculptors, both in France and elsewhere, seems likely to fix this character in the European tradition.

In its formal aspects, then, Chinese art, though it has distinguishing characteristics, presents no serious difficulty to our European sensibility. On the other hand, much of its content is inspired by

PLATE XIV

Stone Sculpture of Bhikshu
T'ang Dynasty

feelings which are not easily accessible to us, though the same may be said of much of our own mediæval art.

Perhaps the most striking difference in this respect concerns the habitual attitude of Chinese and Western artists to the human figure and to animal forms.

We inherit from the Greek a peculiar arrogance about the species of animal to which we happen to belong. We have, therefore, devoted a quite special and intensive study to the forms of our kind; we have developed thereby many specialised sensibilities and a mass of associated ideas which we carry in our " unconscious " ready to vibrate in response to the slightest suggestion on the part of the artist. The Chinese have never, apparently, focussed their attention so narrowly on their own species. They have never lost sight of its relative position in the scheme of nature. As a result we are likely often to feel the inadequacy, and from our point of view, the relative insignificance of their figure imagery, though the sculpture shown in Pl. XIV. suffices to prove that at times they could attain to a noble impressiveness in the human form. But what may well counterbalance this defect is the relatively greater sense in the Chinese of the significance of animal and plant forms.

What, I think, strikes one first is the extraordinary vitality of these creatures. These animals have a life of their own, not a life lent them by us after the patronising manner of so much occidental art, but their own odd, unique and strangely unapproachable life. Arrested by our presence in the course of their own business, they look out at us with stupid wonderment, ready to pass into that bland indifference, which we can catch in their regard, if for a moment we lay aside our inveterate habit of supposing the whole universe to be preoccupied with our affairs.

Here, as in so many other of her contacts with nature, China has reaped the advantage of never entertaining that anthropocentric illusion which the greatest of all Western peoples fixed so early and so indelibly in the European mind.

Indeed, one way of grasping the importance and value of the Chinese attitude is to recognise by comparison how entirely it is opposed to the Greek. The Greeks, indeed, were astute enough observers of animal forms; they could render the results of their purely external observations with clear-cut precision, and they could fit them readily enough into their decorative schemes. But we are conscious that the rhythm is preconceived and somewhat arbitrarily imposed, and that in consequence the Greek artist passed from the literal fact of natural form to the stylised result without ever touching the intimate life of the animal itself. Or, more disconcerting still, we find the animal galvanised into a semblance of human life and displaying qualities with which the artist has temporarily endowed him; he becomes proud, haughty, defiant, heroic, cunning or what not: he poses for us with self-conscious deliberation. No Greek ever took the trouble to understand the bovine simplicity of the Buffalo shown in Pl. XV. B or to consider by what means the Chinese artist arrived at such a creation as the earthenware jar of the Chou period, belonging to the Cernuschi Museum. This jar (Pl. XV. A) is hardly modified from a form which came naturally on the wheel, but by a few touches which destroy its rigid symmetry it becomes what, with the hint of eyes and beak in the lid—and what an eye!—we can accept as a humorously convincing conception of an owl sitting, " warming his five wits," with shoulders hunched and feathers puffed.

The Chinese potter who moulded this work persuaded an owl to become a pot without ceasing for a moment to be himself, without bating a jot of his owlishness. He is not forced to serve an alien purpose nor trimmed to fit into a preconceived pattern. The decorative quality, the transposition into the realm of the imagination, here comes out of a sympathetic comprehension of the thing seen. Such a method is the exact opposite of that stylisation which reduces the variety of nature to an *a priori* order by an external and arbitrary act.

Western art, no doubt, has not been without its moments when such a sympathetic penetration to the inner recesses of non-human life was attained. Sassanian art certainly shows a similar spirit which passes now and then into Byzantine, but far more clearly into early Mahomedan work. And something of it undoubtedly recurs in Romanesque sculpture, though Christian anthropocentrism, even more exacting than the Greek which it replaced, quickly stamped it out in all subsequent West-European art. But more than with any other source of animal design, the Chinese has its closest affinities with that Scythian and Sarmatian tradition whose widespread influence

PLATE XV

—A

Bronze Pot in form of Owl.  Chou Dynasty.          Cernuschi Museum

—B

Bronze Buffalo.  Chou Dynasty.          Stoclet Collection

we are only beginning to understand. Indeed, again and again we are conscious of a distinct and alien influence on Chinese art emanating from this source, which after all had its origin not so very far west of China itself. But what, I think, distinguishes the Chinese animalist from others is his highly developed artistic consciousness. Probably the imaginative sympathy with the inner life of animals is a phase of all early human life; but, generally, it seems to have disappeared before men reached the full self-consciousness of civilisation. In China, on the other hand, the civilised consciousness seems to supervene so early that it does not destroy this primeval understanding with the animal world. These Chinese artists, even the earliest of them, are people more or less of our own kind. They are already fully conscious artists; they speak a language of form which presents no barrier to us. The objects which they created seem to be as clearly made for the leisured contemplation, the purely esthetic enjoyment, which we ourselves give to them, as the works of, say, the Italian Renaissance. We need not fear that they are happy accidents, the unintentional by-products of some other activity. We feel that we share the artist's own delight, that we can establish a communion with his spirit. He reports to us in our own language that dim sense of continuity with nature, the memory of which was lost so long ago by our own ancestors.

In China, that spirit of detachment from the human point of view which enabled the primitive comprehension of non-human life to survive, persists under civilised conditions. The sentiment of intimacy and kinship with animals naturally grows less as the primitive feeling is at last forgotten. Here and there, from the Sung dynasty onwards, we find it replaced by a purely picturesque and external curiosity such as modern European art habitually displays. But even as late as Ming times an echo of that earlier sympathy with animal life occasionally survives.

Not altogether unconnected with this attitude to animals, and at least as strange to the Western mind, is the absence in Chinese art of the Tragic spirit. Whilst their fun is sometimes almost childishly naïve and exuberant, their gravity is never altogether untouched by humour. A Michelangelo is unthinkable in the atmosphere of Chinese art; still more, perhaps, an El Greco, letting himself go whithersoever the exaltation of his fevered imagination carried him. This kind of exaltation, this dramatic intensity of human feeling, seems unknown to the Chinese. Their most exalted religious feeling leads them into a more contemplative mood, one more remote from possible action than ours. It is a mood, too, which admits of a certain playful humour which we are not accustomed to associate with such states of mind.

These characteristics are connected, no doubt, with that happy disinterestedness of which I have spoken. It, too, is the reward of not having fallen into the habit of human arrogance. Since, the Chinese might argue, the world does not revolve round us as its centre, we need not take either the world or ourselves too seriously. We can afford to play. We can play with the offspring of our imagination. They shall be our playthings and our delight. We need not take even them too seriously. If we like to imagine monsters, we will, but, however real we make them, we need not be frightened by them. They are only being terrible in play. And so it comes about that however portentous Chinese monsters may be, they are never tragic, like the progeny of our mediæval fancies. The mediæval mind frightened itself by its own activity. No one could apply the word " Dantesque " to a Chinese creation.

Even the beasts of the Chou dynasty, like the Buffalo (Pl. XV. B), do not, in spite of a certain clumsy ferocity, really belie this attitude. Everywhere I find, underlying the actual invention, this strain of sly, discreet humour. It is consistent with a grave dignity of mien and that weighty austerity of plastic rhythm which is characteristic of the great creations of art.

In later times, this humour, which gives so subtle a flavour to the gravity of the early bronzes, comes more and more to the surface. Already in the work of the L'iang dynasty there is a certain conscious elegance of treatment which begins to betray the secret too much. For the most part the T'ang artists hold their hands, though some examples of monsters show a great exuberance. Finally, in Ming times, the humour has lost all its sly irony, it becomes evident and bursts into a laugh, or perhaps a giggle, in many of the porcelain bibelots of the time. But though the particular mixture of fancy, ingenuity and fun which is the mark of Chinoiserie, is often rather tiresome, it is the outcome of a profound and constant feeling which gives its peculiar flavour to the graver rhythms of the great epochs. It is one aspect of a playfulness and detachment which are inherent in the Chinese spirit.

The Greek who fixed the chains of anthropocentrism upon us gave us none the less its antidote in science, and modern science has perhaps, by its repeated blows at our arrogant assumptions, at last prepared the Western mind to accept the freedom and gaiety of the Chinese attitude. The influence of Chinese art seems to be continually increasing in the West, and nothing could be more fruitful to our art than to absorb something of the spirit—though it is to be hoped we shall not copy the forms—which inspires the great examples.

Chinese art appealed to Western nations originally almost entirely in virtue of its technical ingenuity, its brilliant and tasteful execution, and the " quaintness " due to its unfamiliarity. As we get to know it better, as we explore more and more the great classic periods, we are led to treat it with the same respect and the same concentrated attention which we have to devote to our own great masters if we would apprehend the nature of their states of mind.

G

# FRA BARTOLOMMEO

BAUDELAIRE compared the great names in art to light-houses posted along the track of historic time. The simile, as he used it, seizes the imagination and represents a great truth, but it allows of an interpretation which the limits of a sonnet form forbade him to develope. He takes the lights of his beacons as much for granted as the sailor does the lights of real light-houses. But the lighthouses of art do not burn with so fixed and unvarying a lustre. The light they give is always changing insensibly with each generation, now brighter, now dimmer, and often enough growing bright once more. But we sometimes forget that the lights have to be tended or they grow faint and may expire altogether. For them to burn brightly they must be fed by the devotion of some few spirits in each generation. If that fails for a long period they go out and become one of those dead, ineffectual names which still linger on, obstructions rather than aids to the historical voyager.

In the last half-century Fra Bartolommeo's reputation has, I think, tended to become one of those large, non-luminous monuments. He figures always, of course, in any history of Italian art, but the student tends to greet him with a conventional gesture of respect and to pass on, and he seems to arouse but rarely any warmer feeling. There he appears to stand in the coldly impassive perfection of a well-calculated rhetorical gesture.

There is a certain prim ceremonial air about his great altar-pieces, those well-planned scenic effects demonstrative of an orthodox but uninspired devotion, or if he strikes a tenderer, more intimate note, its sentimental effusiveness leaves us cold.

It is noteworthy how dangerous and difficult is the expression in art of religious devotion. Why is it that the expression of this par-ticular sentiment so rarely convinces any but the most credulous and uncritical minds? It is not merely that the devout are rare among cultured modern men, since we can readily accept from art sentiments

82

of which we have hardly any practical experience. The least amorous and the least jealous find their affair readily enough before Romeo and Juliet and Othello, and the most hardened atheist can share the sentiments of the "Divine Comedy" or of Giotto's frescos. But, none the less, the vast mass of devotional art rings false to the ordinarily sensitive mind. Only by a violent exercise of goodwill could any one find illusion before the imagery of a modern Roman Catholic church or even the stained-glass windows of a Protestant cathedral.

And Fra Bartolommeo was not only a monk of St. Mark's, but evidently a devout one, and probably even, thanks to the dominating influence of Savonarola, passionately and intensely devout. How is it that so little of that passion which illuminates for every spectator the imagery of his great predecessor in the same convent, comes through in the work of Fra Bartolommeo? There is no reason to doubt the sincerity of his feeling, and yet the forms it takes are suspect. This, I believe, is due to the fact that to a great extent the religious imagery of succeeding ages has consecrated in dull conventional repetition the forms of the High Renaissance, modifying them from time to time, it is true, but always in the direction of a grosser vulgarity and a more effusive insincerity. For if we try to divest ourselves of all such associated ideas it is possible, I think, to feel that Fra Bartolommeo is generally extremely straightforward and honest in his expression of emotion. In this matter of reading the sentiment of a picture we are very much dominated by certain generalised impressions. Thus, for us, almost all the art of the fifteenth century appears to have sentimental honesty because we associate such naïveté of form with a corresponding naïveté of mind. But if one takes the trouble to compare Filippino Lippi's "Apparition of the Virgin to St. Bernard" in the Badia at Florence with Fra Bartolommeo's picture of the same subject in the Academia, the result is rather surprising. In spite of the fact that this is even for Fra Bartolommeo a rather operatic conception, Filippino Lippi manages within the more restrained limits of fifteenth-century design to be more sentimental as regards gesture and expression. Filippino's child angels satisfy more fully the modern Christmas-card sentiment than Fra Bartolommeo's agitated and piquant *corps de ballet*. Filippino's St. Bernard shows his ecstasy in gestures of hand and poise of head with an almost maudlin abandonment which from this point of view compares but ill with the *tenue* and restraint of Bartolommeo's.

The fact is that Fra Bartolommeo was one of the first to discover the new conception in art of three-dimensional movement, and the desire to exploit this new power over the rendering of the figure tempted to those emphatic poses which we associate with the theatre, and which have an effect of conventional rhetoric on our minds. One cannot deny that in his great set-pieces he is rhetorical in much the same way as Michelangelo is, but his rhetoric has always a certain restraint and dignity: if it is a theatrical convention it is in a good tradition.

But apart from this, which, of course, does imply a certain unreal emphasis, it seems to me surprising how genuine and direct his expression of sentiment is, and how convincing his types are. It would, of course, be absurd to claim for him that he is one of the great masters of the "characteristic" like Donatello or Signorelli, but, on the other hand, that exalted and ceremonial mood which his great altar-pieces convey is not compassed, as it frequently is, by a mere generalising and smoothing down of all character. His women, in particular, are almost sharply personal and distinct, as full of their own special life as the more individual figures of fifteenth-century art. The air of abstraction which one feels before some of his works comes far more from the unreal and theatrical nature of the general idea than from any lack of vitality and consistence in his characters.

As regards the sincerity and quality of his attitude to life as revealed by the expression of sentiment in his pictures, Fra Bartolommeo compares very favourably with Raphael, who, working along similar lines and in many ways under the monk's influence, gave a far stronger and more unrestrained emphasis to those aspects of feeling which we stigmatise as sentimental. And being much more frankly and vulgarly sentimental, Raphael tends to be more trivial and, the word is hardly too strong, on occasions, silly. Both artists treated the motive of the Holy Family in the same mood of *attendrissement*, and both used on one occasion the rather tiresome conceit of making the infant St. John play with a small cross which he has made of two pieces of wood, and show it to the infant Christ. The poses of the children in Raphael's picture show a simpering affectation of childish innocence which destroys all illusion, whereas in Fra Bartolommeo's the essential vapidness of the idea is almost redeemed by a kind of childish dignity and naturalness in the poses.

Here and there, in the head of St. Simeon in the " Presentation in the Temple " at Vienna, and perhaps in the infant Christ of the National Gallery " Holy Family," one may admit that the emphasis is overdone, but in general it seems to me unfair to accuse Fra Bartolommeo of sentimental exaggeration or of being dully conventional in his devotional attitude. That he is frequently rhetorical it would be absurd to deny, but rhetoric hardly seems out of place in those pieces where, as in the " Salvator Mundi," a theological doctrine is pictorially declared or in essentially theatrical *tableaux vivants* like the " Mater Misericordiæ " at Lucca, or the " Marriage of St. Catherine " of the Louvre.

The position that the last-named picture has occupied in the long gallery of the Louvre is indicative of the comparative neglect into which Fra Bartolommeo has fallen. It hangs, and for many decades has hung, in a particularly dark part of that hopelessly dark northern wall, whilst many a quite inferior primitive basks in the light on the other side. I suspect that, apart from those reasons for this neglect which we have examined and found for the most part ill-grounded, Fra Bartolommeo's very merits count against him. We are still really infected, in spite of the gallant efforts of recent years to attain to a classic point of view—we are still infected by Romanticism, we are a little suspicious of perfection, we still demand that the *élan* of the imagination shall rush the creator into some accidental and unconsidered statement. We demand this almost as a guarantee of good faith and as a proof that he is not too completely in control, that he does not rely on cold calculation for his effect.

Now, Fra Bartolommeo was undoubtedly one of the pioneers and one of the greatest exponents of the most perfectly consistent system that pictorial art has ever produced. In that system all those aspects of nature which had hitherto been explored were used with the fullest consciousness of their effects. Moreover, they were of such a kind as to lend themselves to the most completely logical and intelligible organisation into a strict pictorial unity. When, later on, new aspects of appearance forced themselves on the artist that particular unity broke down and fresh systems of design had to be discovered; but the art of the early sixteenth century in Florence shows the culmination of the complete organisation into pictorial form of a long series of discoveries in appearance which had become by then familiar enough to be capable of perfect co-ordination within the scheme. That system was based primarily upon the plasticity of the human figure, and it required that that plasticity should be as complete and as free as possible. By free I mean free of what one may call the tyranny of the picture plane. In all primitive art the picture plane tends to determine to some extent the artist's choice of pose for his figures, since he finds it always easier to express forms whose greatest extension is parallel to the picture plane. An arm fully extended in that plane is more readily described and more easily recognised than one pointing straight at the spectator, where every part is in the most violent foreshortening possible.

Ever since the discovery of the laws of perspective early in the fifteenth century Florentine artists had been experimenting in the direction of representing clearly and completely movements of the figure at various angles to the picture plane. One can see Paolo Ucello's naïve attempt at it in the figure of the dead soldier lying on the ground in the "Battle of San Egidio," in the National Gallery. Michelangelo and Leonardo in their rival cartoons for the decoration of the Palazzo Vecchio, gave what was probably the first exposition of that complete freedom of plasticity in European pictorial art, but Fra Bartolommeo was following close on their track in this direction. In another direction, equally important for pictorial art, he was himself the great precursor and discoverer. Michelangelo was content when he had given to each figure or group of figures that complete freedom of movement and that fullness of relief. He lacked the specially pictorial feeling of creating the imagined space in which these figures evolved. Leonardo undoubtedly possessed this sense to a higher degree, but even he did not design the setting for his figures with any very closely felt relation between the volumes of his figures and the picture space.

And it was in this respect that Fra Bartolommeo showed the fertility and originality of his genius. Already in the fresco of the "Last Judgment" for Sta. Maria Nuova, which he did when he was only twenty-six, the composition which he discovered forces on the spectator a vivid realisation of the space in which the figures exist. Beneath the figure of Christ seated upon clouds Mary and the Apostles appear seated in a semicircular rank seen in perspective from below. It would have outraged not only Bartolommeo's religious but his esthetic feelings to have subordinated his figures to the scenic effect of vast spaces such as Tintoretto conceived later on, but it is surprising how vivid a sense of space is given in spite of the relative size and importance of the figures. Here was the first idea which Raphael took up and developed into the splendid conception of the " Disputà " in the Vatican, enriching it as usual with qualities which Fra Bartolommeo lacked.

From this point on Fra Bartolommeo continued to add one new and fascinating idea of pictorial plasticity to another. In general his great designs have a symmetrical basis, as was almost inevitable with large altar-pieces in view both of the adaptation to the architectural setting and to the dogmatic themes which inspired him. But upon this symmetrical basis he plays with such freedom and felicity of invention that we are never oppressed by the strictness of the convention. Fra Bartolommeo even gets out of this use of symmetry a quite peculiar and new delight. The general idea of symmetry is far too definitely posed in these pictures for us ever to forget it, but he avoids any close similarity in the corresponding figures of either side. Strict symmetry requires exact repetition, but this he avoids, and gives us instead the most ingenious and satisfying analogues on either side, and in such a picture as the " Virgin between SS. John and Stephen " the eye is perpetually intrigued and delighted by discovering with a happy surprise the exact compensation on one side for every unique form on the other. This may be considered as almost exactly corresponding in visual design to the effect of rhyme in poetry. Like it, it sets up anticipations which are, in happy cases, fulfilled in some unexpected way. By subtle adjustments of direction and curvature of contour the balance is always being undone and restored again. Nothing could be less mechanical than this, and yet, for all its freedom, the rigid logic of a strict architectural unity is never broken, and, one may add, nothing could put a greater strain on an artist's inventive powers or his delicacy of perception.

But, above all, Fra Bartolommeo's discoveries tend to the clearest realisation of the picture space and of the relation of the volumes to that space, their situation within it and the vivid evocation of the circulation of air around them which is, in fact, the consummation of their plastic freedom.*

In a great many cases that space is conceived as circular, and this is indicated by the hollow of an apse and even more vividly by the device of a pavilion with curtains upheld by fluttering angels, whilst the same idea is reinforced by the position of kneeling figures in the foreground.

In the " Marriage of St. Catherine " in the Louvre this conception is carried out with a consummate feeling for the relative quantities and weight of the volumes.  Every volume is as simple and as ample as possible, and yet there is no sense of crowding, no constriction of the ambient space.   In this case the symmetry is violently upset by the single kneeling figure of St. Catherine to the left, but is re-established by the light on the apse to the right which by bringing into sharp relief the silhouettes of the figures on that side creates a strong counter-balancing visual attraction.

Another example of the same idea of grouping figures in a circular space is seen in the " Marriage of St. Catherine " in the Pitti (Pl. XVI.). A comparison of this with the Louvre version of the same subject shows how little the subject and even the general disposition determine the nature of a picture and its effect on the imagination.  By a different choice of proportions, by a different " tempo " in the rhythm and by a difference in the number and size of the main volumes as revealed by the incidence of the light, a completely different mood is imposed on the spectator.  Although symmetry is more adhered to in the Pitti picture it is, none the less, more agitated, more lively, and more complex and varied in its movement.  The severity of the Louvre picture is replaced here by a mood of almost jubilant delight which the music-making angels seem to have aroused.  Other works of the High Renaissance may be more inspired, but it would be hard to find any in which the special quality of masterliness is more apparent.  One is astonished at the extraordinary ease with which Fra Bartolommeo handles the most difficult problems of design.  With what assurance

---

* " Rilievo tanto grande che paiono spiccarsi della tavola," as Vasari puts it.

PLATE XVI

Marriage of St. Catherine. Fra Bartolommeo.          Pitti Palace

PLATE XVII

Altar-piece. Fra Bartolommeo.　　　　Lucca Gallery

he conciliates the most difficult aspects of representation with the exigencies of a rigid pictorial framework! It may be doubted whether at any time in the history of painting so many and such complex elements of appearance were co-ordinated into so close knit, so exacting a harmonic system. When, as happened in the seventeenth century, new and more complex aspects of vision were accepted, the rhythmic system became more elastic and allowed of greater deviations, whereas here the interplay and correspondence of linear and plastic moments have to fit together with uncompromising exactitude.

Once again, in the great enthronement of the Virgin and St. Anne in the Uffizi, a similar theme expresses a quite distinct mood, by reason largely of the freedom of space created above and around the figures.

So indefatigable a borrower as Raphael was, was not likely to miss the point of so splendid a pictorial motive as this of Fra Bartolommeo's, and in his " Virgin of the Baldachin " he gives us his version of the idea.

But perhaps the greatest and most original of all Fra Bartolommeo's designs is that in the gallery at Lucca, which represents God the Father in Glory and two kneeling saints below (Pl. XVII.). Here the picture space is conceived as the unlimited expanse of sky rising from the low horizon of a spreading valley up to the zenith. It is an extremely bold and original invention by which this space is, as it were, filled and dominated by the three figures which are thus given superhuman proportions. The two symmetrically opposed saints are here utterly unlike in almost every particular of pose and contour, and yet the balance is perfectly established. Nothing could be happier than the exquisite subtlety and simplicity of the silhouettes of these two figures upon the luminous sky, even the spaces left between seeming to have a kind of formal significance of their own. Moreover, in these two figures he has carried further a quality which his elder fellow pupil and friend, Piero di Cosimo,* was, I think, the first to conceive, namely, to express the full relief and salience of the volumes by some quality of density and weight in the colour itself. Fra Bartolommeo carries this further and with richer resources both in modelling and in the plastic evocations of the contour. The landscape in this picture is of extraordinary beauty and delicacy of feeling.

* See also " Plastic Colour," p. 215.

It is one of the first of modern landscapes, one of the first in which sufficient breadth and unity of effect is attained for it to express a single intense mood. The date of this picture is 1509, and there can be little doubt that it was to his visit to Venice in 1508 that he owed the stimulus to such a poetical conception of landscape. In Venice he may well have met Giorgione, and, indeed, have seen the Castelfranco altar-piece. It was from thence that he brought back to Florentine art the favourite Bellinesque motive of the music-making angels which Raphael was quick to seize on. And it is in the rare landscape sketches of this period that he is most purely Giorgionesque, as, for instance, in the pen drawing of the Albertina, where we see one of the castellated farmhouses of the Veneto nestling under a crag with trees sprouting from the fissures in the rock (Pl. XIX. B); a motive which we associate with Giorgione and the youthful Titian.

That free lyrical vein which we can guess at here and there under the austere and formal perfection and the dogmatic abstraction of Fra Bartolommeo's great altar-pieces, comes out in all its native freshness and delicacy of feeling in two small panels which have the air of being done for the artist's private satisfaction and as a byplay.

One is the exquisitely beautiful little panel in the Johnson collection at Philadelphia (Pl. XVIII. B). It represents Adam and Eve with Cain and Abel as children, in a landscape which seems to have retained more of Paradise than strict theologians would have desired for the fallen pair. It is in its way a unique work. Here, for once, that dream which haunted the imagination of certain Venetian painters, the union of Venetian charm with the great style of Florentine design, has come true. For the invention and drawing of the figures has all the assurance and ease of one of the greatest of draughtsmen, and the landscape is tinged with that lyrical contemplative charm which the Venetians had learned to express. It is unfortunate that Fra Bartolommeo left it but half finished, so that the want of tone in the figure of Adam breaks the continuity of the design. A curious feature of this picture is that of the high-pitched, thatched roofs in the background. Fra Bartolommeo would not find these in Venice itself nor, I suspect, in the immediate neighbourhood, but they were a favourite motive with Giorgione, who brought them, perhaps, from his native Castelfranco. They certainly figure in the very youthful

PLATE XVIII

B
Adam and Eve. Fra Bartolommeo. Johnson Collection, Philadelphia

A
Creation of Eve. Fra Bartolommeo
Collection of Mme. La Durée

works which belong to Sir Martin Conway, and show the landscape of that place. Did Fra Bartolommeo, one wonders, go up into the mountains, or did he merely borrow the motive from Giorgione's pictures? But, even apart from this, the Giorgionesque influence is very marked.

It appears again in the other small panel (Pl. XVIII. A). This picture was first made known in 1924, in the pages of *Le Musée*. I have not seen the original, which appears from the reproduction to have suffered much in certain places. I should very much doubt if the trees were such mere poles as they here appear. They probably had the sparse feathery foliage with which we are familiar in Fra Bartolommeo's pen drawings. But the composition of the figures and their relation to the landscape seem to me at once very original and entirely successful. The group in the foreground, in spite of a certain awkwardness, which so full a realisation of the exact words of the Old Testament imposes, is very felicitous in its rhythmic flow, and the theme is beautifully completed and maintained in the subsidiary group which represents the later history of the family.

This, as will be seen, is a repetition with slight variations of the group in the Philadelphia panel. The landscape shows again Venetian influence in the thatched barn and the rocky eminence to the left, but it is less Giorgionesque in feeling than the landscape of the Adam and Eve. None the less, something of Giorgione's poetic charm survives in the whole conception of this relation of figures to landscape.

Fra Bartolommeo, who comes in for such hard knocks whenever impetuous artists are denouncing the Academics,* might claim some consideration for these two little fantasies, might claim even for once to have struck his own quite personal note of lyric sentiment.

The only work of Fra Bartolommeo's in an English public gallery is the " Holy Family " of the Mond bequest. Here there is no suggestion of symmetry, the composition is based on the balance of movements in an asymmetric group. This is planned as a single plastic whole. The logic of its sequences is lucid and complete, the movements are freely three-dimensional, and it has the grave impressiveness which comes from such plastic design. But nearly as it shows Fra Bartolommeo to have approached Michelangelo's sculptural paintings, he

* He was probably the inventor of the lay figure.

remained after all a painter; and the treatment of the landscape —though it is still a little too definitely a background—betrays his pre-occupation with pictorial as opposed to purely sculptural unity. The recession of the ruined palace behind the Virgin's head is beautifully planned, and the invention of the great upright of the projecting wall to the left is a felicitous one, and emphasises the continuity of the design. The warm luminosity of sky and distance and the beautiful tonality of the right-hand portion are eminently painter-like. This does not show Fra Bartolommeo at his greatest: he needed for that the more formal architectural motive of a great altar-piece. It is to some extent a compromise between that and the small lyrical pieces which we have been considering. Like them, too, the landscape shows Venetian affinities, being far richer and more what we should call romantic in its appeal than was often the case with Florentine landscape backgrounds. There is, perhaps, even a certain want of unity here, a break between the almost picturesque and certainly inviting suggestions of the landscape and the ultra-Florentine formal completeness of the figure group. Besides this, the colour of the figures is almost too heavy and rich for the more delicate handling of the landscape. For in colour also Fra Bartolommeo shows a similar mixture of influences. He based his ideas of colour and his technique in colouring on Leonardo da Vinci's methods. Those methods were conceived rather with a view to the utmost delicacy of modelling in clear-obscure than to the richness of the colour harmony. But Fra Bartolommeo seems to have tried to graft on to this method something of the depth, intensity and purity of local colour which he had observed among the Venetians. Unfortunately he lacked the perfect instinct for colour necessary to accomplish this. Not naturally a colourist he became extremely interested in colour, with a result, which one often observes in such cases, that the artist is satisfied when he has made each local colour brilliant, warm and glowing, and fails to see that isolated local colours, however attractive to the eye each may be, do not suffice to create colour. That depends entirely upon the intensity and inevitability of their relations one to another. Owing to this fact it is often easier to get into touch with Fra Bartolommeo's ideas of design through monochrome reproductions than before the pictures

PLATE XIX

—A

Study in chalk for Visconti Venesta picture
Fra Bartolommeo.                    Uffizi Gallery

—B

Pen drawing.   Fra Bartolommeo.        Albertina, Vienna

themselves, where, as in the National Gallery example, we are put off by the brick-reds of the flesh, the hot greenish blues, heavy crimsons and orange-browns.

But even with regard to the unpleasant effect of much of his colour we must remember that it is due in part to an attempt to use colour more seriously and significantly than had been done by the artists of the Quattrocento. In this he was following the lead of Piero di Cosimo and trying to push that artist's ideas further in accordance with his own more logical, more methodical nature, but without, alas! the guidance of so sure a sensibility for colour as Piero di Cosimo possessed. But then, Piero di Cosimo was one of the greatest and most original of all Italian colourists. None the less that notion that the weight and density of colour ought to correspond to and support the plastic form was a great step towards the completer colour orchestration of later art.

Whatever may be thought of Fra Bartolommeo's colour there can be no hesitation about his drawings. There he shows all his great qualities of imagination. His unfailing grasp of the large essential elements, his unaffected directness of statement, his exquisite taste in choosing always the simplest, most plastic, least elaborate statement possible, and a sheer mastery and nervous control which has hardly ever been surpassed.

And yet it is surprising to see how far he had to travel from what he learned as an apprentice in order to acquire these qualities. For he was, along with Piero di Cosimo and Albertinelli, a pupil of Cosimo Roselli, one of the most mediocre craftsmen of the Florentine school. In that painter's atelier he learned a peculiarly niggly, fussy, purely craftsmanlike technique of drawing. In the early pen drawings he seems to have conscientiously learned to give to every form as many decorative twists and flourishes as possible with neat, bright, sharp and elegant pen strokes. Drapery, in particular, was carefully taught at Roselli's: only the wretched pupil was taught to put in as many folds as possible and to end each fold with a neat little wriggle which was afterwards carefully shaded. With a pen in his hands Fra Bartolommeo tended always to remember something of this horrible virtuosity, as may be seen in the drawing reproduced in Plate XX. A. Although this is by no means an extreme case it suffices to show how unfortunate that tradition was. Apart from that this design shows with what exquisite mastery Fra Bartolommeo could compose the most complex harmonies of volume and movement. In the drawing reproduced in Plate XIX. A we see how much freer his technique with black chalk was, with what breadth and lucidity he establishes his volumes. It is also an astonishingly original and surprising discovery of a design for a tondo, in which perfect equilibrium is attained in spite of the strong asymmetry. It is, indeed, astonishing to think that in one lifetime a man could bridge the gulf between his early pen drawings and such a work as the " Virgin's Gift of her Girdle " in the Albertina (Pl. XX. B), where in freedom of handling in broad illumination of the essential volumes he anticipates the great masters of the seventeenth century.

Fra Bartolommeo's appeal to sentiment is too discreet and perhaps too limited in its range for him ever to be entirely popular, and even that appeal is somewhat obscured for the casual spectator by the evident consciousness and premeditation of his art. He will, I suspect, always remain something of an artist's artist, but as long as European art looks back to the work of the High Renaissance as the greatest exposition of certain eternal esthetic principles, Fra Bartolommeo's light will not die out completely.

Virgin enthroned. Pen drawing Fra Bartolommeo
Uffizi Gallery

*Photo, Alinari*

St. Thomas receiving the Virgin's Girdle. Chalk drawing
Fra Bartolommeo.
Albertina, Vienna

# THE SEICENTO

I LIKE to assert my claim—as far as I know a well-founded one—to have been the first modern English writer on art to turn a friendly, inquiring gaze towards the masters of the Seicento, whose names still re-echoed, but with a dying sound, at the end of last century. I like, I say, to assert this claim chiefly because it clears me of the accusation of benighted conservatism when I express a more guarded enthusiasm for these works than altogether suits recent converts to Seicentismo. Not but what I welcome their zeal, even if I do not share it, because only a zealous devotion can hope to undertake the arduous task of bringing to life again a whole great period of art which has nearly lapsed through neglect from our artistic conscience. The cause of that neglect, which has lasted for more than a century, is, I surmise, the romantic movement. When Ingres and his circle began to interest themselves in the Primitives the art of Cigoli and Albano was menaced, and though Ingres turned away from his early love the movement did not cease. The rediscovery of Gothic art was only part of a great change in the artistic perspective of Western Europe, and the amateurs and art historians of the nineteenth century found work for a hundred years in disinterring all the buried documents and forgotten pictures which have by now provided us with a fairly complete survey of European art from Justinian's day to the latter half of the sixteenth century. There, as far as Italy was concerned, the roll of art history was suddenly cut short. Jacob Burckhardt, whose influence on the taste of his own and the succeeding generation was paramount, whose Cicerone accompanied us to every museum, stood over us with a warning gesture to prevent our straying into the dangerous byways of the Seicento. The amateur was allowed, even encouraged, by the great authorities of the day to cast a slightly contemptuous glance of patronising approval at one or two of Domenichino's pictures because they recalled the work of earlier and more respectable periods, and Italian art came again to a kind of ghostly revival with Tiepolo and Canaletto.

The seventeenth century in other countries—in Holland, Flanders, Spain and France—still survived. Rembrandt was too big to be left out, though the pundits of Italian art felt free to throw insults at him *en passant*, and Velasquez became too dear to certain great living artists to suffer eclipse. But of Guido Reni and Stanzoni and Carlo Dolci and Furini there was hardly ever a word, and one used to read with a mild surprise in old books of travel impassioned discussions on the relative merits of the " tender Bolognese pencil " and " Roman grandeur." It was, in fact, the accident of my study of Sir Joshua Reynolds's " Discourses " that led me first to look with a more open mind at the works which I had hitherto passed hurriedly by in my search for, too often tenth-rate, Primitives ; so difficult is it not to let purely esthetic impressions be overlaid by stylistic partisanship. But it was Dr. Wölfflin's " Kunstgeschichtliche Grundbegriffe," which first made evident the general principles involved in the change which art underwent in passing from the sixteenth century to the seventeenth. It was he who made clear by analysis the new aspects of vision which underlay the various manifestations of Baroque art.

That analysis is, indeed, of such importance for the study of this whole period of art history that I make no apologies for quoting here, with some modifications, my *résumé* of his book in the *Burlington Magazine* by way of introduction to this essay.

Dr. Wölfflin was already well known to art historians by his admirable book on the High Renaissance. That already showed the independence and originality of his attitude. At the very height of our modern passion for the Primitives Dr. Wölfflin showed, by a careful analysis, that the masters of the High Renaissance, who were then under a cloud, had, in fact, made great advances on their predecessors in the direction of formal unity and expressiveness. Unlike so many art historians, Dr. Wölfflin looks at art with some understanding of the problems of the creator. He does not merely see what there is in a work of art, but he knows what mental conditions in the artist's mind are implied by that configuration. In fact, he begins where most art historians leave off. They are content to show that a picture was produced by such an artist at such a date. He tries to show why at such a date and in such surroundings the picture has the form that we see. It is this method that makes Dr. Wölfflin's work of such vital interest to the artist and art-lover, that distinguishes it so sharply from the vast mass of merely industrious compilations which impede progress by irrelevant facts and darken understanding by nebulous theory. Dr. Wölfflin in this book endeavours to show what was the nature of the change from what he calls " Classic art," the art of the High Renaissance, to " Baroque art," which begins with the seventeenth century and persists to some extent in all subsequent periods, though undergoing occasional reactions towards " Classic " ideas.

He considers the change from sixteenth to seventeenth century art the most decisive revolution accomplished in art since mediæval times. Put very succinctly, it is the change from tactile to visual art. This needs some explanation. All painting is in one sense visual ; in the sense, that is, that painters are confined to visible form ; but the painter may use visible forms to describe more than visible experiences. This is what the painters of the sixteenth century did— they found visible forms to express tactile experiences. The forms they drew tended to record a knowledge of natural form more complete than can be attained by the eye alone, or at all events than the eye regarding from a single point of view ; moreover, they recorded also what could be known by touch. One may exemplify this by the figure-drawing of Michelangelo's followers. These artists tended to diagrammatise all that could be known about the body by every means available, vision, touch, and even dissection.

The Baroque painters of the seventeenth century began a process of detachment from the object which finds its ultimate and logical conclusion in Impressionism. They began to confine their visible records of nature to their visual experience, to exclude as irrelevant all facts which, however familiar, had been obtained by other channels than the actual vision before them.

This change of attitude had innumerable and far-reaching effects, not only on painting, but, as Dr. Wölfflin admirably shows, on sculpture, and even architecture. Our author classifies these effects under the following headings : Linear and Painter-like (*Lineare und malerische*) ; Surface and Depth ; closed and open composition ; multiplicity and unity ; clearness and vagueness, or perhaps better, determinate and indeterminate. In all cases the first term is taken

H

as descriptive of the sixteenth-century art—the second applies to Baroque.

There is nothing new in the idea of the predominance of line in Renaissance art as opposed to the pictorial quality of subsequent painting. It may, however, be a little puzzling to those who have concentrated their attention on the Primitives, since, as compared with, say, Botticelli, an artist like Leonardo already appears to suppress the linear definition of the contour under the influence of light and shade and modelling. But Dr. Wölfflin urges that instead of regarding artists like Leonardo as an intermediate term between Botticelli and Rembrandt, we should consider them as the culmination of the linear. The new use of light and shade developed by Leonardo is not really, according to him, on the way to Rembrandt's chiaroscuro. It is rather a new method of more complete realisation of tactile plasticity. In general Dr. Wölfflin regards the High Renaissance as the logical term of a long process. It is the complete realisation of principles dimly apprehended and only tentatively applied in the preceding art.

Thus, for instance, when we come to " surface and depth," the ideal of High Renaissance composition is a sequence of planes each parallel to the picture plane, as opposed to the diagonal, into-the-picture-space composition of the Baroque.

But we must remember that the great masters of the early sixteenth century, particularly Fra Bartolommeo and Raphael, though the general disposition of their designs tended to lie on successive parallels to the picture plane, were intensely preoccupied with the problem of creating the most vivid sense of movements in depth by the poses of their figures and the disposition of their drapery. In this, at least, they bridge the gulf between Primitive and Baroque.

---

Note.—In considering this question of the third-dimensional aspects of painting a certain difficulty arises from the fact that there are so many distinct aspects of third-dimensional representation, and that these sometimes appear to be in opposition to one another. At least it sometimes happens that artists concentrate their attention on one of these aspects and may be led thereby to neglect others. In particular there is the idea of the complete realisation of a single convex volume like the human figure. When this is represented in

In this connection Dr. Wölfflin pointed out that the Primitives had not fully worked out the parallel-plane formula of design, and they frequently stumbled upon diagonal systems without realising

---

a picture in full sculpturesque modelling we have a vivid sense of the relief of one part as compared with the recession of another, we may even have a clear feeling of the contour as a plane disappearing out of sight and leading to the hidden planes behind the figure, the figure may appear vividly to the imagination as a detached volume which we can in imagination pass round. In fixing thus on the third-dimensional aspect of a single volume or group of volumes we may become almost indifferent to what exactly does surround it. We concentrate on it as a solid mass existing in an imperfectly apprehended space. Such a picture becomes a kind of sculpture on a flat surface, and is well exemplified in the paintings of Michelangelo. On the other hand, we may be more deeply concerned with the relative position of volumes within an imagined space. We may be led to realise comparatively weakly the relief of each volume but very vividly their relations of nearness and farness with one another and with the limits of the picture space. If Michelangelo stands for the one-sided concentration on the three-dimensional volume, Raphael has a clear perception of both the three-dimensional volumes and their reference to the enclosing space, but he does not arouse the idea of motion into the picture space to anything like the same degree as later on Baroque artists like Rubens. Rubens tries to increase both elements to their highest degree. Finally, the preponderance in modern times of landscape where the individual volumes exercise a less important influence on the imagination than the recession from the edge of the imagined space. Recession—distance behind the picture plane—usurped the first place with some neglect of the third-dimensionalism and the solid relief of the separate volumes.

But since the study of atmospheric colour and tone have given them new methods of expressing that recession artists have frequently thrown away also the Baroque methods of diagonal composition, etc., and created the idea of recession even with a disposition of planes mainly parallel to the picture plane.*

* See also with regard to this, " Plastic Colour."

their implication. Just as in modern times some Impressionist artists have often tended to revert to a strict parallelism of general plan without any clear consciousness of its implication and without in any way renouncing their preoccupation with recession into the picture space.

It might be thought that the question of Linear *versus* Painter-like concerned only painting. It is not the least of Dr. Wölfflin's merits that he carries on his argument by parallel citations from sculpture and architecture, showing how a change of outlook which was perhaps originally made by painters affected the sister arts. Thus by placing a bust by Benedetto da Majano beside one by Bernini he shows how the earlier master modelled so as to have a continuous visible contour enclosing the form from every point of view, whereas Bernini, by the interpenetration of his ridges and grooves, breaks up the contour and, as it were, withdraws the emphasis of form towards the centre of his mass. The contrast is as great and of exactly the same kind as between a drawing by Dürer on the one hand and by Rembrandt on the other.

In architecture the contrast is not so clearly evident. Dr. Wölfflin is able to demonstrate, however, to what an extent the Baroque architects worked by visual as opposed to tactile methods, by limiting the possible points of view, by building façades in narrow streets where they must be seen in sharp perspective, and calculating the relief of the various elements so as to produce surprising effects of distortion and projection; or again, in more open spaces, ingeniously directing the spectator's approach so that the flatness and symmetry of the building is not felt, and a more varied, more agitated and more pictorial effect is attained.

The question of open and closed composition is full of interest. Dr. Wölfflin shows how carefully the Renaissance masters designed up to the limits of the frame, the rectangle being accepted and emphasised in the design. The Baroque painters, on the other hand, endeavour to disguise the fact of the rectangle, to suggest or even to force upon the spectator, the supposed continuation of the imagined picture space beyond and behind the frame. They hated the compressed design of the Renaissance, they wanted air and space round their figures. This fact receives a curious exemplification, to which Dr. Wölfflin does not allude, in the enlargement of so many of the canvasses in the Louvre. Though I have never been able to get any exact information as to when this was done, I feel pretty sure that it must have been in the seventeenth century. In any case a number of the great masterpieces of the Louvre have been enlarged in this way, with disastrous results. Mantegna's " Allegories," Leonardo's " Madonna and Child with St. Elizabeth," and Giorgione's " Fête Champêtre," are among the most striking. In every case one can see, by covering up the added strip of canvas, how utterly incapable the Baroque taste was of understanding the principles of Renaissance design.

Dr. Wölfflin gives an amusing instance of this want of comprehension of " Classic " principles by later artists. Even the predominance of Baroque ideas never destroyed the admiration for Raphael's " Disputà," and it fell to the lot of some Baroque sculptor to make a bas-relief terra-cotta copy of it. The design of the " Disputà " depends, of course, on the subtly varied symmetry of two equal halves, the two quarter circles of the blessed on either side of the Trinity in the upper part, and the two groups of holy men on either side of the Host below. Now, to the Baroque artist this symmetry, with its static equilibrium, was unendurable, and this particular sculptor struck upon the genial idea of enlivening the composition by taking a side view of the scene and so compressing one half in sharp perspective and opening out of the other, so that the Trinity and the Host should no longer be in the centre of the composition. The result is, of course, grotesque in the extreme.

Dr. Wölfflin, without ever losing the detached and judicial poise of an historical student, evidently regards the visual attitude of the Baroque as the special contribution of the Northern and especially the Germanic races. There is no doubt something to be said for this idea in that the two greatest exponents of Baroque design were Rubens and Rembrandt, while the reaction, of which more anon, found its home in France. But it is a little unfortunate for this part of his thesis that almost the only great Baroque sculptor was Bernini, and the next was perhaps Puget, and neither of them were Germanic personalities. And as to Baroque architecture, no doubt a great deal can be found in Germany and some in Holland—there is, by the way, hardly any in England—but almost the only Baroque buildings that can be considered seriously as works of art are in Italy. Here, too, Dr. Wölfflin has to appeal again and again to Bernini as the only great exponent in architecture of the essential ideas of the Baroque. It was he alone who knew how to mask and distort the actual forms of construction by unexpected illuminations and by exaggerated perspectives, he alone had sufficient mastery to dispose great architectural constructions as easily as a scene painter disposes his cardboard screens, he alone therefore carried to its logical conclusions in architecture the idea of the purely visual in art.

It must not be thought that the Baroque, in giving up tactile experience and confining itself to visual, lost thereby the sense of plastic relief; by a strange paradox it actually heightened the pictorial expression of mass and volume. For though it stated the facts of plasticity with less completeness, having of necessity abandoned an important means of discovering them, its increased understanding of purely visual indications actually increased its power of exciting the idea of plasticity in the spectator. This suggests, I think, the existence of a principle which may be of great importance in any such esthetic history of art as Dr. Wölfflin envisages, namely, that when once artists have fully explored any aspect of nature and have learned how to express it completely by pictorial means, they tend to retain this power even when they apparently neglect the means by which their predecessors arrived at that expression. The experience has become so clearly understood that it is, as it were, taken for granted in subsequent work. An ancient and highly developed artistic tradition like that of modern Europe is thus full of these elliptical phrases which are perfectly apprehended by all those conversant with art, but which are frequently a stumbling block to the uninitiated.

An instance of this principle is before us to-day. Impressionism is, as Dr. Wölfflin says, the complete logical outcome of the visual hypothesis of the Baroque, and in Impressionism we may say that the visual experience is more or less completely stated. Now, a good many Post-Impressionist artists, feeling that this complete expression denies too emphatically the surface unity of the picture, have attempted to express volume and relief by means of the opposition of almost flat tones. It is surprising how successful in this apparently impossible endeavour some modern artists, Matisse in particular, have been.

They appear to throw away all the means by which plastic relief and recession are suggested to the eye, and yet they can create the impression of it. The relief is, as it were, sub-understood. No doubt we are reminded of its existence by our reading of the whole *mise-en-scène* and also by subtle changes of tone, by the quality and handling of the pigment, so that the apparent flatness of a surface of almost uniform colour has a different meaning to us from the flatness of a purely decorative design.

But though the Baroque idea has dominated pictorial art since its inception till its culmination in Impressionism, its rule has not always remained unchallenged. Again and again in these centuries we find reactions to the " Classical " conception. The Baroque explored the visual field with a new concentration of attention and found how to express its discoveries in paint. It created a new and powerful weapon. Unfortunately this weapon could be used with disastrous effects by vulgar natures. It gave the artist the power of creating " illusion." Now, with great Baroque artists the power of creating illusion was always subordinated to an esthetic idea, but there was nothing to prevent mere practitioners in paint from using it to tickle the fancy of the vulgar, and, in fact, this happened almost at once, so that already in the seventeenth century we see the spectacle of a Gerard Dou supplanting a Rembrandt in popular esteem. The old " Classical " art, though capable of producing very bad stuff, never gave its exponents this terrible power, a power which is at the root of all the pseudo or Royal Academic art of modern times.

Now, this tendency of the Baroque to tumble into " illusionism " must have always disgusted the finer natures among painters. And already, in the seventeenth century, we find two striking examples of this revolt. One is Poussin, who deliberately based himself on the " Classical " tradition. Dr. Wölfflin is quite right in saying that he remains none the less a seventeenth-century artist, that his reassertion of the " Classical " style is no longer " Classical," that the influence of Baroque " visualism " is clearly apparent. None the less he reasserts the essential unity of the picture surface, and designs " closed " rather than " open " compositions, accepting, that is to say, the limitations of the frame rather than denying them. And Poussin has remained ever since the rallying-point for those French artists who have from time to time reacted against popular art and reasserted the principles of pure design.

The other great instance is Rembrandt himself. It may seem strange to cite Rembrandt as a witness on this side, seeing that he is himself not only the greatest but in some ways the most Baroque of Baroque painters. None, indeed, was a greater master of illusionism nor of the suggestion of the depth and continuation of the picture space. None the less, towards the end of his life, we find an increasing tendency towards almost " Classical " dispositions. He abandoned more and more those effects of sharp and violent illumination and the suggestion of vast spaces around his figures. The forms tend to fill the picture space, the illumination becomes flatter and simpler, the distinction between light and shade less emphasised, and diagonal composition is less forced. In spite of this the impression of mass and volume is increased because his vastly increased power of expressing form by the handling of his paint enables him to forego any of these illusionist methods.

This brief survey of Dr. Wölfflin's ideas affords, I think, the easiest approach to the problems of Seicento art. It will be seen, however, that he tended to regard the Baroque as essentially a non-Italian, even a Germanic contribution to the esthetic consciousness of Europe. At all events in painting he turned to Belgium and Holland, to Rubens, Rembrandt, Vermeer and De Hoogh as the chief exponents of the new principle, so that even he did not do much towards opening up the deserted territory of the Italian Seicento. And yet it is that school that provokes some of the most interesting questions about pictorial form and throws a curious light on the subsequent development of European painting.

Great as the influence of Dutch seventeenth-century painting has been on modern art it leaves unexplained many developments, and for these we must look rather to the Seicento proper. The greatest efforts and achievements of the Dutch school as a whole lay in the direction of realism, of the rendering of a particular field of vision with great verisimilitude. In so far as it appealed to the non-esthetic public—and one cannot deny that it did so very largely—its appeal was directed towards satisfying two instincts of the man in the street : first, that of curiosity in any vividly presented image of real life ;

and secondly, the pleasure in the acrobatic skill of the craftsman. It left untouched his emotional life, and in so far as it used illusory methods, did so without exploiting their emotional possibilities to any great extent.

But it was different in Italy. There the idea that it might be possible to interpret any given *coup d'œil* directly in pictorial form was scarcely envisaged. Such an idea was contradicted by the age-long tradition of Italian painting which had always proceeded by an *a priori* construction of objects, each of which might be studied directly from nature, but the relations of which within the picture were dictated by some other principle than their casual collocation.

In Italy, therefore, Baroque methods of composition and particularly the illusory power of strong and sudden effects of light, were employed for the expression of sentiment.

There are few more curious and puzzling problems than those which the expression of sentiment in art gives rise to. Whatever its relation to esthetic experience may be it would be vain to deny that it has occupied a large position in the practice of painting. There is also, I think, a very evident connection between the artistic form at the disposal of any given artist and the kind of sentiments which he is most likely to express. And of these, one of the most evident is the relation between certain violent and unusual effects of light and the expression of what we may call melodramatic emotion.

It is in this relation that the figure of Caravaggio appears as a great and sinister portent in the history of modern art. We may almost call him the first popular artist. The first effective black-leg among painters, the first, that is, to throw over allegiance to the general standards of the profession and to appeal direct to the uninstructed public without first gaining some sort of licence from his fellow artists.

We touch here on a very curious question in the history of European art. It is a mistake to allow a certain tendency to idolise the past, to induce us to suppose that at certain periods all art was good and that the bad art which surrounds us on every side to-day is a modern discovery. The vast mass of artistic production has always been mediocre or frankly bad. But before Caravaggio appeared the bad artist had never thought of setting up on his own, as it were. He had always belonged to the body of his profession, had always done at least lip-service to its principles, and had generally tried to give to his works an appearance of likeness to the work of the good artists of his day. Of course, the moment any artist finds himself without the power to create forms capable of stirring a vivid esthetic response he is vehemently tempted to attract applause by some subsidiary device. He may, like Pintoricchio, overload his pictures with gilt ornament and vivid colour and so win the affection of an uncultured Pope. Or he may, like Benozzo Gozzoli or Ghirlandajo, please his contemporaries by the literal likenesses of their faces introduced into compositions which yet ostensibly appeal to more serious imaginative interests. Or, like Beccafumi, he may seek to astonish by extravagant effects of light and shade and hint at the possibilities of melodramatic art. He may even, like Filippino Lippi, Sodoma and Raphael, begin that unfair exploitation of tender sentiments which we call sentimentality. But in all such cases the appeal to the grosser interests was made, as it were, surreptitiously and under cover of designs which were framed according to other demands. But with Caravaggio we get a man who defies, and successfully defies, professional opinion and does not even pretend to conform to professional standards. We have seen that the elements for such a break had been gradually accumulating, that, bit by bit, the means of expressing melodrama, sentimentality and—the third great interest of the uninstructed—illusion, had been acquired, and, indeed, in the sixteenth century Tintoretto had almost accomplished a similar gesture; but still, I think we may give to Cavaraggio the honour of having been the first purely popular artist, the real founder of the Royal Academy, the Salon, and almost the whole art of the cinema. For that, in fact, is what it comes to—it was in seventeenth-century Italy that that alternative tradition of popular or commercial art was first set up in open rivalry to the old tradition of the profession, a tradition which appealed to other sanctions than those granted by the gross public in recognition for the gratification of its untrained instincts. And since the expression of sentimental and melodramatic emotion provides a slope down which the imagination glides without effort, this new tradition has been, and always, one supposes, will be, by far the greatest impulse to the manufacture of so-called works of art at any particular period.

But it suffers from the fact that it is not really a tradition at all, since it has no constant methods or principles, its only standard being its power of gaining immediate success. Its exponents therefore tend to be as quickly forgotten as they are quickly acknowledged. Whereas the exponents of the ancient tradition express in whatever the pictorial vernacular of their day may be, certain unchanging principles, and take their places in a consecutive, unbroken sequence. Naturally enough, however, the immense success and prestige of commercial art, its far stronger hold on the mass of public opinion, has driven the traditional artist out of the academies and public institutions, and given him the appearance of being a revolutionary.

The Italian Seicento, then, from this point of view, was a crucial moment in the history of art, and in that crisis Caravaggio's act of defiance becomes of symbolic importance. But before we return to that and to the consideration of the general situation of Seicento art, it may be well to discuss a little more some of those preliminary approaches at which I have hinted. What, I think, distinguishes those earlier attempts to interest by the expression of sentimental or melodramatic emotions, which I have enumerated, from those of modern popular art is that they do not break the generally accepted form of pictorial design. For instance, in Raphael's work, however complete and however distressing the expression of sentimental feelings may be, the form in which it is embodied always justifies itself on other grounds, the rhythm does not deviate from what is formally required. In fact, in Raphael's case the formal perfection is singularly complete.

The same is true of the early realists. No doubt a Benozzo Gozzoli had acquired but a feeble idea of form, but such as it is he maintains it intact for all his verisimilitude. In short, these artists, whatever their failings, had style. For I believe we mean by an artist or a picture having style that whatever data are accepted from appearance have been sufficiently interpreted in terms of some rhythmic conception to enter into the imagined reality.

Now, the characteristic of most popular art since the Seicento, and of much in that period, is that in some way we feel that it lacks style. I have chosen a drawing by Bacchiacca (Pl. XXI. C) as being, perhaps, one of the earliest cases of that particular change of emphasis which indicates the break with the great tradition, and hints already, in the early sixteenth century, at modern popular art. It is very difficult to define what it is that makes one feel that this drawing, for all its considerable merits, stands outside the genuine tradition. It is not, of course, here a question of the expression of sentiment, but rather of the description of certain facts of the thing seen, the quality of its realism. It is not merely that it is realistic; it is certainly no more so than some of Van Eyck's or Brueghel's drawings; but one somehow feels that the interest in description has everywhere broken up the rhythmic quality. The general design of the figure is quite satisfactory, though without having any particular significance, and the construction is adequate, so that it is rather by the quality of the actual lines that we are made to feel that the only justification sought for is that of description, that there is a change in the prime impulse and purpose of the drawing from the creation of form to description.*

If I am right, then, we get here the evidence of a new phenomenon in the history of European art. There had, of course, always been many skilled craftsmen with no marked esthetic conviction, but they had hitherto done their best to conceal that fact. Here, for the first time, we have signs of such a skilled craftsman appealing directly to the non-esthetic interests of the public and controlling his form to that end. But so far it is a sporadic phenomenon. The great period of the High Renaissance shows no repetition of it. Whatever the faults of Raphael, Michelangelo and their followers were, they did not lie in this direction. The idea of style became almost an obsession. It was ensued with a desperate resolution even by the less gifted painters. Their failures lay, therefore, in the opposite direction of stylistic self-consciousness and a calculated manner. Something of this tends to obscure Sebastiano del Piombo's work. In him ambition outran the power of his genuine but rather slender talent. Still worse is the effect of this attitude on Vasari, whose reverence for the artist's calling amounted to a religion and to whom the practice of the great masters became an inviolable doctrine. It made him one of the dullest and most meritorious of painters, but fortunately, also, the most enjoyable of all art historians.

* I have put beside this a drawing by Meissonier (Pl. XXI. A) to show to what lengths this new conception was destined to lead in the fullness of time.

PLATE XXI

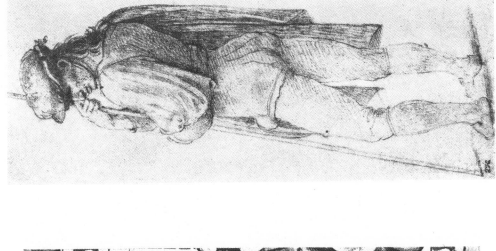

C
Drawing.  Bacchiacca

B
Printed stuff.  "Longchamps."  Dufy

A
Drawing.  Meissonnier

The middle of the sixteenth century in Florence and Rome provides us, therefore, with the spectacle of Academism triumphant—true Academism, that is, which is entirely distinct from Royal Academism. Venice, of course, stood apart from the main current of artistic development, but there remains one great artist who has to be taken into account, namely, Correggio. He certainly carried further the expression of those sentiments which lend themselves to sentimentality. He may even be said to have expressed them with more unreflecting abandonment than ever Raphael did. But he was more fortunate in this, that they implied no clash with his native rhythmic feeling. That, indeed, was so profound and so all-pervading that there is here no question whatever of that conflict between expression and formal requirements which leads to popular art. And, moreover, his rhythmic flow impelled him to make a great step forward in the development of the Baroque idea of design. In that respect he is the great forerunner of seventeenth-century art. In his composition he frequently denies all suggestion of symmetry and abandons all trace of parallelism to the picture plane : the impetuous urge of his rhythm compels to the freest possible movements in depth. In the " Antiope " of the Louvre, for instance, the figure is lying on the ground turned diagonally to the picture plane, so that the eye in following the sequence of its planes is carried forcibly back into the depths of the wood behind, whilst a counterbalancing diagonal movement of the figure of Jupiter brings us back again with a kind of spiral movement, thus closing and completing an asymmetrical but perfectly self-contained rhythmic phrase. Such a picture contains already all the elements of Baroque composition. No less important is his new use of sharp and unusual impacts of light, in the " Notte " and the " Agony in the Garden," which make straight the paths for the melodrama of the Seicento.

One other link has to be established, and it is supplied by Baroccio. He increased deliberately the emphasis on the diagonal disposition of his figures, and carried to its extreme Correggio's fluent rhythm, though with only a fraction of that master's unerring certainty of gesture and fertility of resource. To this he added a kind of vaporous suffusion of every part of his pictures with a golden roseate glow. It is strange, indeed, to what an extent he hinted at effects which were hardly to be exploited till the eighteenth century. For we must here note carefully the remarkable fact that the Italian Seicentists did not carry on directly the movement set up by Correggio and Baroccio. The Caracci in particular, intensely self-conscious and theoretical as they were, erected a barrier against this movement which, being diverted from Italian soil, finds its channel elsewhere. That central current, made up of Correggio's and Baroccio's discoveries, together with the independent discoveries of Titian and Tintoretto, now flowed through Flanders, gaining intense impetus from the genius of Rubens, whence it affected the whole of North European painting and became one of the inspirations of eighteenth-century French art, and, later on, of such romantic French painters as Delacroix.

This explains a certain quality of provincialism in the work of the Italian Seicento. We notice in it a lack of consistency. There are sudden capricious tentatives in various directions, not to mention the violent upheaval of Caravaggio's revolt. How much more central, how much more in the great tradition Rubens appears than brilliant but insecure painters like Strozzi, Crespi and Domenico Feti! Even the Dutch, in spite of their somewhat naïve experimentalism, appear to have a clearer consciousness of their end and to hold a more consistent course.

I can, perhaps, best give an idea of the feeling of uncertainty and incoherence which the art of the Seicento produces by the following notes on two exhibitions of the Magnasco Society, which has undertaken a praiseworthy task in making the pictures of this period better known.

It is interesting to see in these exhibitions that the painters that stand out are precisely those whose names have managed to survive the long eclipse of seventeenth-century Italian painting. Great and prolonged reputations generally seem to have some foundation.

We have still a great deal to learn before we can steer our way easily in the period. What a strange, decaying, and regenerating ferment must have been at work in the artistic circles of seventeenth-century Italy, where Caravaggio was blustering and threatening and killing too, at a pinch, and in the intervals inventing pictorial melodrama, and the Caracci were being refined and saying what was decorous in a picture, and Poussin was silently laying the foundations of French painting with rule and compass, and Dutchmen kept coming

PLATE XXII

The Vision of St. Francis.   Ludovico Caracci        Collection of Capt. R. Langton Douglas
By courtesy of the owner

in and learning how to Italianise, and never letting on about those queer new impressionist notions which they were too instinctive to formulate !   And what a disastrous change has come over the artists' world as compared with that of the previous centuries, when even so impulsive a man as Michelangelo didn't go beyond insulting Leonardo da Vinci !   Whereas here, in the Seicento, we are in a " film " world with high-faluting academies on the one hand and poisonings, bastinadoes, assassinations, and general banditism on the other. With this abandonment to violence and the new emotionalism which prompted it, went, whether connected with it or no, an access of extreme devotionalism and a new extravagance in the expression of religious emotion.   Melodrama and religiosity are the traces left by these social phenomena in the art of the day.

We get in these exhibitions a narrow peep at this seething, turbulent world that followed on the final exhaustion of the notions of the High Renaissance.   What a lot was stirring uneasily there which was to bear fruit of all kinds, good and bad, later on !

Here we can see that oddly mannered and yet original virtuoso Castiglione, who seems to have divined the decorative business of the eighteenth century a hundred years before it was due, for his " Sacrifice of Noah " is far nearer to Boucher than to Poussin ;  and, as though that were not enough, he seems (if one looks at the purely descriptive treatment of the white mare and her pack) to foresee other and more distant triumphs, to prophesy, however dimly, Wilkie or even Landseer !

Here is Ludovico Caracci in his " Vision of St. Francis " (Pl. XXII.) saturated in the traditions of the High Renaissance, but emotionally in another planet, finding an original and interesting composition, and yet, by what curious change of emphasis it is difficult to define, landing plump into the middle of the Royal Academy of the nineteenth century.   Here is Carlo Dolci, in his astonishing " Martyrdom of St. Andrew " (Pl. XXIII.), going even further. He is far more anecdotic, and invents innumerable picturesquely convincing details.   He belongs, one would say, to a less cultured group of R.A.'s—a Millais to Caracci's Lord Leighton—and yet, if one troubles to look behind the general impression, he reveals a power of construction and a feeling for design that most artists might envy.*   Carlo Dolci, indeed, does his

* See Appendix.

best to put us off. How impossible it seems not to pass over with a slight sneer of superiority his sugary, simpering Madonnas and infant Christs playing with wedding-cake flowers! And yet, if one have but the courage and patience one cannot but admit how considerable an artist lies hidden behind that *ad captandum* sentimentality. For once, however, in the portrait of " Sir John Finch," he puts no obstacle in our way. It is a splendidly simple and direct presentment. Here he shows unmistakably the full grip of his draughtsmanship and the rhythmic significance of his design. Before his Madonnas it is excusable if we mistake the smooth alabastrine quality of the painting for the licked sliminess of Bougereau and his kindred. Here we see that his quality is as deliberate, as duly adapted to the expression of his idea as is the quality of a portrait by Ingres. The times must, indeed, have been out of joint when a man of Carlo Dolci's authentic gifts and real sensibility found it convenient to pass under so pitiable an *alias*.

Here is Guido Reni in his " Ecce Homo," once so familiar to us on the walls of the National Gallery, where it remained on loan for many years, just being content to paint better than any one else, and letting his native, but rather sloppy tenderness look after itself. Tiresome as this is, it does not, fortunately, interfere too violently with his peculiarly delicate sensibility, does not prevent our recognising how expressive the actual handling is, nor how unobtrusively perfect, how genuinely felt is the colour harmony.

Here, too, is Domenichino, like Guido, a pupil with the Caracci, who seems to have suffered the least of all the Italians from the strange emotional perturbation of the time. He is the least diverted from the natural and direct expression of his feeling. Here, in Sir Herbert Cook's " Landscape," that expression is so little coloured by the period that if it were only handled with a little less circumspection it might be signed by some quite modern master of landscape, by Derain or Marchand.

It is significant that Poussin, the one really great creative mind that was active in Italy, found in Domenichino the only living artist to whom he could turn for help and inspiration. That, too, gives a measure of the purity and purposefulness of Domenichino's art.

All these painters have managed, as I say, to keep at least their

PLATE XXIII

Crucifixion of St. Andrew.  Carlo Dolci
By courtesy of the Trustees of the Earl of Feversham.

names in the memory of the amateur through the winter of neglect, but there is one painter here, Massimo Stanzoni, who, I think, was well-nigh forgotten. And yet he shows himself in his " Pietà " as one of the most genuine painters of the lot. This picture reinforces the impression which one has already received from the beautiful little " Pietà " which the National Gallery acquired some years ago solely on its evident merit, since at that time no one suspected its authorship. This is a masterly and direct painting, composed with a tense and personal feeling, and not merely with a view to satisfying the requirements of the current convention.

On the other hand, Bernardino Strozzi, the " Prete Genevose," has always forced himself on the most casual spectator by the *brio* of his handling of a rich paste and the certainty and mastery of his rather insensitive relief. Here, in the portrait of a gentleman lent by the Dublin Gallery, he shows himself as the rival and probably the precursor of Vandyck. Here one finds almost all that is left of Vandyck, if one subtracts Rubens. Here is all that languid, anæmic distinction of pose which Rubens, in spite of his feeling for distinction, was too full-blooded to affect, but which became almost the hall mark of Vandyck's portraits. Here are the very gestures, the very airs, the same hands and the same way of showing off their elegance which we associate with Vandyck.

The mere difference in the use of paint in a Strozzi and a Ludovico Caracci shows how little unity of purpose there was throughout Seicento Italy. And what strikes us is that these various and conflicting tendencies are all due to different dispositions and proportions of visual methods already acquired. With the exception of Caravaggio's lamplight effects there is no new curiosity about vision. The new worlds, or too often only the new manners, are sought for between the palette and the canvas ; the painter only looks round his easel in order to find some special case of known visual phenomena ; a new pose of a figure, a new cast of a drapery, never a new valuation of visual elements. Seicento Italian art, for all its search for originality, is enclosed within the then-known world of vision.

Let us now see whether we can classify and interpret a little more clearly the complicated impressions which such a collection of Seicento pictures produces on us. I have said that in the latter part of the sixteenth century, leaving Venice apart, Baroccio's presented the one case of a genuinely progressive idea of design. That he at least was pressing on to the fuller exploitation of Baroque ideas, towards a more continuous, flexible and all-embracing plastic rhythm, and that, strangely enough, instead of being followed up by his compatriots, this movement was diverted to Flanders. As far as I can make out it was the Caracci who erected the dyke that thus diverted the current.

It was Raphael and Michelangelo who first created in the artistic community a full consciousness of the claims of art. Like Wordsworth addressing Haydon, but with more apparent justification, their contemporaries talked of the "high calling of creative art." Art was ennobled.

Vasari's lives give us a measure of this new self-consciousness of the profession. One guesses that the Caracci were deeply impressed by this notion. To them the fluttering, vaporous elegance of Baroccio, his exuberant lyrical sensuality must have appeared rather frivolous and unworthy, his intense but voluptuous devotionalism a little indiscreet. They established a code of pictorial manners. They decided what a picture ought and ought not to present, and they went from one to another of the great masters to find how best to express that very limited range of feelings which they considered worthy and noble enough to be admitted. They were in opposition to the academism of the "Mannerists," whose ideal consisted in the exaggeration of the manner of Michelangelo and Raphael, but they, too, were academic. The academism they opposed to that of the Mannerists inculcated the adoption of a blend of all the manners of the great Renaissance masters. Both contending factions missed alike the future that Baroccio's practice held out to them.

To some extent, then, the influence of the Caracci was away from the development of Baroque art and back to the classic principles of design. Annibale Caracci's decorations of the Farnese palace are doubtless more exuberant and florid than Raphael's work at the Farnesina, more definitely Baroque in the illusionism of the decorative framework of the individual compositions, but they are based on a generally similar notion of composition and disposition of the figures. Some of Guido Reni's works, indeed, done under this influence, almost return to the symmetry and parallelism of Fra Bartolommeo's

PLATE XXIV

B

St. John the Baptist. Guido Reni
Dulwich Gallery

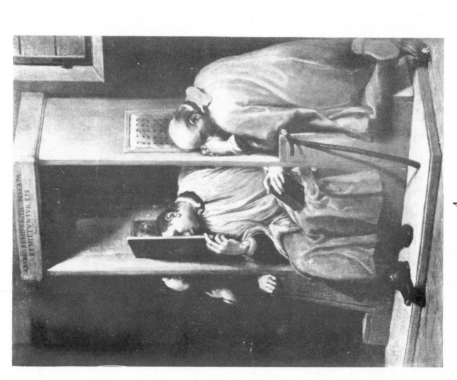

A

Confession. Giovanni Maria Crespi. Turin Gallery

composition. They throw back behind Correggio and the later Raphael to earlier principles. Domenichino, too, reverts sometimes, as in his St. Andrea fresco, to an emphatic parallelism with the picture plane, and this is not without its effect on Poussin.

Guido Reni and Domenichino remain the great justification of the Caracci's methods and teaching. Guido was far more naturally gifted, a more innate painter than any of his masters, and his instinctive feelings forced a more direct and natural outlet through his art. That reflects, of course, and often to a painful degree, the emotional abandonment of the day, and it looks as though the success of his unscrupulous appeals to pathos, in his heads of weeping Madonnas and suffering Christs had led him to exaggerate and stress what came to him only too naturally. Still, like Greuze, another shameless sentimentalist, he keeps almost always his specific painter's quality of handling and his sense of colour relations. What he could accomplish in a restricted scale of greys, olive-browns, olive-greens, and ivory flesh tints may be seen in his " St. John the Baptist," at Dulwich (Pl. XXIV. B), which is, moreover, one of the rare occasions when he struck out a really expressive and original design. Here everything is held together by that constant impulse which underlies style. But the lapses from this in Guido's work are many and deplorable, and show how perilously unstable was the mentality of the time. In a picture in the Louvre of the " Rape of Helen," we find a hundred petty picturesque details in the description of which Guido shows an indecent satisfaction. Here, again, we get just that shift of emphasis from expressive to descriptive form which marks so clearly for us the beginning, at this period, of Royal Academic art.

Still, on the whole, the Caraccesques remain respectable and genuinely academic. But there is, after all, some connection between even the most respectable academism and Royal academism. For academism, by devitalising the art of the great masters, by insisting on precedent and an uncritical respect, really leaves its votaries a prey, for all their careful culture, to sudden lapses into crass vulgarity. That at least will have a flavour, whereas the great art seems somehow to have been deprived of all flavour by a too servile adoration.

The Caracci, therefore, not only checked the natural development of Italian art and left it for Rubens to accomplish, they prepared the atmosphere in which a Caravaggio would emerge. There was much that was genuine in the Caraccian doctrine, but it was so far overlayed with pedantry and dull pretension that the moment had arrived when a skilful craftsman could appeal to the public over the heads of the professors and meet with a rapturous response. And Caravaggio had great native talents, considerable accomplishment, no respect, and a vehement desire for self-assertion. He had all that was necessary to take the decisive step, and the moment was propitious.

Bellori tells two stories of him which illustrate clearly enough this dramatic moment in the history of art. He says that one day Caravaggio was taken by some artists to see two celebrated antique sculptures * when, pointing to a crowd of bystanders, he exclaimed, " See how many masters nature has provided for me and other artists without your statues," and to justify his opinion he called a gipsy girl, took her to his lodgings and painted her in the act of telling a young man his fortune, whereby he gained great applause.

The other story is of the picture once in the Sciarra collection, which represents a rich but misguided youth at cards with a young sharper who is secretly taking a hidden card from the back of his belt according to the indications given him by his accomplice who overlooks the young innocent's hand. This picture was, according to Bellori, the foundation of his fortune, for it fell under the notice of Cardinal del Monte, who, overcome with delight at so new and fascinating a style of painting, took Caravaggio into his service.

Here we have the pictorial anecdote with its crude appeal to irrelevant and non-esthetic interests. This was, in fact, the first " picture of the year," the fountain head of how stupendous a progeny !

The objections urged against Caravaggio's art by his many opponents were of the most futile description, and missed the real point—that his figures were not chosen for their beauty or nobility ; that they belonged to the common people ; and that he did not make backgrounds with perspective vistas. For us, with Rembrandt and Daumier before our eyes, the first point, whatever its apparent relevance at the time, falls to the ground. The second point was due to an

* Probably the " Wounded Amazon," which is indifferent, and the Farnese " Hercules," which is a piece of bombastic extravagance, but there is no reason to suppose that Caravaggio objected to this.

unfortunate misapprehension about the nature and purpose of art which still persists in certain quarters, namely, that the value of a work of art is proportional to the difficulty of its execution. This notion that an artist has to prove his credentials to our admiration by the performance of difficult feats relegates him to the level of the acrobat or conjurer. All that we ought to demand of the artist is that he shall have had sufficient concentration to develop to the utmost his own special sensibility, and that he shall have acquired sufficient proficiency to express its reactions fully. Skill beyond that point is irrelevant and, often enough, impertinent.

In more than one respect, then, Caravaggio's rebellion, however dubious its motives, must claim our sympathy. It was a breath of fresh air in that stifling atmosphere of academic self-satisfaction and pedantry. He at least had genuine, undeniable conviction, as against the tired belief in recipes for the grand style of his adversaries. Moreover, he was not sentimental, there was no humbug about his self-conceit, and he had genuine talent as a painter, a keen observation for certain visual facts and enough imagination to keep in focus his crudely insensitive vision.

Nor must we suppose him altogether deprived of esthetic pre-occupations. No one could at a blow have conceived of a picture in which everything is subordinated to non-esthetic appeals such as our popular artists are now able to produce. These are the result of centuries of development. Caravaggio, if he despised the antique, had at least studied the Venetians and is said to have had a cult for Giorgione, though nothing in his work suggests it. But in any case he was not without a conception of style. His main preoccupation, however, lay, none the less, in non-esthetic directions. What he aimed at was to produce the most vivid shock of surprised acquiescence from any, even the least cultured, spectator. He presented familiar scenes of common life—a gipsy, a man laughing, a party at cards, or else scenes of melodrama, for which the martyrdoms of the saints afforded pretexts.

Even in these interpretations of biblical or hagiographical scenes he contrives frequently to combine melodrama with this familiar and photographic realism. Thus, in his picture of the " Conversion of St. Paul " we see how admirable an impressario for the cinema

Caravaggio would have been.   He has made a very finished representation from nature of a horse in a stable with a man holding its head. He then proceeds to stick into the foreground the figure of a man sprawling on the ground, and, with the help of his limelight illumination, it becomes a sensational religious picture.   No wonder he despised Raphael's cartoons.   In this picture the original design of the man and horse is not without merit, despite the triviality of the observation and the insistence on details for their illusive effect, but the whole design comes to pieces when St. Paul is thus wilfully pushed into the scene, and the parts have no longer any significance in relation to the whole.

The "Calling of St. Matthew" (Pl. XXV.) gives a favourable idea of Caravaggio's astuteness in adapting religious themes to his special manner.   The *mise-en-scène* and the illumination are admirably planned to startle the spectator into expectant curiosity about a vivid dramatic situation.   The sharp actuality of the costumes, the theatrical gestures and the ultra-photographic realism of the expressions are exactly such as are so highly prized in modern descriptive painting.

The ingenuity which Caravaggio displays in thus twisting the data of religious art to his purposes is sometimes surprising.   Even theological dogma is grist to his mill.   In his picture of " St. Anne, the Virgin, and Christ " in the Borghese Gallery he has made use of the text about the Virgin bruising the Serpent's head to portray a domestic event : in a dimly lit room the Holy Family has been surprised by the discovery of a large and very active serpent.   The Virgin, with great promptitude, puts her foot firmly on its head, whilst St. Anne looks on with anxious sympathy and the youthful Christ adds the weight of His body by standing with one foot on His mother's.   He thus skilfully illuminates the dryness of theology with the vividness of a cinematographic presentment.   For whatever the scene, it must be presented in such a way that the spectator would be forced to concentrate all his attention on certain facts, gestures or expressions.

And this concentration of focus on a few moments in the design did lead him to discover new methods of simplification in it and a new treatment of light and shade.   In his design he aimed at large, fully rounded, easily apprehended and sharply marked contours, he disposed his draperies in a few big heavy folds.   In short, he adopted a rhythm which was simpler, blunter, less elegantly contorted and

PLATE XXV

Calling of St. Matthew.  Caravaggio.                    S. Luigi dei Francesi, Rome

involved than the rhythm which the Caraccians practised. The powerful concentrating effect of this rhythm was further enhanced by his new use of light and shade. He conceived the light as coming from a single concentrated point as it does in effects of lamplight or a small window in a dark room, and in consequence, leaving a very sharp, scarcely modulated penumbra between the lighted and shaded portions of a form. He thus cut the whole figure up into two strongly contrasted masses of bright light and extreme darkness. He added to this effect of concentration by adopting in general dark uniform backgrounds against which the figures stood in violent relief.

In all this he was elaborating certain ideas originally suggested by Correggio in his " Notte " and " Agony in the Garden," but he elaborated them so fully and with so many variations that we must allow him the honour of having been the one painter of the Italian Seicento who gave to art a new angle of vision, a new power of expression, and the possibility of a new system of design. What one reproaches him with, is that he used all these discoveries almost exclusively for increasing the effect of his appeal to trivial interests of curiosity or sensationalism, and left it to others to find what esthetic possibilities they contained. In Italy Guercino managed to effect a rather happy synthesis of Caravaggio's light and shadow system with the traditional Caraccian design, but it was in Spain that his discoveries produced their richest harvest, first of all in the works of Ribera. Ribera was a much more serious and convinced artist and a remarkable colourist. He managed even to use some of Caravaggio's most suspect mannerisms, the wrinkles on a forehead or an emaciated limb thrown into relief by the shearing light, without losing, as Caravaggio perpetually did, the unity and detachment of a real style. But perhaps the most curious and unexpected fortune for Caravaggio's inventions was for them to fall into the hands of such an artist as Velasquez, whose sensibility, temperament and character were at the very opposite pole from his. Yet it is impossible not to see how much in the early work of Velasquez is due to Caravaggio not only in the illumination and general rhythm of the design, but even in the treatment of the subject. The Bacchanals, for instance, show just such a transposition of the themes of mythology into the surroundings of contemporary peasant life as Caravaggio invented. There remains, of course, the incalculable difference between Velasquez's distinction, detachment and scrupulous reserve as compared with Caravaggio's blustering Cabotinism.

What, perhaps, shows more than anything else how little of an artist Caravaggio was, in spite of his innate artistic gifts, is that he was so little interested in the new vision of common everyday people and things on which he had stumbled. Nothing could be more striking than the contrast between his realism and that of the contemporary Dutch. With Caravaggio, in spite of the general economy and simplicity of his figure design, any detail of still-life accessories which takes his fancy will receive an emphasis which breaks the unity of the rhythm both in form and tone. Compare, for instance, the still life on the table of the " Supper at Emmaus " in the National Gallery with the still life on the table in an interior scene by Terborgh, and one realises that the Dutch had grasped the possibilities of esthetic harmony in such a realistic vision far more clearly and were exploring these with a deliberate and conscientious disinterestedness altogether inconceivable to Caravaggio. The complacency with which Caravaggio displays his power of literal observation and emphatic description is the very opposite of the scrupulous delicacy and subtlety of perception, the good taste, to put it no higher, of the Dutch. Caravaggio anticipates here the practice of modern popular artists in regarding verisimilitude as an end in itself.

The commotion produced by Caravaggio's revolutionary gesture was immense and was one of the causes of that uncertainty of aim and those sudden fluctuations of manner which we have noticed in the Italian art of the period and which distinguish it so clearly from the more concentrated and coherent evolution of the Northern schools. For there were now two apparently irreconcilable views of pictorial art in Italy. On the one hand, the self-conscious, deliberately stylistic and complex tradition of the Caraccians, and on the other the realistic presentment of Caravaggio with its casual and detailed verisimilitude. Not unnaturally the academic artists were tempted to enliven now and again their exhausted and learned compositions by a spice of that Caravaggian realism which met with so ready a response from the public.

Thus we find later on an artist like Giovanni Maria Crespi

designing sometimes according to the principles of a highly sophisticated harmonic rhythm and at others painting a picture like the " Confessional " (Pl. XXIV. A). Here the planning of the design, the drawing and handling all envisage so clearly an anecdotic effect that it might have a popular success in any contemporary Academy exhibition.

Our revived interest in the painting of this period comes to us, I think, from the fact that even when our gaze was most firmly averted from the later Renaissance and Baroque painters we could not walk the streets of Rome and remain quite indifferent to the surprising beauty and completeness of certain Baroque buildings. And it was with reason that this was so, since the position of Italy in architecture was in marked contrast to that which she held in painting. We have seen that in painting the central current of European development now flowed through northern lands, but in architecture Italy still remained supreme.

Not only did Italy maintain this predominance in architecture, but, strangely enough, in some cases the very men who were executing second- or third-rate pictures were producing masterpieces in architecture. Bernini is, perhaps, the one name that one might put forward as a claimant to high rank in sculpture. But however indulgently we may judge his sculpture, we must admit that in architecture he shows himself as belonging to a far higher rank. The case of Pietro da Cortona is even more striking if one compares the brilliant mediocrity of his painting with his real masterpieces in architecture.

The Rome that we know is to a very large extent the work of those seventeenth-century architects : even what little architectural beauty is scattered about London comes largely from an echo of their work. It is, indeed, surprising what these architects made of the tradition left to them by the High Renaissance. One would have thought that there was indeed nothing more to be done without a sudden break, so complete, so coherent, and so exactly established were the principles of that art. And yet the architects of the seventeenth century, with scarcely any alterations in the individual parts of their construction, gave it a new character. They used almost exactly the same stylistic elements, the same columns and pilasters, the same cornices and mouldings, the same decorative motives, and yet managed to give to the whole a quite new impression. By choosing deeper recessions and more salient reliefs, by introducing convex and concave surfaces in all sorts of varieties, by a less rigidly rectangular planning, by all these and many more devices they developed a whole new architectural language, at once more striking and pictorial, so to speak, and yet, in spite of some florid exuberance, maintaining and even heightening the plastic unity. The fact becomes clear that the " style " in architecture is of little importance compared with the use that is made of it. The great thing is that whatever the style, it should be practised long enough and consistently enough to enable artists to work through their interest in it *as a style* and get to the fundamental business of proportional harmonies. And perhaps no style has ever been so thoroughly worked in this sense as the Renaissance classical style.

None the less, there are already signs in the seventeenth-century Roman architecture of something of that impatient sensationalism to which I have called attention in the painters. Already in Maderno, born as early as 1566, there are signs, in the Palazzo Chigi for example, of a new picturesqueness of surface treatment which is intended to cover a certain poverty in plastic design.

Rainaldi in the main is a great master of severe effects of massive relief, as, for instance, in the tribuna of Sta. Maria Maggiore. He even returns almost to quattrocento principles in the interesting façade of Sta. Maria in Monte Santo, though giving it a new accent by the heavy shadows of isolated projections. None the less, in the Palazzo del Grillo and in certain details of Sta. Maria in Campitelli, he carries even further the hint of picturesque extravagance given by Maderno. The fact is that out of the Baroque the Rococo was being born, and the Rococo was destined to destroy the tradition of plastic design in architecture, and to endeavour to distract us from its loss by the variety and picturesqueness of its surfaces.

Pietro da Cortona, born as late as 1596, shows himself as the most consistently Baroque of this group. It is not without significance that he was a Tuscan and not a North Italian as Maderno and Borromini were, and like a Tuscan he keeps to the great principles of design. It is very significant that the nearest approaches to Rococo experiments occur in his early work, and that as he goes on he becomes more purely plastic.

The façade of Sta. Maria della Pace seems to me one of the great creations of this period. Here a new effect in architecture is obtained by throwing two differently curved convex masses against a concave background. In this way Pietro introduces into architecture something of that complex double plasticity—convex and concave— which is the main business of painting. His façade of Sta. Maria in Via Lata is also a masterpiece of concentrated plastic design by which the utmost impressiveness and mass is given to a small build-ing—only pedants would object to the arched archivolt, where its effect is so happy, so essential to the total unity.

It is, alas ! upon Borromini that most of the modern enthusiasts for the Seicento fix as the great genius of the movement, and if a distinctive and superficial originality is the mark of greatness, no doubt he looms large enough. Here at least we get oddity, extravagance, queerness and novelty pursued as ends in themselves. No doubt Borromini designed some fine works—the façade of Sta. Agnese in the Piazza Navona, for instance—he could not be expected to destroy a fine tradition all at once. But every move he makes, every affirma-tion of his own personality, is in the direction of cheap and vulgar sensationalism. A look at the cupola of the Sapienza will show this clearly. Here everything is meant to attract the eye by its oddity and caprice. The plastic idea is almost entirely lost : sudden, sharp, thin saliences, as in the cornice round the drum, pilasters that give no sense of density or mass to the wall they adorn, give to the whole its papery unreality, its air of being a stage property or a tem-porary building for a world-exhibition. In the lantern there is a return to reasonableness only to allow Borromini to flourish away more extravagantly than ever in the ridiculous spiral business at the top. Even in its origin the Rococo had something of that wilful caprice, that perverse inventiveness, which marked its far more degraded modern analogue, " Art Nouveau."

Thus we see that the architecture of the period presents the spectacle of that solid and consistent working out of certain new possibilities of design the absence of which in pictorial art implied, as we have seen, the dissipation of many great talents which might have come to perfection in a less troubled atmosphere.

In the view here presented of Seicento Italian painting it has been my aim not so much to study it in and for itself—to do that requires a far more intimate knowledge of the period than I possess— as to indicate its relations to the evolution of European painting. It presents, if I am right, the special interest of being a nodal point in that sequence. In that confused knot we may find the germs of some of the most puzzling phenomena of modern painting, especially of the most puzzling phenomenon of all, the existence, side by side, throughout the nineteenth century of two really distinct notions and practices of the painters' craft which have become continually more and more clearly distinguished from each other, and which each claim the tradition of the great masters of the past as their peculiar patrimony. I have tried to find the historical origins of that great and flourishing business of popular art and to show that its genealogical tree cannot go back to the tradition of Cimabue, Giotto, Masaccio and Raphael, but springs from the contest between the pedantic academism of the Caracci and the brilliant charlatanism of Caravaggio. I have also tried to show how the conditions for this situation were already being prepared in the period of the High Renaissance. The essential point of this new departure is the appeal to non-esthetic interests, whence it follows that the emphasis is shifted from the evocative power of formal relations to the purely descriptive possibilities of representation. The *pièce de résistance* of this view of painting is the pictorial anecdote, but the methods employed in that extend naturally enough to por- traiture and landscape. The cinema may be regarded as the apotheosis of the pictorial anecdote, and it is likely enough that it will ultimately supersede altogether painted versions of such themes, leaving to the professors of popular painting the fields of non-esthetic portraiture and landscape. Whether the appeal of these two *genres* will be powerful enough to support indefinitely such expensive institutions as the Royal Academy, the Salon and their innumerable counterparts through- out the world may perhaps be doubted. It would simplify the situation very much if photography of one kind or another, with the possible added control of colour, were able to supply all the non-esthetic gratifications of visual imagery, leaving the practice of painting entirely to those who attempt, in whatever degree, to express esthetic conceptions.

# J. S. SARGENT AS SEEN AT THE ROYAL ACADEMY EXHIBITION OF HIS WORKS, 1926, AND IN THE NATIONAL GALLERY

THE Sargent exhibition is wonderful. That at least was what I heard repeated again and again by the close-packed spectators jostling through the galleries at Burlington House. " The extraordinary number ! That's what one is so impressed by, and they say that he never employed assistants like Rubens, did them all with his own hand." " How wonderful that sunlight on the garden seen through the window ! " " A wonderful piece of work that shimmer on the salmon's tail, and just nothing but the tail of a salmon ! " " And that satin skirt ! " And Sargent's figure seemed to loom in colossal proportions over the social history of the last forty years, in virtue of that untiring industry and that unfailing competence. Wonderful indeed, but most wonderful that this wonderful performance should ever have been confused with that of an artist. That Sargent was taken for an artist will perhaps seem incredible to the rising generation, but I can testify to the fact, for I remember well his exhibiting at the New English Art Club the two sketches of Javanese dancers which I discovered again to my delight in the present exhibition (Nos. 54 and 59). The New English was then the home of whatever serious art England possessed, the home of real artists like Steer and Sickert, and I remember the buzz of excitement at the *maîtrise* of these two figures, though I remember, too, George Moore's warning note : " No artist, but a prince of the *atelier*." Then came " Carnation, Lily, Lily, Rose," which seemed a new revelation of what colour could be and what painting might attempt, and of how it could be at once decorative and realistic. When I look now at the thin and tortured shapes those lily petals make on the lifeless green background, I realise that what thrilled us all then was the fact that this picture was the first feeble echo which came across the Channel of what Manet and his friends had been doing with a far different intensity for ten years or more. This new colour was only a vulgarisation of the new

125

harmonies of the Impressionists; this new twilight effect only an emasculated version of their acceptance of hitherto rejected aspects of nature.

Of course, when the great public has made up its mind and the *Times* has leaders about a national memorial, there must be something there. The only question is what. Those rough, instinctive classifications which crystallise into words often correspond so ill with reality that we find ourselves in hot dispute where no issue is really at stake. And in this matter of the arts we suffer from every form of verbal misfortune. To begin with, the application of art and artist almost exclusively to the art of painting, when artist should be a word of general application to any one who constructs with a view to esthetic satisfaction. The result is that any one who puts paint on canvas is called an artist without consideration of what purpose he accomplishes by this process. Goodness knows the writers are badly off enough, but at least they have some rough classification of those who use words; they can talk of a poet, an essayist, a novelist, a critic, a précis-writer, and so forth. But every painter is an artist, to the hopeless confusion of our understanding.

All the same, as I say, there was a time when this question of what Sargent is, was almost decided in favour of his being an artist in the sense in which Steer and Sickert were, and fortunately still are. So I went patiently through the exhibition to see whether I could get from any of the canvases that particular pleasure which I look for from pictures, namely, the delight in certain visual relations regarded in and for themselves. In Gallery No. V. I did, in fact, discover what I was in search of. A little picture ("Wineglasses") of a surburban French café, a table with two wineglasses in the foreground, a trellised arbour, and sunlit verdure beyond. As a composition it was satisfactory without being in any way remarkable, but the pale grey greens of the foliage made with the warm grey shadows on the pavement and the cooler grey of the table a very agreeable and deliberate harmony— a harmony which was intensified by the discreet notes of dull violet and blue grey in the wineglasses. Certainly if I were shown such a work by a young painter, I should guess that he had something of the special sensibility of the artist, though in the light of all the other works around I can now see that this sensibility was not innate. The picture is signed and dated 1874. It proves that during Sargent's apprentice-ship in Paris he must have caught, in however mild and transient a form, the infection of that curious passion of the artist for the discovery of visual relations that have, goodness knows exactly why, a significance for the spirit. One other work, the study for the Mlle. Gautreau lent by the Tate Gallery, showed that there was a time when Sargent was interested in rhythmic flow of line and, to a less extent, in rhythmic transitions of tone. Since every one of the numerous drawings in the same room proclaimed a total, an almost insolent, indifference to these qualities, one can only suppose that this interest died as soon as it was born.

But, in general, one may say that in all the early works there linger traces of these preoccupations. One finds here and there (" Mrs. Legh," " Edith Lady Playfair," " Mrs. Witton Phipps ") heads that are drawn with some other idea than that of the merely economical statement of the likeness, a real interest in the way the contours flow and at times the adumbration of a definite colour harmony. Or, again, compare the rather early group, " The Misses Vickers," with all those other brilliant and striking groups of members of a family. I do not deny that this is already seen from an essentially non-artistic angle, but there is a reminiscence in the composition of considerations of balance and design ; all is not yet sacrificed to the most striking impression.

But little by little, certainly before the end of the 'eighties, all these preoccupations disappear and Sargent is launched triumphantly into that other world of imagery which is so fortunately unhampered by esthetic scruples. That, indeed, is the explanation of why he could do so many " with his own hand." That hand was a highly trained and obedient servant of his eye, and his eye took in at a glance those salient facts of appearance out of which the average man builds his world ; and, as he never felt tempted to probe sensation deeper for those other relations which only emerge for a disinterested and prolonged contemplation, there was nothing to check his unbounded energy ; nothing to prevent him succeeding, as he did, every time.

We must abandon, then, this futile search for esthetic values in Sargent's work—a search into which the misleading use of the word " artist " has led us. Instead of demanding from him what it clearly was not in him to give, let us consider what it is that he does afford us. We must look at these pictures not as works of art with a value in and for themselves, but as illustrations or reports about other things. An illustrator may be in a way a poet, as Brueghel was, or a dramatist as Rembrandt was at times, or a psychologist as Rouveyre, or a satirist as Hogarth, though in all these cases illustration was accompanied by esthetic considerations, whereas Sargent appears to be a pure illustrator. But as illustrator what does he stand for? The legend is that he had profound psychological insight into character, that he revealed this in all its nudity with a sublime indifference to social conventions. As far as this exhibition goes, this theory is hardly borne out. He can laugh, though ever so decorously, at the pretensions of a Lady Mayoress or at any of those whose wealth has led them to acquire an uneasy footing in aristocratic circles. But for Royalty or for the genuine aristocrat he seems to have felt the same glamour as the great mass of the English middle classes. Decidedly it seems to me he brings no new or individual insight to the interpretation even of social values. Here he moves, and it is one secret of his effect, quite naturally in step with the crowd. One might, however, suppose that the necessities of his profession of portrait painter had imposed upon him the need to suppress his individual predilections, but that these would come out in by-work that he did for his own pleasure. But if we follow him on his holiday travels and examine those rapid and accomplished diaries in water-colour which he used to bring home, we shall abandon such a theory. They prove that Sargent was all of a piece, transparently honest, sincere, and undistinguished in his reaction to whatever caught his attention.

Certainly, on these holidays what he saw was exactly what the average upper-class tourist sees. Everything is as striking as it is obvious. When I look at these water-colours, I seem to hear the buzz of conversation round respectable dinner tables. All those desolating *impressions de voyage*, those desperately commonplace originalities of aristocratic vulgarity which circulate on such occasions, seem to have found not only an echo in Sargent's heart, but a thrilled response. Switzerland—those high meadows seen to the music of cowbells, glaciers beyond, and the purple of the further peaks half hidden in drifting cloud with the blue sky showing through here and there. Italy—a white marble statue against a black cypress—no doves fluttering round, of course—that would belong to a lower social stratum—sunlight on the marble of the Salute, " and, you know, even the shadows seemed as light as the sky "—that narrow canal all grey at twilight and the great clear spaces of sunset sky glimpsed at the end. Scotland—the pink opalescence on the side of the salmon and everywhere, everywhere such agreeable picnics and the siesta afterwards when Sargent, always on the alert for impressions, did his best work whilst the others dozed in the dappled shade.

But to record the motives gives merely an indication. What surprises is the uniform superficiality of the observation. On a vague apprehension of Impressionist practice he built up a formula which always came ready to his hand. This was adequate to the entirely superficial report which he loved to make, and it never occurred to him to penetrate further. The blues of his skies are nearly always the same cobalt, sunlit stone the same burnt sienna, distant mountains the same violet grey. The changes are rung on these just enough to situate the impression, never to exhaust its possibilities.

As an illustrator, then, Sargent's evaluation of phenomena is almost always that of the average cultured Anglo-Saxon. He reveals no vivid personal response, he is satisfied with what is immediately striking to almost all eyes. He is, in fact, always being struck ; what distinguishes him so immensely is his power of striking back, of handing on the blow to the whole vast public.

Sargent's reputation was such that he found himself more than once entrusted with those large schemes of mural decoration which have tempted the ambition of most great painters throughout the ages—schemes which, since they are generally in the hands of public bodies, are hardly ever allotted to those whose gifts might promise a successful issue. Anyhow, commissions such as it was the desperate and vain dream of a Degas and a Seurat to obtain were handed over without a tremor to Sargent. Perhaps no considerable painter was ever less gifted by nature for such an undertaking. What is strange is that this well-read and cultured man should have produced designs so wanting in decorative coherence, filled with such common and inexpressive figures, and inspired with such journalistic pedantry as is revealed in the sketch for the Boston decorations. The answer which he is said to have made to a lady admirer, who asked for the meaning of the design, that they were just " Blokes dancing," whilst it throws a sympathetic light on his character is nearer the truth than he was perhaps aware, for " blokes " these figures remain for all the rays of Aten and other archæological apparatus by which he seems to have hoped to eke out the poverty of his invention. The bronze crucifix is no better. The symbolism of this is as boringly commonplace and undistinguished as the plastic forms in which it is expressed.

But it is time, after so many negative results, that we faced the question of what, then, Sargent does stand for, of what authentic and solid gifts lie behind his vast reputation.

When in a social gathering a new guest enters the room, every one has an impression of his appearance, from which he at once deduces provisionally a number of facts, his social status, perhaps his profession, and a vague feeling of sympathy or antipathy or dubiety ; what we know at such moments is not the man's character, but the idiosyncrasy of his appearance, that whereby he is recognisable. Now, Sargent saw this superficial social aspect of men with extreme clearness, and he had a marvellously accurate sense of proportion so that he could, when he came to paint the man's head, put every feature exactly in its right position relatively to the others.

In front of one of his portraits one feels at once that that is the man's precise social aspect. But Sargent had no psychological imagination, he gives us nothing of what lies behind that first aspect. Then, again, his Paris training had put into his hands, thanks, of course, to his own intelligence in accepting it, a perfect method for recording that appearance economically, methodically, and without any fumbling or hesitation. So that he never muddles or messes a tone ; every brush stroke goes pat into its place, every tone is true enough as representation of the visible facts. It was this splendid method, together with the unfailing accuracy of his proportions, that made him a giant among the Royal Academicians. But he belonged truly enough to their body. Neither his evaluations nor his vision really differed from theirs, it was only his vastly superior capacity for recording them that distinguished him. The result was that he reported to the public those visual facts which interested them, far more sharply and precisely than the older Royal Academy painters. He never missed an effect, he was always striking.

The series of portraits of the Wertheimer family in the National Gallery includes what is perhaps Sargent's best work. Before them even more than before the large and miscellaneous collection of his work as seen at Burlington House I found myself wondering whether my original impressions of those works as they appeared year after year at the Royal Academy exhibitions would be justified and confirmed or not. In those days so general a chorus of praise rose from my fellow critics that I was acutely conscious of the discordant note which my articles struck. In view of the acid and disobliging phrases which rose to my memory I wondered whether I might not be compelled to own that I, and almost I alone, had failed to recognise a great master in the dawn of his triumphs or whether the intervening time would only prove how right I had been. Either alternative seemed to me disagreeable. However, the sight of them relieved me of apprehension. I saw that I had been both right and wrong, and I saw that the dispute between my fellow critics and myself arose from a misunderstanding of the meaning of the words we used. I felt then that what I had said was substantially true; that when I said that Sargent was " our greatest practitioner in paint " I had very nearly hit the mark. But if I had been right from a purely esthetic standpoint I had none the less been wrong in pedantically insisting on that, in exhibitions of what ought to be regarded as an applied art. I had used " practitioner in paint " as a term of abuse, comparing it with the honourable title of artist. I had failed to see that just as there is need both for pure and applied science so there is need for both pure and applied art, and that the art of Sargent is eminently and entirely of the latter kind. It is art applied to social requirements and social ambitions. I see now that this marvellous series of portraits represents a social transaction quite analogous to the transactions between a man and his lawyer. A rich man has need of a lawyer's professional skill to enable him to secure the transmission of his wealth to posterity, and a rich man, if he have the intelligence of Sir Asher Wertheimer and the luck to meet a Sargent, can, by the latter's professional skill, transmit his fame to posterity.

And as we must suppose that it is in the interests of society that a rich man's wealth should be duly transmitted to his heirs, so we may admit that Sir Asher Wertheimer was likewise conferring a benefit on society, both now and in centuries to come, by transmitting his personality and his *entourage*. Viewing the whole matter, then, in this historical perspective and throwing over as irrelevant the purely esthetic point of view, I can see and rejoice in Sargent's astonishing professional skill.

We praise a great doctor though he has added nothing to the knowledge of truth, and we should praise a great applied artist though he has given us no new glimpse of beauty. Therefore, although Sargent is already more fully represented than any living and almost any dead artist in our national collections, I for one welcome the bequest by which the National Gallery becomes the trustee of Sir Asher Wertheimer's fame.

I see that this record of the life of a successful business man of the close of the nineteenth century has a profound historical interest. It was a new thing in the history of civilisation that such a man should venture to have himself and the members of his numerous family portrayed on the scale and with the circumstance of a royal or ducal family, and I see that Sargent has quite peculiar and unique gifts for doing what both his patron and posterity required of him, and that such gifts are by no means common and deserve the fullest recognition.

For Sargent was a brilliant ambassador between Sir Asher Wertheimer and posterity. He managed on the one hand to give to these family portraits the sort of decorative splendour and *éclat* which puts them in line with the princely portraits of the past and which gave just satisfaction to his patron, and yet—and this is surely a supreme merit—he has never flattered him or his family. They are all seen with an almost coldly dispassionate and terribly observant eye. There they are on just the particular social eminence to which they had attained, and not altogether without traces of the meritorious effort of attainment. I used to imagine some trace of irony in Sargent's work. I think I was wrong : he is too detached, too much without *parti pris* for that. But that detachment has enabled him to miss no fact that might have social significance, so that the record of his observations lends itself, if one chooses, to an ironical interpretation. It requires rare gifts indeed to make such a record—a keenness of eye, a skill of hand, and a transparent honesty of purpose that do not often occur to this degree. The record is indeed so well made that it will always be legible, and what is to be read therein will have an ever-increasing historical interest.

To ask to have besides all this works of art is to be too exacting. Indeed, it is asking almost an impossibility. No man who was mainly an artist could have, so to speak, " delivered the goods." No artist could have treated one after another of all these members of the family with almost equal success, with such certainty of keeping to standard. His sensibility would have led him, here into some more penetrating and curious inquiry, there it would have been rebuffed altogether. From an artist, questions of composition and design would demand more anxious research. He could not have been satisfied as Sargent was with a mere general adequacy of presentment. Questions of quality would have held him up, made him repeat passages again and again and, perhaps in the search for some more intimate expression, made him lose all that freshness and *élan* which never deserts so competent a performer as he was.

Sargent had neither the psychological nor the distinctively artistic vision—he had, one might say, no visual passion at all, scarcely any visual predilections—he had rather the undifferentiated eye of the ordinary man trained to its finest acuteness for observation, and supplied with the most perfectly obedient and skilful hand to do its bidding. But his values are never esthetic values ; they are the values of social and everyday life. Naturally, such a vision would never force a man to discover the means by which to record its experiences, and here comes in the connection between applied and pure art. For, just as the man of applied science, having no particular passion for truth, applies the results, discovered by those who have, to some ulterior social end, so Sargent knew how to use for his purposes the discoveries of pure art. And he was not only very skilful in seeing what could be of service, but very fortunate in what lay to his hand. For the dominant influence when he was a student in Paris was Manet. Now, Manet was very intensely an artist, an artist who had a passionate feeling about certain oppositions of tone and colour, and who felt these oppositions in such a way that he had to discover a very abrupt and frank way of stating them. He consequently invented a peculiarly straightforward and concise technique. It was this technique which Sargent had the quickness to see might be turned to quite other purposes, namely, to the rapid and incisive statement of the main facts of representation. For Manet certain relations of tone and colour had a definite esthetic significance; for Sargent they were merely means to effective representation.

From Manet, too, he picked up ready-made, as it were, certain colour harmonies—a chord of salmon pinks, oyster greys, and celadon greens to which he added, as a kind of universal medium, certain cool brown notes. This chord in all its varieties is adequate to his purposes, but he never shows in his statement the positive conviction of a passionate apprehension. It is part of the generally decorative effect of his presentment. Such, as I understand it, is the art of Sargent, a felicitous application of means to an end quite different from that for which they were originally discovered.

I see that one of my fellow critics says that Sargent has ascended Parnassus so high that all can see him. I think he has got wrong in his topography. It is not Parnassus that Sargent has climbed, but another mountain which frequently gets confused with it when viewed at a distance. This mountain has not yet been named. It is very high and has the advantage of never being lost in cloud as Parnassus frequently is. A number of very celebrated artists sit there, and Sargent takes his place on it, how far below Sir Thomas Lawrence time alone will decide.

If only this mountain could be properly named much confusion would be avoided. I for one should not have had that long misunderstanding with my fellow critics in the early years of this century. Moreover, it would save a painful feeling of injustice which rankles unnecessarily in the hearts of many artists. It ought to be as clearly understood in art as it is in science that those who profess the applied branches of these studies have a right to ten times the salary and far higher honours than those who are obsessed by the love of truth and beauty. The latter must also accept the fact that those who are as pre-eminent in applied art as Sargent, may gain, besides present wealth and fame, almost as much posthumous glory as the true Parnassians.

The late Mr. Robert Ross was fond of declaring that all bad artists were nice men; he never said, though he frequently implied, that the converse also held true. Certainly, in all that I have said in protest against the general opinion that Sargent was a great master I have never thought of the man himself with other than admiration. Although I did not know him personally, all I ever heard of him led me to believe him generous and self-effacing; I am sure that he was no less distinguished and genuine as a man than, in my opinion, he was striking and undistinguished as an illustrator and non-existent as an artist.

# LONDON SCULPTORS AND SCULPTURES

## I. Mr. Epstein and the Cultured

OF all the forms of boredom which afflict civilised man, there are probably few more acute or more unvarying than that which results from having, on occasions, to contemplate ordinary works of sculpture. Indeed, so evident is this that it would doubtless be universally recognised, and the habit of erecting sculptures would cease altogether were it not that the bulk, durability, and expense of sculptured stone and cast bronze make them peculiarly suitable for memorials and monuments. But fortunately these objects perform their function without troubling us much—except just the moment after the Royal person has unveiled the object, we are not called upon to give it much attention. It is safe upon its pedestal for the rest of time, and can only exhale a faint exhortation to conventional public spirit which flatters the good citizen and only slightly irritates the bad, who regards the work as a symbol which he and his fellow revolutionists may look forward to the fun of destroying at some future date.

Such, then, being the main uses of sculpture, most of us naturally look upon it as entirely remote from any personal emotion or interest other than that general all-pervading feeling of boredom with which it is so thoroughly imbued. We are brought up to a pious belief that sculpture is an altogether noble and reputable affair. We know the names of the great sculptors of all ages, and yet sculpture has always bored us—till now. And now comes Mr. Epstein, and as we passed round the Leicester Gallery where his work has been on exhibition, each bronze head gave us a new and distinct sensation, a thrill of wonder, surprise, recognition, and, as a result of so pleasant a shock, admiration and gratitude. What miraculous gift was this which could make bronze reveal to us definite, singular, vivid human beings—human beings more definite, more emphatically personal, more incisive in the accent of their individuality, more invasive, at a first glance, of our own consciousness than the individuals of actual life ?

136

Mr. Epstein started from the first with remarkable gifts, but in his early work he was an experimentalist in styles. He ingeniously constructed a kind of archaistic decorative simplification with rude accents suggestive of actuality. Then at one moment, with his insatiable technical acquisitiveness he learned to treat each sitter according to what he felt to be a style corresponding to his or her character—we had the strangest mixture, even in a single series of busts, of Chinese bronzes, early Greek marbles, Aztec, and Rodin. Now at last he has found himself; he has developed a method and a manner of seeing which look as though they were definitive. One imagines that he can go on indefinitely along these lines, increasing the intimacy of his reading of character, the psychological intensity of the mood, the incisiveness and *brio* of the execution. He is surely to be congratulated on having found his own indisputably original and unique artistic personality. There is no doubt about it; it sticks out authentically from all the works, however varied the subjects may be. However completely he seems to abandon himself to the personality he is interpreting, it is Epstein's personality that really startles, interests, and intrigues us. That is the way of the great masters, or at least of most of them; and indeed, when we realise the astonishing assurance, the indisputable completeness and efficacy of these works, the brilliant resourcefulness and certainty of the technique, we must call Epstein a master.

His technical resourcefulness is extraordinary. By frankly accepting the nature of clay modelling, he gets a strangely vivid and exhilarating surface quality. That is to say, he accepts the fact that the head is built up by adding small pellets of clay one after another. He never tries to cover up his traces: one sees how the head has grown centrifugally, how the prominences have gradually pushed outwards to receive the light. Whether we realise this growth from within or not, we feel that the way these pleasingly broken surfaces take the light when once the clay has been translated into bronze is eminently evocative and allows of the utmost accent with the greatest breadth. Were the surfaces which take the light smoothed down, they would lack the glittering variety of light and shade and the sense of mass and resistance that go with that. Now that he has found his style, we can recognise certain definite mannerisms. It would be easy to parody an Epstein.    But the mannerisms are not idle or irrelevant affectations ; they are inevitable steps toward the end he pursues.    Since it is the personality presented as drama that he envisages, he seizes on those aspects of the head which reveal it most sharply.    Generally the head is tilted back so that the chin protrudes and the planes of the forehead, eyelids, nose, and upper lip are turned to receive the fullest light. All these planes are enlarged, and their lower limits either deeply undercut or at least marked by a sharp edge.    In general the features are amplified so as to occupy the whole of the mask, and the mask in turn is pulled out, as it were, at the edges, receding frequently to an anatomically impossible hollow above the ears so as to give all possible expression to the receding ridge of the cheek bone.

In general Mr. Epstein follows the tradition of dramatic sculpture by working with ridges and bosses rather than by the architecture of planes.    For this dramatic sculpture is no new thing, though it has boasted few great masters.    Where Mr. Epstein is perhaps peculiar is in the vehement notation of actuality in the individual head, but even here those who knew Guido Mazzoni's " Pietà " at Modena will recognise that at least one artist of the Renaissance had anticipated a result which seems surprising when we thus meet it afresh and with all the marks of modernity.    Indeed, Mr. Epstein's " Weeping Woman " is singularly like one of the mourners in that group who kneels with hands clasped and mouth awry.    Mr. Epstein's distortions, then, are not caprices ;  they are not made to show how modern he is ;  they come inevitably out of his aim ;  they are necessary to his full expression. Decidedly Mr. Epstein is a master.

But a master of what ? murmurs a still small voice within me which all the turbulence and impressiveness of these works do not entirely silence.  A master of what ?  Of the craft of sculpture, undoubtedly ;  of vigorous characterisation, certainly after a fashion, but even here I should have to make reservations.    Even if we are to regard sculpture as a peculiarly effective form of representation— more than making up for the lack of colour by the palpability of its form—even so, one can imagine a finer, more penetrating, less clamant kind of interpretation of character.    One might tire, perhaps, of the element not only of caricature—since all interpretation of character partakes of the nature of caricature—but of its direction.    One might soon long for something which, even at the cost of being less immediately impressive, wooed one to a gentler, more intimate contemplation—something in which the finer shades were not so immediately blotted out by the big sweep of the most striking, first-seen peculiarities. One would prefer to live with something less vehement in its attack, rather more persuasive.

But this is a question of taste and perhaps of individual temperament, and there can be no doubt that if we are to regard sculpture in this light it is better to have such strong, broad, racy, even brutal characterisation than the merely toned-down, the insipid, the genteel of fashionable portraiture. This at least is alive ; it stirs and moves some corresponding fibres in our nature. This has at least a genuine dramatic appeal, even though, like some greatly admired actors, it seems a little too much preoccupied with getting its effects over the footlights and right to the back of the pit.

But this digression has not stopped the inner voice. It persists : Is he a master of sculpture ? And, alas ! I am bound to say to the best of my belief, No. If I examine my own sensations and emotions, I am bound to confess that they seem to be of quite a different nature when I look at good sculpture from what I feel in front of Mr. Epstein's bronzes. There is an undoubted pleasure in seeing any work accomplished with such confidence and assurance, such certainty and precision of touch ; there is a powerful stimulus in the presence of such vividly dramatised personalities, but the peculiar emotions which great sculpture gives seem to me quite different. They come from the recognition of inevitable harmonic sequences of planes, of a complete equilibrium established through the interplay of diverse movements and a perfect subordination of surface and handling to the full apprehension of these and similar qualities. It may be, of course, that I am so carried away, so disturbed if you like, by all those other qualities of drama and actuality which Mr. Epstein's work displays that I cannot feel this purely formal stimulus to the imagination which is what I seek for in sculpture. But there is the fact as I see it. These busts are for me brilliant but rather crude representations in the round. If these are sculpture, then I want another word for what M. Maillol and Mr. Dobson practise, let alone Luca della Robbia and the Sumerians.

Fortunately for Mr. Epstein, there are a great many people whose imaginations are excited by really capable dramatic representation, and there are very few people who happen to like sculpture in my sense. The majority are quite right to acclaim him as a master, since the gift necessary for such work is a very rare one and he has used it and developed it pertinaciously, and since it does give genuine pleasure. Such work as this is infinitely better than the stylistic, decorative arrangements with which Mr. Epstein started, and in which some of his most celebrated foreign rivals still persist. It is a triumphant expression of genuine feelings about people's character as expressed in their features, and if it does not evince any peculiar and exhilarating sense of formal harmony, so much the worse for the few people who happen to have a passion of such an odd kind.

A later exhibition, July, 1926, of Mr. Epstein's sculptures has recently followed the one here criticised. It shows a decided change in Mr. Epstein's art. It is not in any sense a *volte face* from his former method such as his earlier career occasionally showed. On the contrary, it shows that the surmise which I made in the preceding remarks that Mr. Epstein had found at last his own inevitable personal manner was justified. But it shows me, alas ! that I had not estimated quite as fully as I ought the dangers inherent in that manner ; that when I had looked forward to him as pressing onwards to a more intimate reading of character, a greater intensity of the psychological moment, I was too optimistic. I hardly suspected how insidious was the impulse to increase the violence of the attack, the clamancy of the appeal. I never ventured to hope that Mr. Epstein would turn from being a remarkable illustrator in the round into a sculptor, but I assumed that his illustration was inspired by a genuine dramatic feeling for character. But this last exhibition has dissipated even those comparatively modest hopes. How terribly the blatancy of the appeal has grown, how fast melodrama has encroached upon drama ! Illustration is evidently a dangerous art.

## II. MR. EPSTEIN AND THE PHILISTINES

From a sociological point of view the controversy over the Hudson Memorial is full of interest. It shows us what we had almost come to forget—that the Philistines are always with us.   The Philistine has been quiet for many years, and questions of art have come rather to be quarrels between different groups of artists, or at least of people owing some allegiance to art; and now suddenly the Philistines have woken up and found a voice.   It would be extremely interesting to find, if one could, the causes which have thus stimulated to renewed self-confidence and vocal expression that vast mass of people who generally acquiesce silently in what is done for them.   Is it Mr. Sickert joining the Academy?   Is it the presence of an amateur painter in the Government?   Is it one sign of a general wave of obscurantism and reaction of which one feels the effect in many quarters?   I cannot say; I would consult those who are weather-wise in the spiritual atmosphere did I know such.

But there is the fact—the Philistines are upon us, and we have to close up our ranks.   I have not spared my criticisms of Mr. Epstein's sculpture.   He aims at something which has for me only a minor interest, but he attains his ends with a mastery to which I have always paid tribute.   What he feels he expresses with a virile directness and energy which are admirable qualities.   So against a common enemy he must accept me as an ally, as once before over the nude statues on a Strand building.   We can settle our quarrels elsewhere and at another time; for the moment all who care for art of whatever shade must face the common foe and stop once for all his arrogant attempt to lay down the law out of the abundance of his ignorance and in-sensibility.   I say once for all, but I recognise, alas! that this is pure rhetoric, for his voice will never be completely silent; only, from time to time, the Philistine can be made to see that as he has always made a fool of himself in the past, the probabilities are that he always will.

And what of the sculpture itself?   I am not going to pretend that it has converted me into an enthusiastic admirer of Mr. Epstein's sculpture, or that it causes me any profound emotional reaction.   But it has certain qualities which are almost always absent from our public sculpture.   As a decorative arrangement of forms within a rectangle it shows inventive ingenuity and a sense of proportion. The quantities of relief and hollow, the relative proportions of light and shade are fairly balanced, and the linear rhythm of the design is

well carried through.   By an extremely ingenious placing of the forms
of the birds so as to fit almost exactly (but not too mechanically)
around the form of the nude figure of Rima, Mr. Epstein has been
able to give to the restricted surface a richness of light and shade, a
density and weight which enable it to tell at a distance even in the
full sunlight of a summer's day.   This just estimate of scale and of
the intensity of relief necessary for a given situation, particularly out
of doors, is hardly ever attained in our public monuments, and merely
to have achieved this should entitle Mr. Epstein to high praise.
Whether you like this or not it is a legible design, whereas our sculptors
nearly always mumble and blur their statements from timidity and
want of conviction.

Besides this patent decorative quality we can recognise a definite
imaginative purpose, a clear personal attitude in the conception of
the figure of Rima.   She is imagined as a human being with something
of the haggard shyness and strangeness of wild things.   This is
certainly no tired repetition of a conventional formula, but a vivid
and individual creation.   To me the effort to convey by such emphatic
illustration a poetic idea is unsympathetic, but no one can deny that
the sculptor has achieved his intention.   It is thus a work primarily
governed by a poetical idea and expressed in vigorously decorative
forms.   What I regret is that among those, to me, minor concerns
the distinctively plastic imagination has not found any place.

There is a poetic idea and a decorative idea, and these are
thoroughly fused ; there is not, so far as I can see, a plastic idea.

The general design of the sanctuary seems to me successful.
The long rectangle of stone which brackets the sculpture and the two
plain rectangles on either side is well proportioned to the space of
lawn in front of the long stone-bordered pools.   But this commend-
able elevation has not received any adequate plastic execution.   The
stone rectangles are too thinly and smoothly finished, the edges are
too mechanical and abstract.   What was needed was either some
surface treatment, some blunting of edges, or even some play of light
and shade which would have given a density and volume to the stone-
work sufficient to carry the richness and weight of the sculptured slab.
The usual mistake of our men of taste is here shown, the mistake,
namely, of thinking that simplicity can be achieved by mere abstraction

and negativity. True esthetic simplicity can only be achieved by a rich and fervid sensibility working through the complexity of the matter to an ultimate unity. Such dead and mechanical simplicity as is shown here is less offensive, but no more moving to the sensual imagination than mechanical enrichment. I wish Mr. Epstein himself had cut these plain rectangles straight from the rough stone. Then they might fittingly have enshrined his relief, for the whole would have had a truly related surface quality. This would well have repaid the extra labour and cost.

So much for the sculpture itself. A word more about its vociferous critics. What fascinates me about the Philistine is his extraordinary sensitiveness, the ease with which the slightest surprise puts him off his balance and out of temper. One may almost say that whenever a work of art has sufficient accent for him to become aware of it, he sees red. It is not so much certain kinds of art that he hates. He hates any art of which he becomes aware. He is only contented and peaceful when, as he jogs his way, he can pass public monuments and statues without having any sensation at all. He has a blind traditional feeling that monuments have got to be there; they are part of the age-long prescription of public ritual, but, since they must be there, let them be as nearly as possible invisible, let them in no way rouse him from the day-dreams of his instinctive life. Then, and then only, is he content. But the expression of any idea of which he becomes aware rouses him to a passionate fury of denunciation. The Royal Academy has evolved in response to this feeling on the part of the average man. It attends to this inexplicable but apparently inevitable convention of art, but it keeps it well out of the way of any real interest, it produces something entirely anodyne and innocuous. And so the Philistine is a pampered being. Would that he could reflect for a moment, if such an effort of sympathetic imagination were possible to him, on the hard fate of those of us who have had the misfortune to be born with certain susceptibilities which, in our madness, we have cultivated by years of study to a considerable acuity, and imagine what heroic self-control is ours, as we walk about the streets of London, as we pass the statues in Parliament Square, or gaze on the ruined surface of Westminster Abbey, or dodge a taxi behind the Edith Cavell monstrosity, or contemplate the outside of the Victoria and Albert Museum, or see any one of the hundred thousand horrors to which the streets of London expose us.

We do not stamp with rage, we do not cry and shriek, we do not accuse the authors of these things of Fascism or unnatural vice, we behave with exemplary calm and patience, and yet we suffer far more in our sensations of discord and disharmony than it is possible for those who have never trained their senses in such matters. But watch the Philistine in his intemperate rage. There has just closed a show of some of the finest modern French pictures which have ever been seen in London at the Independent Gallery. It was a selection of picked masterpieces by the men whose work is acclaimed all over the civilised world, and yet there were to be seen there respectable old gentlemen stamping like naughty children on their catalogues, invading the private offices of the gallery to insult the proprietor, and carrying on like an hysterical woman in the lift. Really, before asking the artists to mend their morals, we have some right to ask our censors to look a little more to their manners.

Decidedly the modern Philistine is a pampered being. There have been times when his feelings were rudely disregarded by tyrannous gentlemen of taste and education. But in the fullness of time he has come by his own. We now bow to his power, we admit that being in so huge a majority he has a right to have nearly everything arranged to his taste—look at the lounge of any big hotel and see how carefully his whims are consulted. We admit that ninety-nine out of every hundred public buildings and memorials should be of the requisite ineptitude. But has the Philistine no compassion? He has in London hundreds, perhaps thousands, of pieces of sculpture totally devoid of all significance; cannot he allow us one little corner of Hyde Park, past which his daily business does not take him, where we can, in leisure moments, contemplate something which is, to put it at the least, decorous, intelligible, and respectful of past tradition?

### III. THE PHILISTINES AND THEIR STATUES

As fundamentalism has driven men to the study of evolution, the row over Mr. Epstein's relief has prompted me to look more curiously at London's statues. There can be no doubt that on the whole the Philistine lords have arranged things very skilfully so as to avoid any disquieting artistic impressions occurring in the streets and spaces of their capital city, and I should hardly venture to disturb the reigning harmony by calling attention to the few statues which have some artistic purpose, did I not know that they are too familiar to the Londoner ever to be seriously regarded.   The moment which I have chosen, the season when every one is out of town, is propitious, too, for such inquiries, since it is the one season when one may stand and gape at a statue and only pass for an American visitor instead of being suspected of lunacy.

Most cultured Londoners when challenged to mention one good statue in their metropolis point to Charles I. in Trafalgar Square. The seventeenth-century pedestal of this monument is one of the few exquisitely proportioned structures in London.   The baroque decoration of the two rounded ends is also very happy, owing to a good original design which has been singularly improved by the curious accidental enrichment wrought by the acid smoke of London on Portland stone.   By this chance the original plastic idea has been enormously enriched and emphasised, and it has gained a rare variety of surface quality.   The statue of the unfortunate king is, however, hardly worthy of this splendid pedestal.   It has, of course, something of the decorative quality which was traditional in all Renaissance bronze work.   The sculptor has made use of the creases in the leather jack-boots, the details of the mane and tail, and even the veins of the horse, not to mention the details of the armour, but all these are treated in a tight and literal manner and are imposed on a feeble and uncertain plastic theme without any consistent or well-held rhythmic idea.   On a small scale it might make a charming *bibelot* for the mantelpiece.   As it is, the feeblest of Italian Renaissance sculptures would make it look foolish.

Far better as an example of the peculiar decorative effect of bronze which the Renaissance evolved is Grinling Gibbons' statue of James II. behind the Admiralty.   The pseudo-classic pomposity of the imperial pose and the affectation of the Roman costume are easily forgiven for the sake of the exquisite clarity and incisiveness of the imbricated corselet, and the various graven and modelled ornaments for which that costume provided an excuse.   But the head and bare

L

limbs have also a nervous precision and accent which no other English sculptor has quite equalled. The general effect resembles that of the Italianising French sculptors of the later seventeenth century, but I doubt if any of Louis XIV.'s artists had quite the refinement of taste that Gibbons shows.

Far less decorative than either of these, but more convincing as a plastic idea, is the George III. in Cockspur Street done by Wyatt in 1836. It is a matter-of-fact affair enlivened by the rather conventional rhetorical pose given to the horse, but it is an honest and capable piece of sculpture. Wyatt has made happy use of the king's ridiculously small bullet-head. By means of the peruke he has joined this knob to the rounded shoulders by an unbroken curve which counters and contains the strong opposing diagonals given by the horse's checked movement. One guesses that Wyatt for the purposes of sculptural design has under-estimated the cubic capacity even of that royal head.

Another respectable equestrian statue of a purely conventional type is the William III. erected in 1808. Placed as it is among the beautiful plane-trees of St. James's Square, this is certainly a pleasing object.

All these are at least passable works, they are not artistically scandalous or disgraceful, but they are hardly capable of arousing more than a feeling of mild approbation.

Rodin's group of the Burghers of Calais is altogether another matter. This makes a bid for something much more impressive, and asks to be judged by higher standards than its decorative amenity. It is, however, unfortunately placed. Although the pedestal on which it is mounted is itself very praiseworthy in design and proportion, it seems to me much too high for the sculpture. I believe Rodin approved of the present emplacement, but it is known that his original idea was to have the group only a little raised from the ground, and I cannot doubt that this was the right conception. Placed where it is, behind the end of the Houses of Parliament, it does not detach itself sufficiently from the multiplicity of mouldings and windows which cover the face of that building. This work is not only far more ambitious than any other sculptural monument in London, but it is so infinitely more achieved than almost everything which it has to

compete with that one is inclined by the comparison to too favourable
a view.   Here, undoubtedly, is a master, one who has a clear conception of forms and the power to realise them.   But that conception
is not essentially a sculptural one.   Rodin's concern is with the expression of character and situation, it is essentially dramatic and
illustrational.   In this composition he has tried to present the dramatic
situation of the surrender of Calais to the English.   He has given us a
group of different types of sturdy characters worn out by famine and
delivering themselves to death, together with the diverse states of
mind that the situation provokes in them, some defiant to the last,
others broken with age and disillusionment, others lamenting their
premature death.   If we allow for a certain rhetorical emphasis which
is perhaps inevitable in view of the necessity of striking an arresting
note from the first—since the sculptor of a public monument has to
calculate for the mood of bored indifference with which we habitually
approach such works—if we allow for this rhetorical bias, we must
admit that the types are well chosen, the poses often striking, and the
movement of each figure convincing in its consistency and flow.
We must add to this the one really sculptural quality which Rodin
possessed, namely, the quality of his surface.   For there is a " sculptor's
quality " as there is a " *qualité de peintre*."   If we analyse what we mean
by this I suppose it comes to saying that all the minute unconscious
movements of the hand as it manipulates either paint or clay conform
to some deep instinctive rhythmic urge.   It is this that gives the
vibration of life to a surface, transmutes it from dead matter into a
medium of the spirit.   One cannot deny this quality to Rodin.   In
any sculpture gallery if we catch sight of only a fragment of Rodin's
actual handling—he is by no means always responsible for the actual
execution of his later works—we are attracted to it by this emanation
of vital force.   And in the Burghers of Calais this quality is fortunately
evident.   Look, for instance, at the tense and nervous modelling of
the taut muscles in the man holding the key of the town to the right
of the group.   It has the palpitation, the possibility of movement
and change of life itself.   Or again, in the broad incisive handling of
the heads the same admirable quality is apparent.
      I believe this was the first complex group of figures that Rodin
attempted : that it was done in direct answer to the challenge of the

critics who grudgingly admitted his capacity to model a single figure but denied to him the power of co-ordinating a larger whole. In view of the extreme unfairness with which Rodin's earlier works were received—I remember well the howls of indignant rage and the guffaws of the idle public before his Balzac, which remains, to my thinking, his supreme masterpiece—it is unpleasant to have to agree with the critics. But there it is. Rodin's rhythmic sense had only a short range. It was confined to his nervous organisation. In the larger relations it broke down. So here this group remains a crowd. Each figure has been separately conceived, and then they have been moved about until they fitted together with as little inconvenience to one another as possible. At least, that is the impression one gets. There is no controlling rhythmic idea, no *liaison* between the different parts, no interplay of planes, no estimation of the relative quantities of unbroken surfaces to intricate and agitated ones. An unco-ordinated monotony and uniformity of quality pervades the whole. It hangs together by its dramatic but not by its plastic unity. Rodin could achieve texture, he could not achieve architectural structure. He could not hold and vary his rhythm throughout a sustained phrase. He could only repeat his short phrases over and over again.

As far as I know the specific pleasure of sculptural design, in which Rodin just fails us, can only be found by the Londoner before one work exposed to the public gaze.

The situation and aspect of this statue are so comically incongruous and unexpected; it has so much the air of a meteoric intrusion from other worlds, that a mythical explanation has to be found for its appearance. It all began, it is said, with one of the many occasions when " the Lord waxed exceeding wroth with His people, the people of London." But it so happened that being also " exceeding wroth " with a number of other people in different parts of the world, it did not suit His purposes to hurt them in their most sensitive spot by a financial crisis. He therefore considered in what way He could punish them most severely and continuously without interfering with the general course of events, and in the end He condemned them to possess and expose perpetually to the public gaze one work of genuine sculptural design. The people of London were at first staggered by this verdict, but they are an ingenious and resourceful people and they had often played the game of hiding an object in a clearly visible situation and they knew that the best results were obtained when it was placed in so conspicuous a spot that every one overlooked it. So they found a place in the very heart of Philistia where more Philistines would pass within a few feet of it every day than in any other position in the whole of London town, and where it would yet remain completely unknown.

So far, I think, the Philistines were playing the game with as much fairness as success, but I regret to add that they cheated a little over the question of mounting the statue. They erected it on one of those granite drinking-fountains where you press a knob and a little water trickles into a tin mug. About sixty years ago benevolent people were very fond of erecting these objects. They apparently believed that it really was thirst that drove people into the public house. So far all was quite correct. Where the cheating came in was in getting a certain J. Edmeson Archt. to design a canopy in elaborately convoluted cast-iron of quite surpassingly hideous form and decorated with very cast-iron patterns, and in making the said canopy fit so closely over the head of the statue as to obscure it considerably, not to mention the tiresome interruptions to the view which the supporting columns interpose.

So there, on a triangle of pavement behind the Royal Exchange and a few feet from Threadneedle Street, inside its cast-iron cage and on top of the red polished granite fountain where no stockbroker ever drinks, sits London's one really good, I might almost say first-rate, statue.

An inscription runs as follows on a granite slab below it :

" Erected 1878 at the expense of John Whittaker Ellis, Alderman, William Hartridge, Esq., Deputy, supplemented by a vote in Wardmote, also by donations from the Drapers' Company and the Merchant Taylors' Company."

I do not know whether Mr. Ellis, Mr. Hartridge, or Wardmote dictated the subject to the sculptor, but it was one that any sculptor might justly accept and it was peculiarly adapted to bring out all the qualities of Dalou's genius. For the figure of Maternity suckling a baby and holding an older child to her knee with a protecting gesture is signed Dalou 1879.

Here, at least, we are in the presence of genuine sculpture. There is nothing the least curious or interesting or decorative or in any way striking about it. The treatment is as traditional as the subject. This is just a mother like hundreds and thousands of mothers. There is no marked poetic or dramatic idea to help us out. We can get no pleasure here from anything but the special quality of sculpture, the harmonious counterplay of a complex system of planes and movements. It is only when, as here, the sculptor has himself felt intensely the continuity of the movement throughout every part, that he can communicate this special effect to our imagination. It is just because this group of three figures with all their complicated and corresponding movements depends entirely for its effect on realising continuity, that the actual setting of the statue is so unfortunate. In trying to apprehend the inevitable relation of the woman's back to the movement of the arms, we are continually disturbed both by the excessive shadow in which the upper part is lost, and by the columns which cut across the forms. But with a little patience the rhythmic scheme becomes evident, and we can feel the specific exhilaration which this clear sense of a vital order permeating a complex of volumes and planes arouses.

There is, of course, a further quality in sculpture which it is difficult to explain or analyse, namely, that of surface quality. The question to be solved is, if we consider a bronze statue, how far the surface should suggest the sudden and complete resistance to touch of actual bronze, and how far it should suggest the quality of flesh or drapery. The power to imitate in bronze a totally different substance is one of the stock marvels of sculpture to the unsophisticated. The imitation almost to the point of illusion of flesh, lace, velvet, or hair produces in the mind of the barbarian of modern civilisation a vivid shock of wondering admiration, but this can hardly be counted an esthetic quality.

From the esthetic point of view, the determining factor must rather be some intimate correspondence between the larger rhythmic movements and the minute changes of direction which are due to the " handling " of the material, and which arouse in the mind the idea of some particular kind of surface. With certain hieratic and rigid movements we might almost require to be reminded of the unyielding resistance of the actual metal, with other rhythmic systems such a surface might arrest the movement too sharply. When, as in most Renaissance bronzes—as, for instance, in the James II. already mentioned—the decorative aspect of the material is exploited, we also need the sharpness of edge and the flatness of facets to which bronze specially lends itself ; but in general we may say that for the richer and more complex rhythmic ideas, a rigid unbroken surface tends to be too schematic and abstract. A certain suggestion of play in the surface is almost as necessary as the " nervous " line in a drawing. But the exact degree of this play or " atmosphere " of the surface must depend on the general rhythmic feeling and the type of curvature of the modelling.

Dalou's treatment of surface is evidently deliberate and consistent. He chooses for his drapery a thick soft material which takes full rounded folds, and this is in accord with his feeling for flesh. Here, too, full rounded forms predominate, but they are never flaccid or inflated. One may perhaps compare his treatment to that of della Quercia among the Italians of the Renaissance, but he is a della Quercia become aware of what the eighteenth century contributed—its variety of surface quality, its more conscious and nervous sensuality. But that is all that Dalou has borrowed, there is no eighteenth-century *mièvrerie* in this ; it has the frankness and candour of an earlier art with that subtlety superadded.

More and more as time goes on Dalou begins to stand out from the ruck of nineteenth-century sculpture. How poor beside his generous and ample manner do the brilliant, stylised, photographic effects of Carpeaux show ! How genuine he is beside the conscious stylistic borrowings of Alfred Stevens !

Dalou was an exile in London during and after the war of 1870, and it is to that fact that we owe this one really moving piece of public sculpture. He left here, too, the admirable tondo of a bacchanal scene in the Victoria and Albert Museum. But the Maternity of the City of London is a more impressive work. It is, indeed, one of the best of his that I know. Perhaps one day the iron tabernacle which disfigures and conceals our one masterpiece might be removed by a vote in Wardmote.

### IV. MR. DOBSON'S SCULPTURE

The question of the relative superiority of the arts of painting and sculpture has always been canvassed among artists. It is not, perhaps, a very profitable discussion, but it enjoys a surprising vitality. Leonardo da Vinci was a hot partisan of the painter's art, and used as his trump card the superior conditions of the painter's craft. He compares the sculptor, working in a barn in dirty old clothes and covered from head to foot in stone dust, with the painter, sitting in a finely furnished room, in ease and comfort and wearing his velvet robe. There is something a little shocking to the modern mind in the idea of such naïve social ambitions in so great a man. We have suffered enough from the gentlemanly artist since his day to be less impressed by his good manners. The attacks seem to come mostly from the painters who turn to sculpture from time to time or when their eyesight is beginning to fail, and do so with the slightly contemptuous gesture which Renoir expressed to Rodin who, when asked by the latter why he had taken to the sister art, said : " I'm too old and feeble to paint any more ; I have to do something easier."

There is, after all, a truth in this. Sculpture is from one point of view much easier than painting. The sculptor interprets the solid forms of nature in solid forms. He is spared that complicated projection of solid forms on to a flat surface. The sculptor, if he has once grasped imaginatively the relation of two planes to one another, has no more to do than to shape his clay or stone to that. The painter has to discover the different distortions of each plane due to its appearance from one particular angle of vision, whereas the sculptor is allowed an all-round vision. It may be due to this much greater simplification of the general problem that sculpture seems to be *par excellence* the art of primitive peoples and of early civilisations. It would seem that for the sensibility and mentality of these stages of civilisation sculpture was the simplest and most attainable expression for the sense of visual form. Think of the complexity and richness of sculpture of the negroes as compared with their purely decorative, geometric ideas of form on a flat surface ; or of the high attainment of twelfth-century sculpture in Europe at a time when painting could only command the most elementary and abstract conceptions. In the later stages of civilisation, with a more sophisticated mentality, sculpture seems to become progressively more and more difficult.

It may be that when once we have lost the blind courage of ignorance, when once the mind has become fully conscious of the problem it poses, sculpture appears altogether too formidable. For, though we live in a three-dimensional space, our minds and our imaginations are not really quite at home in it. We move about only on the flat surface of the earth : it is only the various directions upon that surface that are fully present to our consciousness ; we should be bewildered had we to choose between all the possible movements of translation that are open to birds and fishes. And so we instinctively approach even solid objects in plane and elevation. We cling to these flat aspects as being the most familiar and the most readily intelligible. And almost all European sculpture is haunted by this need to conceive in terms of successive elevations. It seems almost as much beyond the human imagination to conceive form without reference to a flat plane as it is for our mathematics to calculate the interaction of three bodies in space.

And this inability to grasp fully and readily three-dimensional relations has affected Northern art even more than the art of the Mediterranean peoples. Our architecture is continually hampered by it, and sculpture has always had among us a precarious existence. It has been least neglected by the public when it has borrowed most from the pictorial aspect of things—when it has used form to paint, as it were, in light and shade ; when, moreover, it has used these means to emphasise, not form itself, but the psychological or dramatic associations which it may arouse. It is only when it belies its own nature and becomes picturesque that it finds a ready acceptance. If a young artist with a feeling for sculptural design were to realise fully all these considerations, he would show almost superhuman courage and tenacity if he were to persist in being a sculptor in twentieth-century England.

Perhaps Mr. Dobson did not know at the start what he was in for when he set out to be a sculptor, and a sculptor who would confine himself to purely sculptural plasticity. Whether he knew it or not, his having pulled through to some kind of recognition is one of the happiest omens for English art of to-day. For whether we like his work or not, we must admit that it is true sculpture and pure sculpture, and that this is almost the first time that such a thing has been even attempted in England. This may seem an exaggerated statement, but when one considers the poverty of sculpture of any kind in England, and how much of what there is has been devoted to sentimental photography in stone and bronze, it will not seem *a priori* improbable. It is perfectly true that now and then artists of striking personality have used sculptural means of expression, and perhaps none with more conspicuous success than Mr. Dobson's contemporary, Mr. Epstein. One might even concede that Mr. Epstein expresses in solid forms a richer invention and a more vivid imaginative outlook, but for all that he is not playing the same game. We have now a good many painters who are trying to express themselves within strictly pictorial limits ; we have as yet only one sculptor who has adopted a similar attitude to his art.

Starting thus with no native tradition behind him and with such a problem to face, Mr. Dobson has set about his task with wise deliberation and a clearly thought-out practical plan. There are, roughly speaking, two avenues of approach to a complete work of art. The artist may work through his sensibility towards the perfect organisation of form, or he may attack the organisation of form deliberately, and, when once he has mastered that, allow his sensibility to give body and substance to what began as an abstraction. By either route the way to a perfect fusion of the two elements, which is essential to a complete work of art, is generally a long one—that is why so many artists only achieve their real expression late in life—and what is done by the way, will always be rather a work of promise than of fulfilment. The influence of Cubism on modern art has caused many, perhaps the majority, of the younger generation to adopt this second route— to begin, that is, by a conscious study of organisation. Mr. Dobson is no exception to this. In all his early work we feel this deliberate consciousness of the formal problem, and it is only of late that he has felt sure enough of his control to begin to express the result in terms of a more intimate and sensual contact with life. His invention of plastic schemes was always happy, even if it was not always new and personal ; but in the earlier work one felt that the idea was never fully embodied. It remained, in part, an abstraction. Mr. Dobson

PLATE XXVI

Bronze bust.   Mlle. Lydia Lopokhova.   Frank Dobson

is far too methodical to be in a hurry. He has had the patience to learn one thing at a time, and, moreover, to allow time for what he has laboriously and consciously acquired to become an unconscious habit of hand and eye. His plastic ideas have become richer, more complex, more stimulating, by the variety and freedom of the movements involved, and they are more and more fully externalised. The cold dogmatism of the early Cubist essays is yielding to a more vital and sensitive apprehension. We are less and less conscious of the scheme, more and more of the uniqueness of the result. His sculptures begin to take on that air of reality and individuality without which a work remains, after all, only a kind of theorem.

It was, I think, in the bust of Mlle. Lydia Lopokhova (Pl. XXVI.) that Mr. Dobson first came through his period of apprenticeship. Here, for the first time, his feeling for the possibilities of balanced sculptural systems was strong enough to allow him to start without any *a priori* conception. For the first time he could be sure that out of the living figure, and by using what was most characteristic of it, he could yet find an inevitable and patent harmony of direction and plane. The movement here is no vague or abstract rhetorical gesture, but bears the unmistakable accent of a definite and unique personality. It has, in fact, the quality of life, and yet, complex and unexpected as it is, it builds for us a completely satisfactory and clearly balanced formal system.

Naturally enough, when Mr. Dobson has treated the figure as a whole, or in such groups as his sketch for the Cardiff Memorial, the problem has become more complicated and he has now and again returned to a more abstract and generalised statement in order, as it were, to make sure of himself. Thus, in a small marble of a nude figure lying down he has been absorbed mainly by the problem of organisation. It is from that point of view a most satisfactory work ; the analogies of the various forms of the figure are clearly brought out and the different quantities of the masses are beautifully and inevitably related.

In a more recent seated nude he has attained a similarly perfect organisation of an even more complicated interplay of contrasting movements, and has yet kept not only the naturalness and ease of the pose, but a more vivid sense of life in every part.

More advanced still from this point of view is the admirable little clay sketch of a three-quarter-length figure (Pl. XXVII.), where the comparative simplicity of the plastic scheme has allowed the artist scope for a freer and easier handling and more play to his sensibility. Here at last the scaffolding is all taken down and we are no longer conscious of the process by which this became formally organic. Here is the art that conceals art.

The same may be said of the charming bronze, " Head of a Girl," where a very living and rather unexpected movement has been most ingeniously and subtly compressed within the narrow and exacting limits of the bust form.

One cannot doubt that Mr. Dobson is reaping the advantages of a severe academic training—in the good sense of that much-abused word—which he has so deliberately and courageously gone through. Whatever his future work may bring, one may now feel sure that it will never degenerate into the formal incoherence of the photograph in the round or into that exuberant decorative expressionism by which a good deal of modern sculpture seeks to make itself interesting to those incapable of response to plastic design.

PLATE XXVII

Study of nude.  Frank Dobson

# BOOK ILLUSTRATION AND A MODERN EXAMPLE

BOOK illustration is a battle ground, a no-man's land raked by alternate fires from the artist and the writer, claimed by both, sometimes nearly conquered by one, but only to be half recaptured by the other. One day, perhaps, when we have constructed some kind of esthetic applicable to all the arts alike, some principles will be laid down to settle the dispute, but for the present it must rage. The question even whether true illustration is possible at all has never been satisfactorily answered.

Is it conceivable that one man should express a certain mood in words and another should find forms expressing an identical one? Hardly, one supposes, since no two men ever can quite coincide in their emotional reaction. No one doubts that where facts only are at issue this coincidence is possible, the illustrations to a scientific treatise or a trade catalogue can clearly be perfect, but where the writer is an artist and the illustrator an artist there must be divergence. These questions are stirred again by Mr. E. McKnight Kauffer's illustrations to " Burton's Anatomy of Melancholy."* Two distinguished literary critics have expressed themselves upon these illustrations, one with vague dissatisfaction, the other with unqualified contempt, and yet to me they appear not only entirely delightful for their decorative charm, but quite peculiarly adapted to their purpose in relation to the text. So that this time, at least, the battle is set. Whilst I claim for them decorative charm I am, as it were, on my own ground, which perhaps my literary *confrères* would not dispute, but when I suggest that they are good as illustrations, I am advancing into the disputed territory. What I am claiming, however, is only this, that a quite peculiar literary situation has allowed of a peculiar solution.

To clear up the issue let us return to the general question. There is no doubt that a book may be decorated—initials, borders, *culs-de-lampe*—these may be always admitted if they are good of their kind; they do not provoke any question with the writer. It is only when

* " Burton's Anatomy of Melancholy." Nonesuch Press, 1926.

157

the artist's forms have a further significance, suggest ideas or feelings by what they represent or by symbolical or expressionist methods, that they impinge on the text. It is only then that the question arises, first, can it be done at all? and secondly, has the artist in question done it? It seems to me that real illustration in the sense of reinforcing the author's verbal expression by an identical graphic expression is quite impossible. But it may be possible to embroider the author's ideas or rather to execute variations on the author's theme which will not pretend to be one with the text, but rather, as it were, a running commentary, like marginal notes written by a reader. Now, such marginal notes may, as we know, be horribly exasperating or they may be illuminating, according to the writer and also the nature of the book. A writing of close-knit texture and concentrated unity of effect—a lyric poem, for example—should have its margins clear of all, even the best, comment, since nothing must distract us. In such a work there are no interstices, no pauses where the commentator can decently put in his word.

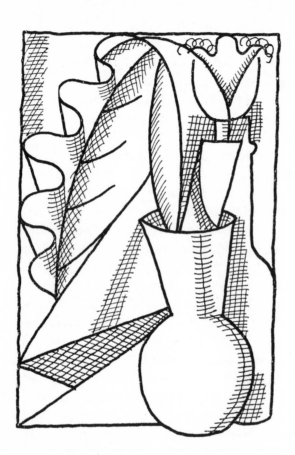

But if the book be of a rambling, easy-going, cut-and-come-again nature, there are hundreds of places where we may turn aside and chat with our invisible fellow reader. And of all such marginal commentators the draughtsman is the most discreet, for he is inaudible, he never puts an actual word into your head which might get confused with the words of the author. He merely starts a vague train of thought by the image which he puts before

you in one of those pauses which the author's discursiveness allows. Though even so, of course, the question of whether he be welcome or not will depend upon his tact, his appositeness and the absence in him of impertinent self-assertion.

Now, it appears to me that " Burton's Anatomy of Melancholy " is of all books the most illustratable in this way, and far more illustratable now than when it was written. Also, it appears to me, though here I speak in fear of my literary friends, that Mr. McKnight Kauffer has proved himself the most charming, the most sympathetic, and the most witty of interrupters.

But first, as to the decorative quality of his drawings, their aptness to the text regarded as a purely formal matter of black and white, or rather grey. To begin with, the typography of the book seems to

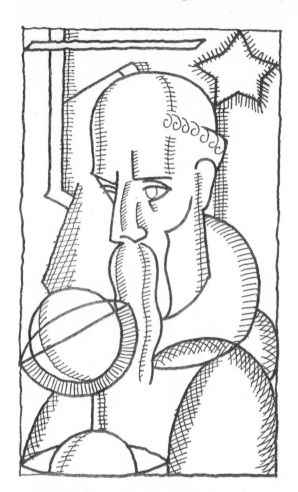

me admirable. The general effect of an ancient folio is preserved without any affected archaism, all is clear, lucid, well planned, and admirably printed on very good paper. Mr. Kauffer has clearly appreciated these qualities in his drawings. He has determined that in every way they should conform to the general effect of " colour " of the printed page. This means that he has had to maintain a certain average density of tone in his drawings, nowhere allowing too heavy or too closely placed darks, and nowhere becoming so thin as to leave a " hole " in the page.

A further consideration must be that of the rhythm of the drawn line—or one might almost say its *tempo*, since the quality of the drawn line depends so much on its pace. And here the printed page presents to the draughtsman a difficult problem. The rhythm of ordinary free draughtsmanship is nearly akin to that of the written word, but it is not at all naturally akin to the printed. The letters of our print, though originally based on written forms, have become far more rigid and exact, and have, if we imagine them drawn, a slow and excessively precise movement. Anything so exactly precise as the printed letter would be intolerably dead in drawing. Now, the early Italian illustrators did, in their wood blocks, find almost the exactly right kind of rhythm for the printed page, but it is no easy matter for the modern artist who uses zincotype line blocks to draw for that process anything equivalent to these early woodcut outlines. The first artist who tried it at all extensively was Aubrey Beardsley. He fell into the error of a far too insensitive mechanical precision.

WOODCUT FROM "THE DREAM OF POLIPHILUS."

His line, whatever its decorative quality may have been, was eminently inexpressive, insensitive and dead. And here Mr. Kauffer seems to me to have succeeded beyond any of his predecessors. He has drawn his main outlines with some kind of reed pen which allows of slow, steady movement without losing impetus and without much change of thickness. He uses this line with much freedom and variety, now with a firm and bold precision, and now more tentatively and tenderly.

M

But he has also seen that where a book is as large as a folio the open outline does not quite " hold up " to the grey of the print, and he

plays about on this fine solid drawing with thinner lines crossed at right angles or dotted or in thin, regular, corkscrew curls, producing in this way the most charming interplay of diverse textures and something that almost suggests the idea of colour.  So much for the nice adjustment of his technique.  In the spacing of his designs, the ordering of his volumes, the balancing of his directions, he seems to me to show real invention and the finest sensitiveness to visual values.

I have said that Burton is more suited to illustration now than

when it was written. We do not read Burton simply, nowadays, for it is in intention a learned medico-psychological treatise to which its author has given a quite fictitious appearance of scientific method

by dividing it into headings of " causes," " prognosticks,"
" symptoms," " cures."   No doubt this may have taken seventeenth-
century readers in, it will not do for us, and no one to-day goes to
Burton for counsel or pharmaceutics ; we read him for the delicious
flavour of his Renaissance pedantry and quaint humours, and for the
sonority and flow of his prose.   We do not, then, take him at his own
valuation : we may love him, but we could never avow to him the
reasons of our love.   Now, all this gives the illustrator of Burton a
peculiar position.   We cannot ask of him to be more reverentially
submissive than we are ourselves.   He must enjoy Burton's flavour
to the full, but he is guilty of no ill manners if, after all these centuries,

he now and then takes us, rather than the author, into his confidence ;
if he now and then whispers to us in a voice which the old man cannot
overhear, " Isn't he a delightful old buffer ?   Let's keep him at it ! "

It is in this spirit of affectionate raillery that Mr. McKnight
Kauffer has commented Burton, and in order to do it he has compounded a quite peculiar
brew of artistic motives.  I
should never have guessed
that the ingredients could
have mixed so well into so
exhilarating a potion.  We
have seen already that the
" Dream of Poliphilus "
and the old herbals give the
special note of " colour "
of these illustrations, but
there is nothing too literal
in his use of these models.
To these, then, treated in
the freest way, he has added
of all things modern Cubist
practice.  What is really
upsetting is the perfect
fusion of these elements.
He has drawn from Cubism
a new and quite unforeseen
possibility.  We are so little
accustomed to rest con-
tented in the contemplation
of abstract visible forms, as
compared, for instance, with
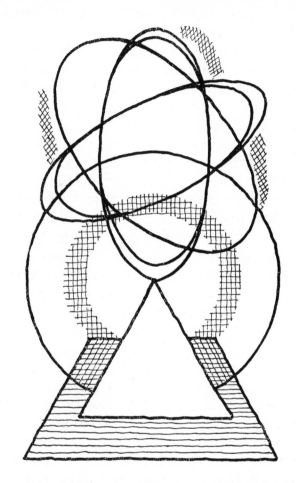
our readiness to contemplate pure auditory shapes, that Cubism
which set out to discover purely formal relations has always tended
to suggest some accidental significance.   People have insisted on
reading into it symbolical or expressionist meanings, and many artists,
such as the Futurists, have exploited it in that direction.   Nothing
could be more delightfully witty and apposite, therefore, than the

peculiar and quite distinct use which Mr. Kauffer has found for it. He frankly lets it correspond, as it so easily does by reason of this fictitious symbolism, to the half-magical and cabbalistic flavour of Renaissance science which had not yet run clear of Alchemical and mediæval lore.

The peculiar charm of much Renaissance science, and of Burton's in particular, is that it takes on so much of the quality of a work of art. It does not really supply information as it pretends to do, it only lures the imagination on into a mysterious region where the whole secret of the universe lies, always just over the next range of hills. Just so Mr. Kauffer's Cubistico-cabbalistic forms set the imagination free, we feel that if we could only pore long enough over these diagrams to understand them and then read very carefully all the authors Burton quotes, we should really hold the clue in our hands. And yet all the time our intellect knows well enough that it is only letting the imagination loose on a long tether; that it will come back to us breathless, delighted but empty handed. And we know, too, that it is really no use poring over Mr. Kauffer's diagrams, he has just been helping us in the subtlest, wittiest way possible to have our little game with the ultimate nature of things.

And beside this pseudo-scientific witticism of Mr. Kauffer's goes a pseudo-archaistic pedantry which I find equally delightful. With just as light and playful a touch as he handles the pretensions of Burton's science he handles also the art of his day. He knows all about Renaissance designs, but he has the self-confidence which all genuine artists feel when confronted with past art. It is not for him something sacred and absolute to beget a slavish copy or a skilful pastiche; it is an inspiration and a point of departure for his own art. He gives to these Renaissance pillars, columns, pyramids and arcades, a quite fresh flavour, so that while they remind us of the past they have the vitality of a contemporary creation. His pedantry is as full of enjoyment and poetic zest as was Burton's own. In that he is much nearer to the men of the Renaissance, to Brunelleschi and Donatello, than are any of their too abject worshippers of to-day, or rather of yesterday, since the high-water mark of such unintelligent industry was touched at the end of the last century.

In his illustrations of medicinal herbs Mr. Kauffer follows with

a delightful freedom the herbals of Burton's time, but gives to his drawings a more deliberately decorative quality, though often by means of a freer balance and a less strict symmetry. His landscapes are generally reminiscent of the " Dream of Poliphilus." Two in particular strike me as curiously happy—that which illustrates the effects of hot desert air in producing melancholy where we look over the battlements of an oriental town to the desert dotted with schematic palm trees, and that which illustrates the lonely places beloved of the melancholic, where a lonely church stands on shattered rocks beside the sea. In this Poliphilus and Picasso seem to shake hands across the centuries, but though both are alluded to the design has its own special half-ironical, half-poetical charm.

It was an inevitable tribute to Burton's vast knowledge of the classics that Mr. Kauffer should give us the portraits of the great men, the writers and philosophers of the ancient world. In these he has shown a curious power of taking the traditional portrait busts and giving them the oddest twist. They are at once schematic and decorative and full of life and character. The character, it is true, is sometimes underlined almost to the point of caricature. Aristides, for instance, is irresistible in the inflexibility of his wooden-headed rectitude. Alcibiades is almost as amusing in the up-to-date Oxford manner of his elegance. Now and then, perhaps, one may feel that Mr. Kauffer's light-hearted humour is pushed too far. The " Mars and Venus " is frankly comic, but ever so prettily so, and in his occasional naughtiness he adapts himself to Burton's own peculiar mixture of it with pedantry and ingenuity.

A great part of the pleasure which these illustrations give comes from the fact that in spite of all the knowledge of past art and of quite modern practice which they evince, in spite of their admirable planning and balance, they have an air of freshness and spontaneity, as though they were drawn with something of the same exuberant and easy eloquence with which Burton rolled out his catalogues and long-drawn phrases.

I doubt if any true illustrations can have the timeless quality of the great efforts of creative art. Probably these drawings of Mr. Kauffer's will date—the peculiar effect on us of their mixture of modernity and humorous antiquarianism cannot last. But Burton himself " dates." It is precisely because he dates so charmingly that we read him. I believe Mr. Kauffer's drawings will themselves date as agreeably and give to this edition of the " Anatomy " a unique and distinguished position.

By way of comparison let me cite another interesting modern example of book illustration, where the problem set to the illustrator was very different. Certainly few modern book illustrations have

WOOD ENGRAVING.   DERAIN.

seemed to me hitherto so stimulating as those executed some time before the war by M. Derain for "L'Enchanteur Pourrissant" of Guillaume Apollinaire, published by Kahnweiler. Here, as I say, the problem was different in that the text pretended to a concision and completeness very different from Burton's rambling manner. "L'Enchanteur Pourrissant" is evidently based on Flaubert's "Tentation de St. Antoine." It takes us into a world of extravagant imagery in which Merlin, the Lady of the Lake, Behemoth, Delilah, Cadmus and various animals mythical and real take their parts in a quasi-philosophic phantasmagoria. There are a few happy images and pleasing phrases scattered about in this rather precious and stilted production, but it cannot be regarded as a very important work of literary art. Derain has, in consequence, taken it rather lightly as a jumping-off place for his own free imaginative constructions which have, in fact, a more authentic air than Guillaume Apollinaire's. He has taken no less bold liberties with the printed page. This was executed in a very agreeable though slightly affected modern type, the main character of which was the absence of accent, the equal, pervading, pale greyness of the resultant page. Against this Derain has opposed woodcuts in which massive blacks and pure whites predominate. There is no greyness at all. The woodcuts, as a result, are of a totally different weight from the text. There has been no attempt at treating text and illustration as part of a single whole, so that I am perhaps doing more than justice to the illustrations by giving the examples here reproduced on separate pages without confrontation with text. None the less, one may, I think, admit that in this case the illustrator has justified his claim to play the leading part in the whole production, for he has given a new and completely successful interpretation to the art of wood-cutting. He has treated it indeed with an almost unheard-of freedom of handling. Instead of taking the pen drawing as the point of departure, which has been the method of procedure almost from the beginnings of the art, he has regarded the gouge as the essential instrument of expression. He shows, I think, a wonderful instinct for conceiving forms directly in terms of the gouge-stroke on the wood block, with the result that his sensibility comes through to us unchecked. It is like having an original poem instead of a translation. Derain has rightly concentrated first of all on the decorative disposition

WOOD ENGRAVING. DERAIN.

of his blocks of white and black, their enrichment of the page, but his forms have none the less a surprising life of their own, and the extreme simplification of his statements has a witty quality and one that stimulates the imagination. The illustrations might, in fact, lead one to anticipate more from Guillaume Apollinaire than he was able to provide. The opportunity for what might have been a completely successful case of modern book production was just missed here. With so remarkable and original and also so dominating an illustrator as Derain the typography should have been adjusted to the colour and weight of the artist's woodcuts. In that case the text alone would have been left to play an agreeable but secondary *rôle*.

# SPECULATIONS IN LANGUEDOC*

FROM Montpellier to Toulouse is a matter of a few hours in an express train. In that short time one has gone from the eastern capital of Languedoc to the western; one has also gone over an imperceptible watershed—easily tackled by the Canal du Midi—from the Mediterranean basin to the Atlantic. But the change of civilisation and culture is out of all proportion to this slight separation in space and time. There are two Midis, and they are quite unlike. Provence is, perhaps, the most intelligible land that there is—intelligible, at least, to the cultivated European, who has inevitably, by one means or another, such continuous references to the Greek spirit; for Provence is even more Greek than Roman. The bent must have been given to its civilisation before Rome came along. Otherwise, how explain the fact that Roman architecture and Roman sculpture are so much finer and more sensitive in Provence than in Rome itself? Even those who, like myself, will hardly cross a street to see the remains of a Roman building, knowing beforehand how like the latest stunt in fashionable modern architecture it will prove, have to admit before the Pont du Gard, the Maison Carrée, and the Nymphæum at Nîmes, and even before the touchingly naïve but ever so sensitive little arch at St. Remy, that Roman art could become expressive when its exponent had some other qualities than Roman efficiency and drive.

Yes, surely, Provence is still, not only Pagan, but decidedly Greek, and yet here in Toulouse neither Paganism nor Greece is thinkable. The Romans, of course, were here for ages, but as no Greek influence had preceded them they must, one guesses, have been here in some purely efficient Anglo-Indian manner. At all events, Paganism, if it ever flourished here, is dead, deader far and more unthinkable than in the Ile de France, where Romanesque and early Gothic are so apt to give a hint of its presence.

* *Nation and Athenæum,* 1924.

In vain one repeats to one's self that Toulouse lies south of Florence itself; in vain one sweats incessantly night and day; the idea that one is in the Midi will not take hold. The town belies its latitude and bids defiance to its climate. Some squalid Belgian town might have furnished the model for the newer streets—flat façades, windows neatly picked out in red brick from the drab cement front, elaborate and beastly cast-iron balconies, and no play of light and shade, as often as not no outside shutters. Or in older parts one seems to be in a part of Paris built in the Empire style when it was already out of fashion. An Empire without precision, blunt, heavy, and tired, with all the ornaments cast in putty and stuck on. At times there comes a whiff of remembrance from some North-country manufacturing town, from Leeds or even Bradford. Only now and again, when one catches sight of the blazing sunlight on the bare brick walls of an old church tower, something in the brown-red of the brick, with the grey patina of the Southern light upon it, recalls a vague memory of Bologna. The town smells worse, and has apparently fewer drains and more cesspools, than any Italian town I know, and yet it is obviously immensely rich, flourishing, and even learned, if one may judge by the numbers of students of all nations and all colours that frequent the cafés. For all that, it seems to lack any definite expression, unless just this inextricable tangle of contradictory motives is what it expresses. But how illegible the result is ! No one character dominates; always the contradictions frustrate its effect.

And yet it would be absurd to deny that Toulouse has somehow created a special art with its own special flavour. It would be absurd to deny to its inhabitants a certain originality and creative energy. For one thing, their Gothic architects invented and exploited the peculiar Tolosan arch—in which the two curves of the arch are replaced by the two straight sides of a triangle. It is a singularly ugly and unpleasing invention, but it is original. But the strangeness of Tolosan art begins straight away with the Romanesque. One enters the vast basilica of St. Sernin by the south door, and there on either side are two sculptured bosses. How on earth, one wonders, came these Hindu figures here? Of course, they are not Hindu, but how otherwise describe their rounded, inflated forms, their pasty modelling, their intricately convolved and flaccid rhythms ?

Inside, on the ambulatory wall, are placed a number of stone bas-reliefs, full-length figures of angels and saints, also of the end of the eleventh or early twelfth century. Here, too, are the same heavy, fat, rounded forms; here, too, there is the same want of any clear accent. They look as though they had been hammered out of lead, not cut in stone. They are caricatures of Byzantine forms, with perhaps a lingering reminiscence of the last degradation of Roman craftsmanship.

No doubt, then, the Romanesque art of this region has a character of its own, and nothing could bring out more clearly the contrast between East and West Languedoc than a comparison of these figures with the sculpture on the porch of St. Gilles near Tarascon. That porch, both as architecture and sculpture, is, I think, as fine as anything that this great creative effort of the twelfth century affords. The relief is everywhere perfect; the salience of pilaster and arch is as frank and clean as in the finest Greek architecture. It is, indeed, more Greek than anything; only in the animal sculpture it has a strange vitality, a perception of the peculiar character of the species which goes beyond the Greek imagination, and recalls early Chinese and Persian interpretations. But, what is more noteworthy, there is nowhere a hint of other than Pagan sentiment, whilst here in West Languedoc, at Moissac, all the spiritual terror of the Middle Ages finds expression in the tortured poses, the emaciated faces, and the writhings of the damned. And though the work at Moissac is far finer and more sensitive than that at Toulouse, it belongs to the same family.

The mediæval sculpture is equally contradictory of one's anticipations. It, too, has only Northern analogies. In the museum are a number of over life-size figures. They are carved in stone and painted. They are encumbered with the clumsy and grotesque costume of the fifteenth century. Features, expression, gesture, all show a sharp, literal, and slightly comic realism. They remind one of Claus Sluter and the Belgo-Burgundian school, but they have none of the dramatic passion and idealism which excuse a little the over-emphatic accent of their too actual forms. These Tolosan figures are the expression of a more literal, more banal, but no less incisive spirit. Still, it is only by what they lack that they can claim kinship with Southern art—

they have no sense of classic equilibrium and repose, and they have only so much style as a traditional craftsmanship imposes.

The impulse to create is marked enough in this centre of Languedocian culture, but how unenlightened it is by any clear sense of style ! It may seem almost too fantastic to relate with this ancient history of Tolosan art the fact that so many of the worst modern painters hail from this place and are called back to their native town to decorate its Capitol.  There Jean Paul Laurens, Benjamin Constant, and their kindred spread themselves to the delight of Tolosan shopkeepers, whilst the accomplished Puech, in the intervals of sculpting American parvenues, carves ideal figures.

If ever we get at a psychology of artistic creation as opposed to the psychology of esthetic apprehension, we shall have to count this urge towards production as one of the determining factors.  But we shall have to recognise that it may become disastrous if it outruns too far that sensibility which, without it, may perish and leave no record behind.  It is possible that some of the most esthetically gifted people have never expressed themselves for want of this creative energy, whilst the world is filled but too full by the insensitive productivity of the merely creative.  For the production of the greatest art there is needed not only great sensibility and creative energy, but also the synapsis between them must put up just the right amount of resistance to hold back the sensibility from too immediate an outlet in creation.

Originality and creative energy, then, we must grant to the Tolosans —and perhaps they find their best expression in the architecture. Here, too, nothing is perfect or shows a consciousness of the idea of perfection, but now and again by the sheer vehemence of self-confidence of its creators they strike out impressive ideas.  St. Sernin itself is one of the most ambitious of Romanesque constructions. Its mere size is impressive, and here and there it rises almost to greatness.  The effect of the transepts is completely successful.  The large, well-proportioned openings of the triforium, leading the eye into the spacious vaulted gallery which runs round it, have something of the imperial and courtly splendour of the architecture of Justinian's reign.  For a moment one is reminded of Ravenna—yet one more of the many conflicting reminiscences which this strangely mixed culture brings to mind. But outside the surfaces are never quite happily treated. The general conception of the east end, with its many apsidal endings which form a kind of inflorescence, as though they had budded out one from another, is fine, but the architect failed to get the full advantage of his plan, and frittered away his surfaces with a profusion of thin engaged columns which contradict the circular movement of the walls.

The original Romanesque tower may have been good enough and well-proportioned to the building it dominated, but in the thirteenth century they added two more stories with the ungracious triangular Tolosan arches, and not only spoiled the external proportions, but by the increased weight necessitated the added supports at the base which do much to spoil the interior effect. Again this terrible ambition to be impressive at all costs, this importunate facility of creation.

One at least of the Gothic churches, the Jacobins, does something to justify the experimental eagerness of the Tolosan architects. It is a great, gaunt, brick building with huge unmoulded arched recesses going nearly the whole height of the outside, and a many-storied campanile. But the great originality is in the interior plan. It is, in effect, an immense long hall of great height with an apsidal end, and divided down the middle by a row of circular columns which run their huge unbroken shafts right up to the spring of the roof. It is a curious idea thus to block the central view of the place usually and appropriately destined to the high altar, but it is none the less very impressive by its skilful exaggeration of the impression of the high suspension of the twin-vaulted roof on either side of the row of columns.

Here at least an architectural idea which reminds one of Northern examples—of certain brick churches in the Netherlands—gets a clearer, franker expression from that logical precision and clearness of statement which we associate with Mediterranean culture.

# VINCENT VAN GOGH

THERE may very well be some picture dealers still left in Bond Street who remember a young Dutch assistant at the Goupil Galleries who came every day to work, like every one else in those days, in a top hat. This particular top hat covered a shock of obstinate red hair, a receding brow over fixed, intense, but rather furtive eyes. The face showed a type half peasant, half criminal. This was Van Gogh in the 1870's. Presently he disappeared from the scene, and scarcely any dealer in Bond Street gave him another thought until in 1910, when he had already lain for twenty years in his grave, his works dazzled, astonished and infuriated all cultured England at the Post Impressionist Exhibition. "And," as one of the dealers who so remembered him said to me, "he used to be such a modest, retiring young man." He was, of course, a modest, retiring young man; but he was also a saint. He was the victim of the terrible intensity of his convictions—his conviction that somewhere one might lay hold of spiritual values compared with which all other values were of no account. This obsession drove him out of Goupil's, drove him to the Gospel and into a seminary for Protestant pastors; out of that again, to be a lay preacher and missionary; out of that again—for he made the fatal mistake of carrying out Christ's teaching literally—into sheer vagabondage and art; and then the terrible pressure of the obsession and his growing violence of character drove him into the madhouse and at last to suicide, but not, fortunately, until, with incredible determination and courage, he had taught himself to find an expression in paint for the desperate violence of his spiritual hunger, and left a body of work the mere bulk of which might well have occupied a lifetime, though there were barely ten years between his beginning painfully to teach himself to draw and the fatal pistol-shot. If, when he was still going every day to Bond Street, he could have compared prophetically the quiet, uneventful lives of his *confrères* during those years and his own tragic Odyssey, if he could have put ten years of squalor, starvation, ecstasy, madness, suicide and posthumous fame against the quiet, uneventful, successful life that would have resulted if he had stuck to his job, would he, one wonders, have chosen as he did? Probably, for this insignificant Dutchman had the heroic fire in him. But, in fact, the very idea of choice was incompatible with Van Gogh's nature. One pain at least was spared him—the uncertainty of trying to weigh the consequences of an act against the force of an inner impulse. Everything in his life was settled for him by the irresistible compulsion of inner conviction. The violence of that internal conviction was so extreme that hardly anything from the outside world could penetrate to him or leave its mark on his agitated spirit. No objective judgment of the outside world was possible to him. Even in art, where he was to prove his exceptional powers, he was quite unable to the last to attain any objective standards—unable to understand why he should not admire equally Meissonier and Cézanne. In this sense of the pure subjectivity of his experience he was mad from the beginning.

He was mad, but he was also a saint. In all the turmoil of his inner life the one dominating supreme impulse was a passion of universal love. It was the Christian idea of a love so all-embracing that it could scarcely attach itself to any individual; it was for all men and even for all things. And the tragedy of his life lay precisely in this, that only in his painting could he find any sort of expression for this love. When he approached people the very intensity of his feeling obstructed and distorted its expression, and instead of attracting and soothing them he infallibly irritated and repelled. By a peculiar irony of fate his feelings translated themselves in speech and manner into the opposite of what he meant. His love made people avoid him, and the utter self-abasement and humility, which his love inspired, translated itself into arrogance, harsh judgments and violent acts.

Only with quite poor, humble people could he hope to come to terms, and with them his contacts were superficial, since they could not share his intense spiritual life. For the rest, his devouring hunger for devotion and self-surrender was always stifled by the repulsion he aroused. Even Theo, his brother, whose goodness and patience were without bounds, could only approach him at rare moments. Otherwise, he was alone.

The account of Van Gogh given above is, in the main, an outline of the extraordinarily moving and beautiful tragedy which Dr. Meier-Graefe wrote some years ago.*   It is the tragedy of a saint who only found the way to peace through suicide.   Already in the bare statement of the facts of his life one feels something of the quality of a work of art.   From beginning to end it seems to move with a fatal acceleration to its desperate close.   Dr. Meier-Graefe has found a way to tell the whole story of his life as it presented itself to Van Gogh. It is as though the poor madman were going over it in soliloquy.   So fully has he identified himself with his hero that one hardly notices when Van Gogh is speaking in one of his letters and when the writer is interpreting for us what he must have thought.   We thus get a life seen from within outwards, and it was precisely so that Van Gogh was forced to live by reason of that incredible inner energy.

Any one who has read Van Gogh's letters will have felt that here was a personality more beautiful and more interesting than anything it accomplished.   For Van Gogh was not primarily an artist, and his personality only burst its way through into a tortured and difficult expression in paint because it met fatal obstructions elsewhere and was bound to find some outlet at whatever cost.

When once one realises this, one sees why Van Gogh's pictures are not the least like other pictures.   Their origin is different ; they are the outcome of a different kind of emotion towards the visible universe from that which governs the creations of most painters. Vincent's paintings are pure self-expressions, hardly at all the expression of a specialised reaction.   The strange thing is, not that as pictures they are so imperfect, but that judged by purely visual standards they are so free from aberrations.   The purity of Vincent's nature was so absolute that, puzzled and slow-witted as he often seemed, he was incapable of making just the sort of mistakes that one would have expected.   One would have supposed that this profoundly religious nature, whose one longing was to devote himself to humanity, would, when he turned to painting, have lost himself in some of those many delusive by-paths that offer themselves to the modern artist ; that he would have conceived of some terrible new kind of *tableau à*

* *Vincent Van Gogh.*   By Julius Meier-Graefe.   Translated by John Holroyd Reece.   Medici Society, 1922.

*thèse*, some horrible pictorial didacticism of the kind that Tolstoi recommended. But as Dr. Meier-Graefe pointed out, in an admirable passage on taste—though taste, in the sense in which the connoisseur and the man of the world uses it, was utterly abhorrent to this passionate anarchist—his creative energy made his judgment infallible. He saw through the falsity of Emile Bernard's anæmic exercises in religiosity, he realised that his own love was so universal that he had no need to choose subjects in order to express himself; he saw that his religion could find expression far more clearly in a picture of old boots, of a chair, of a brothel than in any religious subject.

In an exhibition of his works given at the Leicester Galleries in 1923, we had, for the first time in England, an opportunity of seeing something of the extraordinary artistic adventure which this strange being accomplished in the incredibly short time between his first devoting himself to painting and his tragic end. It is characteristic of his intensely personal and subjective talent that at each period he manages to convey so much of his beliefs, his passions, and of their effect on his temperament. Perhaps no other artist has illustrated his own soul so fully, and this all the more in that he was always the passive, humble and willing instrument of whatever faith held him for the time being in its grip. What strikes one all through his work, and with a fresh astonishment every time one sees it, is the total self-abandonment of the man. He never seems to be learning his art. From the very first his conviction in what he has to say is intense enough to carry him through all the difficulties, hesitations and doubts which beset the learner. He works, as a child who has never been taught works, with a feverish haste to get the image which obsesses him externalised in paint.

One could see that he must have always worked at high pressure and topmost speed, even if his large output in so few years did not prove it. That far exceeds in quantity the output of Cézanne's forty years of unceasing labour. Van Gogh had no time and no need for that slow process of gradually perfecting an idea and bringing out of it all its possibilities. He was too much convinced at the moment ever to doubt, and he was too little concerned with the fate of his work or of himself to mind whether it was complete or not, so long as he had, somehow, by whatever device or method that might come ready to his feverish hand, got the essential stuff of his idea on to the canvas. This is not the way of the greatest masters, of the great classic designers, but no one can doubt that it was the only way for Van Gogh. And so the fiery intensity of his conviction gave certainty and rhythm to his untrained hand.

What astonishes one most in the series of his pictures is not only the rapidity of the work itself but the rapidity of the evolution which he accomplished. His early painting of a " Pair of Boots " is a still-life study in which the influence of his early Dutch training and his enthusiasm for Israels are still apparent. This belongs to the year 1886. The latest work seen at the Leicester Galleries is the " Cornfield with Rooks," done at Auvers just before his death in 1890. And the difference of spirit between these two is immense.

In between lies Van Gogh's *Annus mirabilis* 1888, the year of his sojourn in Provence, of his comradeship with Gauguin and his first tragic outbreak. And in that year he had not only to sum up, as it were, all his past endeavour, but to accept and digest the influence of so dominating a character as Gauguin's. We see him in the " Zouave," frankly accepting Gauguin's oppositions of flat, strongly coloured, lacquer-like masses, but this is the only obvious evidence of Gauguin's effect on Van Gogh's art. The " Sunflowers," now in the Tate Gallery, is one of the triumphant successes of this year. It has supreme exuberance, vitality, and vehemence of attack, but with no sign of that loss of equilibrium which affects some of the later works. It belongs to a moment of fortunate self-confidence, a moment when the feverish intensity of his emotional reaction to nature put no undue strain upon his powers of realisation.

This is a harmony based almost entirely upon yellows. Against a pale, almost lemon, yellow background the heads of the sunflowers show as dusky masses of heavy burnished gold. Yellows indeed, and pure positive chromes at that, take a preponderant place in Van Gogh's colour scheme. Such a use of yellow is rare in European art. It occurs frequently in Italian paintings of the fourteenth century, and then seems almost to disappear from the palette. It was in Van Gogh's case doubtless due to Oriental influence, since it played so large a part in Chinese decorative design of the seventeenth and eighteenth centuries.

Van Gogh was in a sense a colourist, but in a very peculiar sense. He seems to have had a special sensitiveness to colour. It produced in him a kind of intoxication. But his feeling was mainly due to this almost purely physiological response. His reaction was far more nervous than mental, by which I mean that it was rather the lower than the higher nerve centres that were involved in his response. His reaction to colour, as to so much else, is elementary and childlike. He was altogether incapable of seizing the complex interrelations and correspondences of such profoundly meditated colour structures as Cézanne built up with a kind of intellectual sensibility.

In the " Sunflowers," as so frequently in Van Gogh's art of this period and as in most of Gauguin's work, preoccupation with the arrangement of the silhouette is very apparent. And, moreover, the source from which both artists got the idea—the Japanese print—is evidently disclosed.

It is a curious fact that both artists who owed so much to Cézanne found in his work the suggestions which led them in a direction the very opposite to that which Cézanne pursued. Cézanne's great preoccupation was always with construction in depth. With regard to the contour, what concerned him almost painfully was its function as a disappearing plane. That is the opposite of Van Gogh's interest in the contour as silhouette, as part of the organisation of the picture on a flat surface as a decorative unity. This was, no doubt, in part due to the influence of Japanese prints aided by his desire for pure positive colour. But even here Cézanne gave a sort of justification, since his perpetual anxiety about the contour led him sometimes, in despair, as it were, to reassert it with a line, often, I think, with the vague intention of returning to it later on. But Cézanne's contour lines fulfil a very different function from those even, heavy outlinings of the whole contour which suited well enough Van Gogh's primitive conceptions of form.

That interpretation, or perhaps misinterpretation, of Cézanne had far-reaching consequences on the development of subsequent painting.

One of the most original and, I think, one of the most entirely successful pictures of Van Gogh which figured in the Leicester Gallery exhibition was the " Yellow House at Arles " (Pl. XXVIII. B). Perhaps nowhere else did he express so fully the feeling of ecstatic wonder, the intoxicated delight with which he greeted the radiance of Provençal light and colour.   Here he shrank at nothing in order to find a pictorial phrase in which to sing of the violence of the sun's rays upon red-tiled roofs and white stone walls.   To do this he has saturated and loaded his sky, making it, not indeed the conventional cobalt which is popularly attributed to Mediterranean climes, but something more intense, more dramatic and almost menacing.   How utterly different is Van Gogh's reading of Provençal nature from Cézanne's contemplative and reflective penetration of its luminous structure !   Here all is stated with the crudity of first impressions but also with all their importunate intensity—and they are the first impressions of a nature that vibrated instantly and completely to certain dramatic appeals in the appearances of nature.   In striking contrast to Cézanne, too, is Van Gogh's indifference to the plastic structure of his terrain, which is treated here in a cursory manner.   The artist's interest was entirely held by the dramatic conflict of houses and sky, and the rest has been little more than an introduction to that theme.

But in the daring simplicity and vehemence with which that theme is stated we get a measure of Van Gogh's originality and an explanation of the great liberating, though also perhaps destructive, influence which his work exercised later on.

The canvases of the succeeding year, 1889, show another rapidly accomplished evolution.   The brushwork becomes more agitated, or rather the rhythm becomes more rapid and more undulating, and all the forms tend to be swept together into a vortex of rapid parallel brush strokes.

An example of this period is the " Cypresses " at the Tate Gallery, in which all the forms appear to be quivering and rushing upward with a flame-like motion.   The agitation of his own mental state—he was at this time in the asylum at St. Remy—has by now become the real theme of his art.   His vision of nature is distorted into a reflection of that inner condition.

Still, once or twice even at this period of frenzied vehemence the inner agitation and the outward vision came to terms and produced works of an unforgettable intensity.   The finest of these, and perhaps of all Van Gogh's work, is the " Ravine," now, I believe, in America.

PLATE XXVIII

*A*

Le Ravin. Van Gogh.                    By courtesy of the Leicester Galleries

*B*

The house at Arles. Van Gogh.          By courtesy of the Leicester Galleries

In this picture, by some fortunate conjunction of influences, all the agitated vehemence of his handling serves only to give vitality to the structure of the rocks ; and here, under the dominance of a more steadily held impression, Van Gogh has been able to persist until the loaded paint has become fused into a substance as solid and as precious as some molten ore shining with strange metallic lustres.*

In the " Cornfield with Rooks " we get a glimpse of Van Gogh's last phase of almost desperate exaltation. Here the dramatic feeling has become so insistent as to outweigh all other considerations. There is no longer any heed given to questions of formal design, and Van Gogh ends, as one might have guessed from his temperament that he must end, as an inspired illustrator.

Perhaps after all it would be truer to say that all along he was much more an illustrator than a plastic artist. All through we have seen that the dramatic appeal is the first consideration. It is significant that his first enthusiasm was for Israel's sentimental commonplaces, and that he was, a little later on, sufficiently moved by one of Gustave Doré's *ad captandum* inventions, a picture of prisoners tramping in single file round a dismal prison yard, to execute from it a finished oil painting. It is true that through his heavy handling there transpires an altogether new intensity and sincerity of feeling. He turned bad secondhand sentimental drama into a genuine dramatic expression, but the emphasis is none the less psychological. It may have been merely the accident of his constant association with French artists in Paris that changed for him the choice of his pretexts. Most illustration depends on the psychological significance of the persons or situations delineated in contradistinction to plastic art where the implications and associations of what is represented are irrelevant. Van Gogh learned from those plastic artists around him the habit of regarding almost any vision as a possible basis for design. But his whole nature impelled him to regard even the most indifferent object, a pair of boots or a chair, as charged with dramatic significance. It is only, therefore, in his approach to nature, in the motives he chooses, that he appears plastic. In reality he is an illustrator. Those convictions of dramatic

* Another treatment of the same valley, which lies just behind the lunatic asylum at St. Remy, is seen in Pl. XXVIII. A. This has not nearly the same subtlety of treatment, but is none the less a very striking composition.

significance which even the most trivial scene might excite in his exasperated mentality, modulated every line, tone and colour which he put down, into conformity with themselves. And this dramatic feeling was generally accompanied, perhaps even initiated, by his forcible reaction to brilliant light and colour.

The extent to which he was possessed by those dramatic moods gave him an astonishing conviction and impelled him to the most novel and daring innovations in the use of his medium. He could not wait to drag out of oil paint its subtle possibilities of expression. With reckless fervour he forced it somehow or another to convey his insistent feeling, and he was often rewarded beyond what one could have predicted, and the heavily loaded, tortured impasto takes on at times a strange, almost crystalline beauty.

But his innovations were not only technical in this narrow sense. The violence and elementary character of his responses to the appeals of vision led him to disregard the want of ordinary accomplishment which his short and late apprenticeship had imposed, and to brush aside all the subtleties and complications with which the painter's craft had become invested in the course of centuries.

He returned to a more than primitive simplicity of statement and built his images with almost the schematic bareness of a child's drawing. Within those limits, however, his conviction gave him a masterly precision and sureness of touch.

It was this peculiarity of Van Gogh's genius that made his influence on the next generation so considerable. His power of communication was so great that it was impossible even for the most casual spectator not to be arrested by it. The very fact that it was so elementary gave it an impressive force in a sophisticated society. When Post Impressionism dawned on our astonished world in 1910 it was, I think, Van Gogh who was the most overpowering revelation. Artists in particular felt that here was the authority for altogether new perspectives. His example inspired them to venture upon innumerable experiments, most of which were doomed to failure, but had at least a healthy effect in making new creations seem possible. It relieved artists of the pressure of discouraging pessimism which the criticism of the day imposed on the world as a mark of fastidious good taste. It destroyed in them the prestige of a culture which preached the doctrine that all real works of art were already enshrined in museums, and that the best that could be hoped for from the modern artist was the multiplication of skilful pastiches. Perhaps nothing short of Van Gogh's blatant anarchism in art could have served this end. Certainly in Paris the attitude of the " *Fauves* " in the first decade of the century was largely due to his influence, though it was doubtless reinforced by the strange discovery of the *douanier* Rousseau. It is doubtful, certainly, if Cézanne's influence alone would have prompted artists to such new experiments as Cubism and all its offshoots and successors. Nor, one guesses, would Matisse have ventured quite so far from the habitual norm of European painting without Van Gogh's inspiration.

Now that art has settled back more or less into the old lines of development, that exhilarating moment of reckless experimentalism begins to wear a rather strange look. But from time to time when one compares one of those highly accomplished and eminently polite products of the reformed " *Fauves* " one has a faint regret that with all their new-found accomplishment they have not managed to retain more of the daring confidence in their own convictions, even their own caprices, of earlier days.

It is well, perhaps, at this moment to recall with gratitude what Van Gogh's saintly self-immolation accomplished for us, for, to tell the truth, his work visibly declines in importance. He was the exact opposite of those artists like the early Corot, Sisley and Seurat, whose work continues gradually to unfold the full richness of feeling hidden beneath its superficial unimpressiveness some decades after the artist's death. Van Gogh staked all on the first shock of his attack, and as we recover from that we look in vain for further revelations. Certainly he was a more remarkable man than he was artist.

# SEURAT

THE acquisition by the Tate Gallery through the Courtauld Fund of Seurat's " Bathers," the purchase by an American for a high price of the " Grande Jatte," the acquisition by the Louvre of " Le Cirque," and lately an exhibition of his works at the Lefèvre Gallery, all show that Seurat is at last coming into his inheritance. That he has not already done so long ago may at first sight seem surprising. It is due partly to the special character of Seurat's genius, partly to the accident that, just when he might have emerged, Cézanne, himself long overdue, occupied the field to the exclusion of every rival. But now that Cézanne's contribution has gradually been assimilated by the artistic consciousness of our day, it is evident that, if we set aside Renoir and Degas, whose work had long been accepted, the other outstanding figure of later nineteenth-century art is that of Seurat.

None the less he will, I think, always make rather a limited appeal. There was in his personality the strangest combination of an extreme sensibility and a devouring intellectual passion. He had, indeed, what is perhaps a good thing for an artist, more intellect than judgment. He had a passion for reducing the results of sensation to abstract statements, such, for instance, as his well-known formula of the effect of lines in composition, namely, that gaiety is given by lines ascending from the horizontal, calmness by horizontal lines, and sadness by descending lines. Gaiety, by the by, is about the last quality one would predicate of his " Cirque," which is a deliberate demonstration of the effect of ascending lines. Such abstractions go but a very little way towards explaining the effect of so complex a thing as a pictorial design, still less can they be made much use of for the creation of such a complex. But it was a peculiarity of Seurat's intense love of method that it was by working along such lines as these that he was able, as it were, to lay by in pigeon-holes those actual sensations upon which his sensibility was nourished. Thus

188

he proceeded perpetually by analysis and classification working out separately and in turn the effective qualities of line, tone and colour. When he came to synthesise, the process almost appeared to him to be a mere logical deduction from the classified data of sensation—a deduction which could be stated by perfectly ascertained and pre-conceived methods. He is even said to have carried these so far that he was able to work all night in a feeble gaslight covering his huge canvases with his innumerable dots of colour, so exactly was the effect of each of the colours which he had previously mixed, ascertained.

Nothing can be imagined more deliberate, more pre-ordained than this method, nothing less like that divine afflatus of inspiration with which artists are often credited. And yet inspiration is the word one has to use before such strangely original conceptions as his landscapes declare. Who before Seurat ever conceived exactly the pictorial possibilities of empty space? Whoever before conceived that such vast areas of flat, unbroken surfaces as we see in his "Gravelines" could become the elements of a plastic design? And yet nothing less "empty," pictorially speaking, can be imagined. There is such a tense, imaginative conviction in these subtly-built-up statements of surface that one can well believe that Seurat's own definition of the art of painting, as "the art of hollowing out a canvas," was so evident to him as to make the effort of the imagination in cutting away so much material proportional to the vastness and emptiness of the space thus excavated.

And this work is accomplished solely by reason of such a delicate sensibility that it can perceive and hold firm almost infinitesimal changes of value. It is by the accumulation of these almost invisible gradations that the result is obtained. That incredibly laborious technique of a minute pointillism was perhaps the only possible technique that would admit of such subtlety of variation. This, indeed, seems to me to have been of even greater importance to Seurat's aim than the extra luminosity claimed for it. It alone allowed of a sufficiently slow and tentative approach to the final statement, it alone made evident the slightest changes of tone. Often, indeed, the whole structure of a design is held together by those slight changes of tone which are due to illusion, as when one sees the sky just a little darker where it comes against the edge of a white sail or a building. And yet, for all this close adherence to observation, how unlike anything natural these pictures are ! How utterly fixed and immovable everything is ! His pictures are alive, indeed, but not with the life of nature. He will paint air and almost nothing but air filled with light, but there is no breath in his air. If his designs live and breathe it is by the tension of the imaginative concentration which they reveal and impel us to share. Seurat is of the lineage of Poussin, and he is as austerely aloof and detached as he.

Seurat's ambition was as vast as his disinterestedness was complete. He attacked and carried through with a kind of inspired and yet ant-like patience the most terrifying pictorial problems. To conciliate those fleeting evanescent atmospheric effects which the Impressionists had noted in their rapid and fluent manner with the exacting canons of classic composition and to realise this completely on a large scale by the slow accumulation on the canvas of myriads of minute dots of colour might have deterred any one but a fanatic. And indeed there must have been something of a fanatical devotion beneath the rigorous intellect and reserved manner of this strange young man.

It was in the " Bathers " that he made the first grand demonstration of his new ideas. The scene is laid on the banks of the Seine just outside Paris. In the hot summer afternoon boys recline or sit, naked or partly dressed, on the bank with cast-off clothes and boots scattered on the grass, whilst others are playing in the water. This scene, which for most people contains the hint of some kind of lyrical beauty, is seen by Seurat with an almost inhuman detachment. How natural it would seem to accentuate the beauty of the naked forms by choice of pose or of lighting ! How easy to mitigate the banality of boots and trousers ! But here everything is given with the same even, unrelenting unemphatic precision of statement. There is no bias whatsoever. The hot haze of the summer afternoon whitens the luminous sky, half veils the distant factories and bridge, and plays over the luminous bodies in the foreground, and no one could render this enveloping with a more exquisitely tremulous sensibility, a more penetrating observation or more unfailing consistency, than Seurat; but, none the less, every contour of the ungainly shirt tucked into the half-drawn-up trousers, or of the boots and socks, is rendered with the same unchanging attention. Yet the effect is neither of lyric beauty, nor of banal or ironic realism. Seurat's aim lies behind and deeper than all such attitudes to the scene. It would be hard to find any word uncoloured enough to describe the mood this evokes. It is like that which comes to us from some of Piero della Francesca's monumental and motionless groups. It is a mood of utter withdrawal from all the ordinary as well as all the poetic implications of things into a region of pure and almost abstract harmony. For that, indeed, is the secret of this great composition, the compelling harmony of all these forms, the so evident inevitability of all its correspondences and correlations. Boots and trousers lose their everyday banality when they are implicated in so close-woven a texture of formal harmony, however relentlessly their shapes are defined. One is forced even to rejoice that boots have tabs, so evidently do they here become the key to a whole sequence of rhythmic phrasing. And no less does the beauty and charm of the summer sunshine sink into the background of consciousness and become only another part of the colour organisation. But yet, in spite of the exactitude and rigour of its harmony, this picture retains also something of its quality of immediacy, of a thing that was actually seen and seized on by the imagination in a single ecstatic moment. It is just that quality that Seurat's passionate research for abstract principles and scientific method might, one guesses, endanger. With him the balance between sensibility and doctrine was a delicate one. If the doctrine were to cease to be amenable to constant correction by the sensibility it might become the predominant partner ; demonstration would replace inspiration and theory passion. There was certainly a tendency for this to happen towards the end of Seurat's short life. That his sensibility would have regained the upper hand I do not doubt, but the balance sometimes inclines against it. The fact is that his method—he always called it " *ma méthode*," and any suggestion of infringement of his claim to have originated it moved him to something as near to self-assertiveness as his reserve and self-possession admitted—his method became increasingly his great passion, until he came to regard his pictures almost as demonstrations of its validity.

In the " Bathers " the method was not yet fully developed. The colour was put on in small dabs broken across by dabs of other colours, but those colours were always mixed on the palette to give the desired tint. He had not yet analysed the colours into more or less pure notes which should make up the required tint by means of optical mixture. Such a complete analysis implied, of course, much smaller units of colour, and this was finally attained by the juxtaposition of small round dots of the pure colours necessary to produce any required resultant.

The " Grande Jatte " was the first application of the method in its amended and final form. It presents a world from which life and movement are banished, and all is fixed for ever in the rigid frame of its geometry. The " Poseuses " (Pl. XXIX.), which was the most important work of the Lefèvre exhibition, follows closely on that. It is not so ambitious, but even more than with that, one feels that it has never quite been " seen." The " Grande Jatte " was created by assembling innumerable separate studies, an assembly in which everything took its place according to the principles of harmony which Seurat had elaborated. In the " Poseuses " the same method is employed. Seurat has made the same model pose in back, side and front views in a corner of his room, one side of which is completely filled by his painting of the " Grande Jatte." One feels that the poses have been found in order to fit a preconceived geometric scheme. Certainly the position of every single object and every part of the contour of every object has been ascertained to an almost incredible nicety. One cannot move a button or a ribbon without disaster to this amazingly complete and closely knit system. Since Poussin surely no one has been able to design in such elaborate and perfect counterpoint. But I come back to my feeling that here the harmony has been arrived at almost by trial and error, by a perpetual adjustment and readjustment. I do not mean, of course, that such arrangement and adjustment of one thing to another was the result of any merely intellectual calculation. It needed in order to succeed nothing less than Seurat's impeccable sense of proportion, of quantities, of tone and colour values, and his marvellous sense of balance of direction. What I mean is that, none the less, one feels that at no moment did the rhythmic idea flash into the artist's consciousness as a melody suggests itself to a musician.

Les Poseuses.  Seurat.

By courtesy of Messrs. Reid and Lefèvre

Still there it is, a wonderfully strange and original composition almost disquieting in its fixity. It is a very epitome of its author's theories of analogy. The analogies run through it even to the minutest details, analogies of form and analogies of colour. In colour, for instance, the violets, greens and reds of the " Grande Jatte " find their analogies in the wall, the mounted drawings and the green garment or bag so carefully hung upon it, and in the bright rust reds of the sofa and parasol.

The main idea of the composition is of two long uprights, one, the central nude, the other the seated nude prolonged into the two upright figures of the " Grande Jatte." The picture is thus divided exactly into two equal halves, a bold application of Poussin's favourite practice. One half is occupied by the " Grande Jatte," the other by the nearly blank wall at right angles to it. This right-hand half has, instead of a third upright, a pyramid into which the seated figure is almost forcibly fitted. The original idea of the central standing nude is to be seen in a very beautiful drawing published in M. Coquiot's book. It was standing firm with both legs together. But Seurat felt the need of an analogy, in the left-hand half of the picture, to the pyramid in the right, and has made the model's right leg stick out so as to be almost exactly parallel with the left-hand side of his pyramid, in order to do so. There can be no doubt to my mind that this was right from the point of view of the perfection of the composition, but it has led to a certain meagreness in the drawing of this figure. The volumes here seem wanting in fullness, especially as compared with the surprising beauty and ease of the nude to the left. Just with regard to this central figure something too literal, something of the unassimilated fact, seems to have persisted. It lacks the great style of most of Seurat's drawing.

It is for such reasons that I cannot share the widely expressed opinion of my fellow critics that this is a greater masterpiece than the " Bathers." It no doubt represents a further stage in the development of Seurat's method, but it is too much put together, it has lost something of the conviction and immediacy which had not yet been subordinated to his science when he did the " Bathers," and which still persists in the landscapes of the last period. I cannot doubt that if he had lived Seurat would have found a way to put his

o

completed method at the service of his sensibility. What revelations his early death deprived us of !

Certainly " Les Poseuses " show once more that strange aloofness of Seurat's spirit which we noted in the " Bathers " ; but it is less remarkable here where the deliberate arrangement by the artist of the models in the studio gives already a certain air of unreality to the thing seen. But the same characteristic of Seurat's attitude awakens an almost disquieting feeling before the later " Jeune Femme se poudrant," which was shown by Mr. Paul Rosenberg recently in London. This is, indeed, one of the strangest pictures I know, so utterly remote is the point of departure from the place to which Seurat carries us. It is as though he had made a bet that he would take the most intractable material possible and yet mould it to his ends. This impossible woman, in the grotesque *déshabille* of the 'eighties, surrounded by every horror of gimcrack finery of the period, might have inspired Daumier to a grim satire, or Guys to an almost lyrical delight in its exuberance, or Degas to a bitter and merciless epigrammatic exposure, or Lautrec to an indulgently ironical scherzo ; but Seurat passes over all such implications with an Olympian indifference, he treats the subject with religious solemnity and carries it into a region of abstract beauty. No Byzantine mosaic, however solemnly hieratic, could be more remote than this from all suggestion of " La vie Parisienne." The design is affirmed with an almost oppressive decision. We are forbidden to imagine the slightest tremor of change in these impeccable contours. By incessant revision the position of everything has been ascertained down to the minutest fraction. At first it seems to be all surface—contours revealed by spots of pure but elusive colour—and then these almost imperceptible changes of colour build up for us solid volumes bathed in a faint glowing light. There is scarcely any tone contrast, no definite light and shade, and yet in the end these volumes assert themselves with overpowering completeness. For all its decorative flatness, for all its theoretical and abstract colouring, this is intensely real, but for all its reality nothing of the original theme, of the thing seen, remains untransformed, all has been assimilated and remade by the idea. And perhaps this complete transmutation of the theme by the idea is the test of great art. It means that in proportion as

PLATE XXX

Le Port.  Seurat.                                    By courtesy of Messrs. Reid and Lefèvre

*A*

Port en Bessin.  Seurat.                            By courtesy of Messrs. Reid and Lefèvre

*B*

a picture attains to this independent reality and inherent significance the element of illustration drops out altogether and becomes irrelevant.

Near by, in the French Gallery, there hung a large composition of Picasso's, representing a " Mother and Child," to which he had given colossal proportions and a preternatural massiveness of limb. To a prolonged gaze these seemed to become but airy trifles beside the immutable fixity of Seurat's woman.

The landscapes seen at the Lefèvre Gallery all belong more or less to the period of complete pointillism, though in some cases Seurat's earlier method of small swept brush strokes persists underneath the fine network of dots. Each in its entirely distinct way is, to my mind, a complete and irrefutable discovery. They are all primarily designs of specially conceived spaces filled by specially interpreted luminosities and colour vibrations. How perfect Seurat's insight was into such appearances and how nice his control of expression, can be realised when we compare the opalescent pearly greys of the " Courbevoie " with the flaming whiteness of the " Gravelines " and the dither of sunlight in " Le Port " (Pl. XXX. A). But as beautiful and surprising as any is the " Port in Bessin " (Pl. XXX. B), where the shadows of still clouds hanging over the sunlit sea make an exquisite arabesque, picked up again by the patterns of the turf on the weathered down in the foreground. When viewed at a short range this appears as an almost flat pattern design, but retire to the other end of the room and the planes stretch to infinite distances, with almost the effect of an illusion.

It is one of the peculiarities of the pointillist method that tones which are so near together as to be indistinguishable close at hand become strongly contrasted when viewed from farther off. It is this that enabled Seurat to keep the surface of his canvas so unaccented and yet to produce an almost exaggerated salience and depth of relief. Several of these landscapes have fortunately retained their original frames, flat pieces of wood covered by the artist with his interminable spots of colour. Again, we see his mastery of effects of contrast and his exacting logic. The argument, one sees, must have gone somewhat thus : the function of a frame is to cut off the imagined picture space from the actual space of the room. To do this there should be an equal contrast between frame and picture at every point. But with a gilt frame the contrast cannot be equal at every point. It is strong where the gilt comes against a dark mass in the picture, weaker where it opposes a light, not to mention the even greater differences of colour contrast which this uniform gold implies. Seurat, therefore, set to work so to paint the frame as that, at each point, both colour and tone contrasts should be equal, and one cannot deny that he has succeeded to perfection. Hardly less remarkable is the fact that a precisely similar technique in frame and picture produces in one case a solid flatness, in the other the illusion of recession and distance.

Seurat's artistic personality was compounded of qualities which are usually supposed to be opposed and incompatible. On the one hand, his extreme and delicate sensibility, on the other a passion for logical abstraction and an almost mathematical precision of mind. On the one hand he accepted the whole body of Impressionist discovery about appearance even to the point of stating those phenomena which, even while we observe them, we know to be illusory, on the other hand, the mere statement of appearance which so preoccupied the Impressionists has no importance whatever for him. Appearance as revealed by Impressionist researches is nothing to him but the raw material out of which he builds, and his building is so purely logical and architectural, so precisely balanced and so nicely proportioned that the final result is utterly remote from appearance. The question of verisimilitude hardly occurs to one, so little can we refer his pictures to anything outside themselves, so completely does the created reality hold us by the laws of its self-contained system.

No doubt, at all times in the history of art we find that newly discovered data of appearance become the basis for new ventures in design with a consequent modification and extension of the esthetic sensibility. What is rare and what makes Seurat's genius so surprising is that in the few years of his activity he was able, starting entirely *de novo* with the large body of new data which Impressionism supplied, together with his own additional observations on irradiation and the physiological effects of contrast, to create out of that, altogether afresh and without any guiding tradition so extraordinarily complete an esthetic system, together with a new technical method so perfectly adapted to its expression.

# ON SOME MODERN DRAWINGS

THE arts of drawing and painting have always been closely associated. Most great painters have been great draughtsmen and most great draughtsmen have done great work either in painting or sculpture. They are nevertheless distinct methods of expressing an artist's feeling about form, and they have reacted upon one another in many various ways.

Whatever conception of drawing is prevalent at any particular time tends to hold the painter's art in a certain direction, but at times discoveries in painting have forced drawing into new channels. On the whole, since drawing is the simpler medium, capable of interpreting fewer aspects of appearance, it tends to be the more conservative of an habitual manner.

The artists of the Renaissance devoted a consecutive and persistent study to the expression in drawing of the forms of the human figure, and finally evolved, both by direct observation and by observation interpreted in the light of anatomical research, a concise and expressive system capable of describing in very legible terms the general aspect of the figure in varied positions. Indeed, they had so thoroughly mastered these phenomena that they were able to construct the figure in situations which it was impossible actually to observe, as when they delineated nude childish forms fluttering in the air over the Virgin's head, with a surprising verisimilitude.

The forms finally elaborated by Raphael, and still more by Michelangelo, were indeed so complete and consistent and so fully satisfied the demands of the artistic expression of the time that they became, so to speak, stereotyped. Succeeding generations of artists, feeling that there was nothing further to be got from observation of nature, ceased to look at it, and learned instead from Michelangelo and Raphael, or at least got their formulas so fully by heart that they only saw nature through them.

One of the characteristics of this view of the figure was that a certain selected group of anatomical facts were regarded as fundamental

197

and necessary. Any drawing of the figure, it was thought, must at all costs display clearly the knowledge of the facts. An amusing instance of this is that in all the figure-drawing of the sixteenth century the umbilicus is shown with extreme precision and emphasis. And this became so much an essential of artistic faith that artists indicated it even when the figure was covered with a clinging drapery.

The result was that it came to be regarded as of the utmost importance that the artist should express a number of facts, some of which had been discovered by other means than pure vision. Vision was distorted by outside knowledge. Anatomical knowledge almost inevitably affects vision. A familiar instance of this is seen in the contour of the calf of the leg. Anatomy shows us that there are here two main muscles which overlap, the upper one folding in about halfway down the calf and leaving the other one to continue towards the heel. This overlapping of two convex forms produces a long, slightly curved line. That curve is, so to speak, indeterminate—it is difficult to the observer to state exactly where and to what extent it deviates from a straight line, although it is quite clear that it is not straight. It even seems, owing to the strong bulge of the upper muscle, that, where that ceases, the convexity is succeeded by a faintly concave curve. Now, artists like Utamaro, who had no anatomical knowledge, do frequently give a slight concavity to this curve, but with the Renaissance artists this would have been an unpardonable solecism. Every artist must clearly declare that double convexity, whatever the actual appearance, however imperceptible to the eye, regarding a particular model in a particular situation, that might be. Such knowledge of non-visual fact, then, clearly makes easy a definite interpretation of an indeterminate and puzzling appearance, and may point the way to a clearer perception of the phenomenon, but it also tends to fix and limit the observation and prevent the sensibility, obsessed as it is by a known formula, from reacting freely.

There can be no doubt that to any one who looks with unprejudiced eyes, Utamaro succeeds in expressing a more intense and personal reaction to his female figures than did any of the Italian mannerists, whose main preoccupation was to show their familiarity with certain sacred facts of anatomy.

This Renaissance system of figure-drawing is a curious instance of a phenomenon which occurs again and again in various aspects throughout the history of art, namely, that although the whole object and purpose of the work of art is the expression of the artist's peculiar sensibility—his own special reaction to vision—both artists and amateurs find this so exacting that they continually invent methods of avoiding the effort which this experience by the artist and its acceptance by the amateur entails. They seek to establish some code of shibboleths whereby the true artist can be unmistakably and demonstrably recognised and welcomed with becoming enthusiasm. The indication of the umbilicus at all costs was one of these ingenious shibboleths, and the whole system of Renaissance figure-drawing was compact of similar devices.

And as, since Renaissance times, the art of drawing has been the basis of artistic training, this stereotyped formula has become the mainstay of the student's curriculum. It has obvious advantages for the purposes of instruction, examination and the awarding of prizes. But, since artists persist in coming forward, the formula has undergone various changes, been added to here and there, been made more flexible and more expressive in different directions. Rubens, Watteau, Ingres, to take a few instances, have all had their say in the matter. But, in the main, this conception of figure-drawing has formed the backbone of artistic training ever since Michelangelo and Raphael consecrated it.

It has been shown elsewhere * that the main development of painting throughout the seventeenth century, and again in the nineteenth, was in the direction of freeing vision from the disturbing influence of knowledge gained by other means ; but all the time drawing has tended to restrain painting in this movement, to give the young artist always as the point of departure the statement of vision interpreted in the light of non-visual experience, or of such visual knowledge as can only be acquired by examination from different points of view. But in the seventeenth century in Holland the new interest in a purely visual interpretation was so strong, and academic doctrine so weakly established, that the greatest and most original of Dutch masters, Rembrandt, dared to claim for drawing also a new

* The Seicento.

freedom of expression, did, in fact, establish a new and alternative language of graphic statement.

But to the pure visualist, or Impressionist, as we may conveniently call him, drawing presents, as compared with painting, a peculiar difficulty. The drawn line does not directly record any visual experience. It describes a contour, and that contour is presented to the eye as the boundary of one area of tone seen against another area of different tone and colour, and throughout its length there will be continued slight variations in this contrast. In drawing this sensational datum is, as it were, summarised and symbolised by a line which contrasts equally with the white paper on either side of its thickness. We have to accept this as a kind of summation of all the infinite number of points at which the sensation of one coloured area ends and another coloured area begins. Supposing these two areas are formed by a flat piece of paper lying on a flat table, this summation of the points is fairly adequate and the outline represents well enough the sensation. But in the majority of cases the boundary of one area in contrast to another represents for us the limit of one convex volume against a remoter and perhaps concave area. In such a case each point of the contour becomes the section of a line which is passing away from the eye at right angles to the plane of the paper, and from the point of view of the evocation of the plastic relief of the volume it is the fact of its disappearance that is important. And herein lies the chief problem and difficulty of the art of drawing. For whatever reasons, the imagination is only strongly affected through vision by the vivid realisation of plastic forms, and the great trouble with the drawn contour is that it tends to check that realisation. For one thing, the drawn line tends to carry the eye along its course; indeed, there here comes in, to conflict with this plastic expression, one of the very beauties of the art of drawing, namely, the interest excited in us by the rhythmic flow of the line as we follow its movement along. For the drawn line is a perfect record of a certain gesture, and all gesture, as we see in the dance and the drama, has a strong evocative power over the imagination. In handwriting, where the lines do not even suggest plastic relief, our whole attention is fixed, in so far as we contemplate it esthetically, on these traces made by gestures, and we deduce from them very strong impressions of the character and mood of which these gestures are the outcome.

This purely abstract rhythmical attraction of the line is still more potent in a drawing, and we may call it, by analogy with handwriting, the calligraphic quality of a drawing. But, as we have seen, this very quality tends to divert our attention from the cross-sections of disappearing planes and fixes it on the continuous movement of their summation in the line. It is one aspect of the eternal conflict in the graphic arts of the organisation on the surface of the picture and its organisation as an ideated three-dimensional space occupied by volumes. The conciliation of these two opposing tendencies, accomplished by innumerable different devices at different periods, may almost be said to be the material of any intimate technical criticism of pictorial art.

Now, with regard to this rhythmic flow of the line we must note one psychological fact; namely, that perfect rhythmic continuity and coherence is only attainable by human beings when their activity is at least partially unconscious. To fix the attention on any gesture is to deprive it fatally of that specific quality of rhythmic unity. It is unnecessary to detail the innumerable instances which will occur to every one of this curious phenomenon, but I suppose that any one who has learned to play the piano will agree that the full rhythm of a musical phrase can only be expressed when familiarity with the instrument and the act of reading has made it unnecessary for the attention to be concentrated on each note in succession—when the phrase is apprehended as a single whole and is, as it were, handed over to the unconscious mechanism for execution. The phrase " practice makes perfect " is an expression of this truth.* The frequent repetition, then, of any form tends to make possible its rhythmic or calligraphic expression. This is the method in the case of handwriting, where the shapes of letters and even words have, by constant repetition, become ingrained in our nervous system,

---

* A curious and rather unexpected confirmation of this occurred to me recently when at the request of Mr. Robert Bridges I studied a collection of scripts and handwritings from the esthetic point of view for a tract on Handwriting issued by the S.P.E. I found that the best, free (*i.e.* almost entirely unconscious) handwritings were far more beautiful than even the best of the formal scripts, where in spite of familiarity a certain amount of deliberate and conscious endeavour was made to attain regularity.

and can be called forth without any idea of these shapes rising to consciousness. A somewhat similar result is produced by the training of students in that system of figure-drawing which derives from Michelangelo and Raphael. The student repeats so constantly certain sequences of typical curves in a somewhat similar order that they become unconscious habits, and, according to the individual's capacity, rhythmic.

But there is another method by which the artist may withdraw his consciousness from his gesture sufficiently to allow of his line being rhythmical. This is attained if, before an actual appearance, he becomes so concentrated upon the interpretation of a contour as to be unconscious of what goes on between his hand and the paper. The ideal of such a situation is that he should actually never look at the paper. This, of course, is a counsel of perfection, since, under such circumstances, although the hand is likely to express the rhythm admirably it will fail to do so with correct proportions. Nevertheless, some artists do make admirable notations in this way. Or, if the vision be one aroused in the " inner eye " by the artist's imagination, he may draw with his eyes shut. Here, again, the rhythmic quality is likely to be excellent, but the proportions are almost sure to go astray.

It seems to me possible, then, to distinguish two ways of arriving at rhythmic drawing through the gesture becoming freed from conscious attention. One, which I call the calligraphic, because it is arrived at by similar processes to those of rhythmic handwriting, the other the rhythm due to the concentration on the actual vision.

Now, the tendency of calligraphic rhythm is to be flowing and easy in proportion as it is composed of relatively simple and uniform curves. This degenerates in the hands of mannerists into a succession of full, rounded, unbroken curves which come easily to the hand. The artist achieves thus a certain vulgar, insensitive elegance, and impresses us by the bravura of his perfectly executed but obvious gestures. Tintoretto may be taken as one of the greater masters whose drawing shows this quality.

On the other hand, the tendency of the Impressionist painters, using the term in its widest sense, has been to concentrate on the vision and to express relief by subtler, more complex, less uniform

PLATE XXXI

A

Drawing.                                        Adrian Brouwer

B

Drawing.                                        Dunoyer de Segonzac

curves, and also by far less continuous lines; since their pre-occupation is rather with the plasticity and varying emphasis of the contour than with its continuity. This may be seen to perfection in Rembrandt's, and very strikingly too in Brouwer's, drawings (Pl. VI. and Pl. XXXI. A), where the volumes are indicated by broken lines which, by their continually varied quality, suggest the variations of contrast which the line is intended to express in various parts of its course. Rembrandt, particularly in his preoccupation with volumes, frequently gives several slightly different versions of the contour for fear of preventing us by any one too precise and over definite statement from realising the movement of the disappearing planes.

It would be foolish to over emphasise too much the distinction which I have here indicated between calligraphic and Impressionist drawing. Undoubtedly the freedom of hand of the calligraphic training, if it has not produced too fixed a formula, will serve the artist's turn when he is concentrated upon the vision, and it is not irrelevant that Rembrandt had one of the most beautiful, if not the most beautiful, handwriting that we know. But it is none the less true that drawing in the hands of some seventeenth-century Dutch painters became a more elastic medium, capable of recording certain aspects of vision which had hitherto been inaccessible to it. But of the two methods in vogue in the seventeenth century it was the old Italian one that predominated in the eighteenth century, and has remained the basis of art training till recent times.

What I wish to consider here is, what are the effects on the art of drawing of the changes in painting which have followed from Cézanne's influence on modern practice or from such other influences as have supervened in the last twenty years. Cézanne himself (Pl. XXXII. B), in spite of a totally different rhythmic bias, is, as a draughtsman, of the kinship of Rembrandt. With him the expression of the volume is of supreme importance, and even more than Rembrandt he dreads any single final statement of the contour, and rather adumbrates its exact situation than defines it. But, like Rembrandt, his contour is freely broken and expressive of changes of quality being here more, and there less, emphatic and precise. His drawing is Impressionist in its emphasis on the interrelation of planes in his refusal to isolate any form from its ambience. On the other hand, in his painting the emphasis on the volumes and the fullness of their relief marks his work off from contemporary Impressionists, and it was this which struck most his immediate successors, Van Gogh and Gauguin. These both began to emphasise more completely the separate volumes, to articulate more clearly and in more easily legible phrases the surface continuity of the picture. With Gauguin this tendency was greatly increased by his love of savage art with its naïve assertion of the individual object. This led him finally to a conception of drawing which was in some ways the opposite of Cézanne's, to the inclosure of the volume—of, say, a nude figure—in an unbroken, almost unvarying contour (Pl. XXXVI. B). But this did not lead him back into the Italian method, because his view of the figure was not based on the expression of anatomical knowledge, but on the acceptance of a more immediate impression of the appearance. Instead of interpreting that appearance in terms of anatomical structure, he endeavoured to approach it without *parti-pris* as a mere visual phenomenon. This was, no doubt, in part due to Cézanne's influence. He it was who first made artists uneasy at the too ready familiarity with a known interpretation of vision and drew them back to a more naïve and instinctive receptivity to sensation. The effect of Gauguin's method was to cause a new interest in the surface organisation of the picture, to increase immensely the feeling for its aspect as decoration. This movement had influence in proportion as at that time a general malaise and sense of fatigue had been brought about by the endless repetition of the old Impressionist formula in which surface organisation had been abandoned entirely in favour of recession. Gauguin, in fact, went back to an almost Byzantine simplification of the problems of drawing.

Almost the same may be said of Van Gogh,[*] who even more than Gauguin accepted the influence of the recent revelation of Japanese colour prints. In many of his works objects are outlined with a heavy, continuous painted brush stroke which is scarcely impinged on by the subsequent painting. It was this reassertion of the continuous contour, this disregard of the contour as a disappearing plane, which led to a considerable revival of the art of drawing. But among

[*] *Cf.* Van Gogh, p. 178.

PLATE XXXII

—A

Drawing on plate.  Ninth century Mahommetan

—B

Water-colour drawing.  Cézanne

the artists who accepted the new influence this did not lead back to the old calligraphy of the schools. It was based on oriental influence from Japan, upon Gauguin's records of Polynesian native art, and before long upon reference to negro art which began to attract attention by its surprising novelty and unexpectedness to European eyes and by its peculiar sensitiveness to certain unfamiliar aspects of form. To these influences one may add, perhaps, a renewed interest in Byzantine art which everywhere manifested itself with the breakdown of the Renaissance tyranny. The reference to all these primitive and unfamiliar arts gave a totally new aspect to the expression of form by drawing. The outline reasserted itself vigorously as against Cézanne's modified Impressionism, but with the rejection of the old calligraphic formula it accepted with an almost childlike naïveté the immediate impression of the model. No anatomical facts were any longer held sacred; the figure might, according to circumstances, be envisaged from totally different points of view, values of direction and movement were allowed to impose themselves even to the extent of violently distorting proportions and contradicting even the best-known anatomical facts. Meanwhile that unconsciousness of gesture, which we have seen to be always a necessity of rhythmic harmony, was attained, not by familiarity with any known type—since this would have contravened the new demand for naïve freshness of response—but by concentration upon the vision to the point of forgetting the paper. This concentration, be it remembered, was not upon the contour as a disappearing plane, but as a continuous gesture.

Matisse's early drawings show this new aspect of the art of drawing to perfection. In the drawing of a nude (Pl. XXXIII. A) we see this indifference to correct anatomical fact, and to proportions. He has not attempted to correct anywhere the first naïve spontaneous response to the thing seen: thus he leaves the monstrous disproportion of the oval of the mask. The line records his response to the apprehension of the movement of the head. In fact, the imaginative apprehension of the whole balance of movements becomes the main thesis rather than any apprehension of the exact forms of the various volumes (of the limbs and trunk) which together compose this complex. But we note that although the actual proportions of the figure are freely disregarded, there underlies these distortions not only a clear sense of balance of movement, but of the volumes created by the lines. The volume of the trunk and its relation to the legs and arms are very evident.

We note also that by thus surrendering himself to the immediate impressions of vision and sacrificing everything to the freshness of his response he has attained a singular beauty of linear rhythm. It is the beauty of an extremely free and unconscious gesture. It is elastic, as it were, at every point to his continually varying response to the quality of the contour. The line is highly rhythmic, but with so free a rhythm that it cannot be expressed in any known system of curvature. It bears to the calligraphic line of the schools the relation of an extremely free prose rhythm to a strictly prosodic one. The extreme subtlety of Matisse's rhythm, which, if it seek authority, must rely rather on oriental than European examples (Pl. XXXII. A), was the cause of a great deal of misapprehension. Many people to whom it was unfamiliar mistook it for the almost total absence of rhythm which occurs in the attempts at drawing made by people without any sensibility to form or skill of hand. At the Post-Impressionist exhibition one indignant spectator was even moved to send to the papers his own version of a Matisse drawing. The result was, to any sensitive eye, as far removed from Matisse as it was from Ingres.

Many of Matisse's later drawings show a decided return to the anatomical and proportional correctness of the European tradition. In these, as it appears to me, he frequently loses altogether the native distinction of his line, and with that his sense of the significance of values of movement, with the result that the figures are altogether lacking in the vitality of the earlier work. But even now, wherever the rapid notation of a whole scene is his object, Matisse recovers all his spontaneity, the expressive grace and freedom of his gesture, and his instinctive grasp of movement and volume (Pl. XXXIV. B).

Picasso also has a strong innate rhythmic feeling. Like Matisse's, this is elastic and free, but his gesture is more continuous in its flow ; its alluring grace is more an innate quality of the gesture itself than the result of an acute sensibility to the impression. He is more *a priori* and abstract, and is therefore more liable to envisage the decorative beauty of the drawing itself than the expression of a definite reaction. For, in fact, his reactions to vision are both diverse and

PLATE XXXIII

B

Modigliani

Pencil drawing.

A

Henri-Matisse

Pen drawing.

Pen drawing.    Picasso

Pen drawing.    Henri-Matisse

uncertain. He seems unable to embrace these different tendencies in any single integral expression. Thus he varies from envisaging a psychological end, and that too sometimes touched with sentimentality (as, for instance, in his early, " blue," period *) to such purely plastic constructions as his Cubist designs. In fact, he seems so little able to bring these ends into a single focus that he carries them both forward on parallel lines. Thus his interpretation of vision is rarely profound. Sometimes he will seize on the pretext of insignificant details—a button, the fringe of a chair cover, the mouldings of a mantelpiece— to serve a decorative end, sometimes he will find therein the excuse, and little more than the excuse, for a nearly abstract and *a priori* plastic construction. But whatever the end in view in his drawing, he uses that modern free linear rhythm with such ease and elegance that we are sometimes lulled into a premature acquiescence.

At times he confines his line to the even, slow *tempo* of a tracing, as though wilfully depriving it of any suggestion of nervous sensibility, and relying entirely on the balance of directions and movements to create the volume, arriving thus at the very antipodes of Cézanne's drawings, and approximating, though from a totally new direction, to calligraphy. Undoubtedly the calligraphy, if we venture so to call it, is of the strangest, most novel kind (Pl. XXXIV. A). It is as though out of confidence in his extraordinary nervous control, he set out to bid defiance to the laws of nature, as though, knowing that rhythmic gesture requires a certain momentum in the hand, and therefore a certain rapidity of movement, he made a bet to get rhythm without that and by means of a movement so slow that it lacks momentum. And also he determines that the rhythm shall have nothing of the mechanical monotony that usually characterises such movements, but shall be of that new, free, " oriental " type which Matisse attained by a rapid unconscious movement. Does he or does he not win this extravagant wager ? I confess I am left always hesitating as to the answer. But even if he does I scarcely feel that it is worth while thus to sacrifice those elements of expression which depend upon accent and variety in the line.

Rouault, though he admits psychological interests more constantly and more whole-heartedly than any other artist of the modern

* The early etching (Pl. VII. A) gives the measure of this marked psychological preoccupation.

tradition, has discovered a fully integrated and intensely personal method of expression. Rouault, indeed, is, as I have already suggested,* peculiar among modern artists in that with him psychological and plastic values are both at issue, and even appear to have both co-operated in determining the form. His use of line is also peculiar. In the first place, his contours are often broad washes of the water-colour brush, curiously resembling in this some early Chinese examples. They seem to be often final revisions or even alternative statements of the contour or as suggesting violent accents of shadow. But, in any case, they are of so surprising a freedom, with so agitated and vehement a *tempo*, that they never check plastic movement by arresting the eye on the contour.

His rhythm is no less peculiar to himself. It is rugged, with sudden angles and staccato movements, without the elegant flow of Matisse and Picasso. It has the power of evoking by its broad indications of structure and plastic volumes the strangest psychological entities (Pl. VI. B). His art is of the nature of tragic caricature, and it is therefore not altogether surprising that he often uses closely similar means to those employed by Rouveyre.

In the extreme complexity of modern art it is difficult to trace all the interacting and interlacing influences which leave their record in the drawn line. We have to some extent followed the fortunes of that extremely free rhythm of which Matisse provides the most striking examples, but the practice of the Cubists has worked in an opposite direction. The former, insisting on the freest, most immediate response to the impression, produced a rhythm of indefinable subtlety; the Cubists, on the other hand, basing themselves in part upon certain *obiter dicta* of Cézanne, sought to reduce form to certain almost geometrical elements, to resolve the infinity of nature into a combination of a few recognisable and regular curves. In contrast to the free " prose " rhythms of Matisse, they reverted to a monotonously regular and fixed " prosody." It is typical of Picasso's dualism that he who pushes the free rhythm at times to such strange extremes was also one of the founders of the new geometrical system of drawing. Only, be it remarked, the native elegance and delicacy of his nervous organisation gives even to his most rigid constructions the vibrant

* Some Questions of Esthetics, pp. 24, 25.

play of vitality which some of his followers either despise in their dogmatic intolerance or despair of attaining.

This must not be presumed, however, of Picasso's friendly rival in the elaboration of the Cubist doctrine, Braque. He has, if possible, a more delicate and exquisite sensitiveness of touch which ingratiates him even in his most austerely geometric constructions, and which, gaining ground upon the impulse to abstraction, has made his design progressively more and more seductively elegant.

Another draughtsman, Modigliani, who came under the spell of Cubism, was also gifted with an instinctive rhythmic feeling which tempered the monotony of his abstract ovoid curves. The example which I have chosen (Pl. XXXIII. B) shows him as more than usually responsive to the subtleties of his immediate impression, and only in the eyes, hair, and part of the dress reasserting with a bravura, which is slightly out of key, the claims of his abstract system. Still, even the very sensitive oval of the mask is doubtless supported and held together by a sub-understood reference to the type curves.

Let us turn now to some draughtsmen who have never come so definitely into the direct line of the Post-Cézannian development, although subtly influenced by the general esthetic ambience. Maillol was a painter before he became a sculptor, and his drawings, though they subserve his sculptural aims, have none of that too positive assertion of the tactile as opposed to the visual aspects of form that frequently marks a sculptor's drawings. Maillol's drawings show an intense concentration upon the realisation of the volumes, in all their plenitude, and of their relation to one another. In his concentrated and impassioned suspense he loses all consciousness of the gesture. There is never with him the slightest suspicion of any trace of self-satisfaction or self-assertion. No hint of bravura ever interposes between us and the plastic idea. In his general conception of the figure he departs but little from the traditional European type as realised by the Greeks and developed by the great masters of the High Renaissance. But his approach to this conception is not through that traditional calligraphic system of drawing described above. He discovers it afresh as decisively as Gauguin discovered the Tahitian type and by a similar abandonment to his visual impressions. Only

P

his sensibility has a much longer wind. His exploration of all the implications of the volume is far more patient and prolonged, and the simplicity at which he finally arrives is never summary or arbitrary, never obedient to *a priori* and merely decorative needs. His sensibility is always at work, always fully concentrated on the plastic idea which the model evokes. In the nude here reproduced (Pl. XXXV. B) he has arrived at a statement of extreme simplicity with the most evident interrelation of the volumes. But that simplicity is at the antipodes to any *a priori* geometric schema. The contour, for all its broad and easy movement, is tense with the plastic content which it embraces, and so definite is the evocation of the movement of planes that even in the thighs, where there is nothing but white paper, we carry these movements on in imagination and fill in for ourselves the almost imperceptible indications of the drawing.

Bonnard descends directly from the older pre-Cézannian Impressionist tradition modified by the need to discover a more significant organisation of the picture surface and a possible formula for mural decorative design to which the older Impressionist formula had proved itself inapplicable. Besides this, Bonnard (Pl. XXXV. A) has always been a remarkable illustrator in his lithographs and drawings for books. He discovered a very peculiar and original style of drawing which conciliates in a surprising way all these diverse ends. His method has been to keep everything, as it were, in solution, to avoid as far as possible any positive statement, to rely on suggestions. It is almost as though instead of stating anything, he evoked it by a witty allusion. Thus, in the curiously fluid continuum of his texture we catch at hints of all that has moved him, the psychological situation, given by infinitely subtle but pointed accents, dispersed here and there, and the plastic relief, again given rather by innumerable isolated indications ; whilst, finally, all these cohere in a decorative weft as of some oriental carpet of shimmering and elusive complexity. In Bonnard's case, to divagate for a moment from our present inquiry, I find an interesting confirmation of my suggestion as to the conditions favourable to the mixture of the arts, for all these ends are pursued with a certain playful lightness of touch. Neither psychological nor plastic constructions impose themselves too weightily. Neither seem pushed to grave or important

PLATE XXXV

B

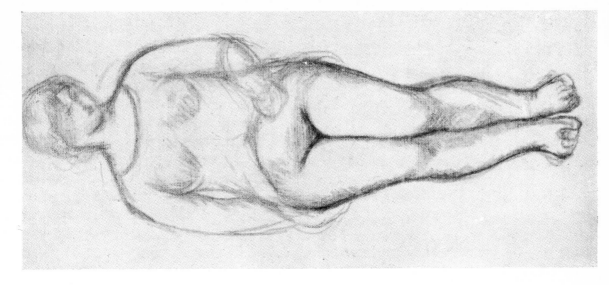

Maillol

Drawing.

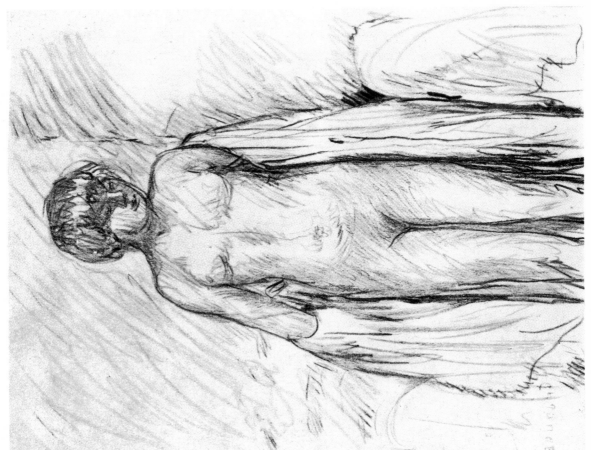

Bonnard

Drawing.

A

issues. They play into one another's hands in much the same way as the words and music of Semele.

But to return to his drawings. They show an extraordinarily acute and witty quickness of perception. He is able to seize the minute decisive indication of the turn of a head, the glance of an eye, the pose of a hand, which has significance for evoking his playfully indulgent mood. His plastic evocations fit nicely into this. He feels the form in its large, easy aspects, and refuses always to define it too clearly, leaving here, too, a certain play to the imagination. Even here he will not press too heavily. He is almost as much concerned with the surface as with the volume. If we compare his nudes with Maillol's, Bonnard remains much more on the surface. Maillol is concentrated upon the volumes and their tense interplay. Bonnard glances at these and has an eye, too, to the quality of the epidermis. In a drawing of a child's back, for instance, the slight indications of modelling give us, even more than the underlying plasticity, the fluctuations of light upon the delicate skin. There is always the same playful and allusive lightness of touch.

Among the younger painters Segonzac is one of the most remarkable as a draughtsman. At one time, in his drawings of Isidora Duncan and the Prize-ring, he followed the practice of the continuous contour with a free, loose rhythm. It is doubtful whether this was at all suited to his specific feeling for plasticity, which is concentrated on the feeling of density and weight of the volumes rather than on values of movement. In his later drawings this feeling finds a more appropriate expression. As we saw, Rembrandt and Brouwer had discovered a method of drawing which disregarded the formulæ of the Renaissance tradition, and recorded more directly the plastic evocations of vision. Segonzac arrives, as was not unnatural to a modern draughtsman, at a curiously similar method. The nude reproduced here (Pl. XXXI. B) shows with what freedom from all calligraphic preoccupations he follows his response to plasticity, with what indifference to any constatations which are irrelevant to his apprehension of the volumes.

In England we have in Sickert one of the few survivors of the pure Impressionist tradition of drawing. In Duncan Grant (Pl. XXXVI. A), the master of a singularly pure and melodious linear rhythm. He has adapted to his personal feeling the free " oriental " rhythm, and uses it with a great effect for indications of movement.

Such, then, are some of the new and very varied forms which the art of drawing has taken in response to the many new experiments in pictorial design which the art of our time has undertaken. In the main we note the complete abandonment of that system which persisted more or less from Raphael's time till the latter half of the nineteenth century. The art of drawing has by now become as freely experimental as the painter's art. It no longer exercises that conservative pressure which it still retained throughout the changes of the early and middle nineteenth century.

PLATE
XXXVI

—*A*

Le Train Bleu.  Water-colour drawing.  Duncan Grant

—*B*

Drawing.  Gauguin

# PLASTIC COLOUR

CENNINO CENNINI, writing in the fourteenth century, gives us a full account of the methods of the painter craftsman of his day. Among other things, he describes how to make the preliminary drawings. He gives many alternative methods, of which the most typical and usual kind was done on a paper carefully prepared with a special surface of dull, pale green or reddish colour. On this the outline was drawn, then it was shaded, and finally the lights were put in with white laid on in small washes or hatched strokes. The object was thus interpreted in three tones, the light, the medium, which was given by the coloured paper, and the dark. When the artist came to the painting of, let us say, a drapery, he followed a precisely similar process. The whole mass was laid-in in the local colour—red, blue, green, or whatever it might be ; this was then shaded by darker tints of the same colour, and the lights were hatched in in semi-transparent white washes which allowed the local colour to show through. The method of painting, that is to say, was closely linked with the method of drawing. In both the fixed framework was the continuous outline to each figure, and each space thus delineated was filled by a local colour which was modulated in parts by intenser colour to give shadow and elsewhere by white to give light, the transitions in both cases being softened off by lighter hatchings. In its simplest form this approximated to the illuminated drawings in manuscripts in which the *rôle* of colour was mainly decorative, its reference to natural appearance scarcely going beyond that of following the local colours of nature, such as flesh tints, the green of trees, the blue of sky, and this only in the most generalised way. Except for this, colour was hardly regarded as expressive of any feelings about the visible three-dimensional world of actual life. So far as these were given it was by the general disposition and character of the forms. Colour was essentially an addition, an ornament and embroidery of the linear design calculated to make it more attractive but not more expressive.

From that day to this one may trace a gradual tendency towards a view of colour as an inherent part of the expressive quality of form, a tendency to recombine into a single indissoluble whole all the aspects of form instead of proceeding by the schematic division into line, shade and colour. That tendency has doubtless suffered many fluctuations, but on the whole it has persisted.

But even for Cennino Cennini's day we must make some reservations. The method described above was doubtless the accepted method of the schools, it was what every young painter craftsman learned by years of apprenticeship until it enabled him to turn out a perfectly finished and richly ornate altar-piece with the same certainty and competence as the armourer could turn out a suit of armour. And inevitably the greater number of painters were of this kind. But even then the great creative geniuses, though they learned only this method, instinctively applied it to ends which went far beyond the illuminator's ideal. Duccio, for instance, even before Cennino Cennini's day, was compelled by his instinctive feeling to give such differences of weight and density to his various local colours that they do in effect take a fixed position in a three-dimensional space ; they are not merely on the surface of the picture ; they are at such and such a distance within it. Nothing is more striking than the difference between the great masters and the craftsmen in this respect : the craftsmen always hugging safely the decorative surface, the masters already conceiving spatial and plastic relations so clearly that they cannot allow decorative considerations to interfere. Now and then, no doubt, the childish delight in pure ultramarines and vermilions will interrupt the process. Simone Martini, for instance, sometimes tumbles back into pure illumination, but, on the whole, the greater men at least make sure that colour will not interrupt the expression of volumes and spaces. Even Fra Angelico, professional illuminator though he was, and having an almost childish delight in pure primary colours, none the less manages, by the delicate choice of weight and saturation, to situate them within the space and even to suggest their atmospheric envelopment ; whilst in his landscape he sometimes hits with astounding exactness the precise values which evoke the idea of deep recession.

From this point of view one of the most remarkable Primitive painters, if one can call him a Primitive, is Piero di Cosimo.   In general effect his pictures resemble those of his contemporaries. That is to say, the scheme is built up of clear, strongly marked local colours, but he gives to these so great a variety of saturation and weight, and adjusts these variations with so subtle an insight into their situation in the picture space that his pictures arouse a vivid sense of recession and of the envelopment of his volumes in a luminous atmosphere.   If, in the National Gallery, one compares Piero di Cosimo's " Cephalus and Procris " with, say, Botticelli's " Mars and Venus," one notes how much more resistent to the eye, so to speak, are Piero's figures, how much more clearly they detach themselves from sea and sky, and we can measure thereby how great an advance Piero di Cosimo made in the direction of colour plasticity.   Perhaps, however, he already benefited to some extent from the theoretical advance which marks the next stage.

That new step towards the identification of colour with form was made when it was recognised that local colour underwent profound changes in passing from the lightest to the darkest portions.   And that these modifications were not merely of degrees of lightness and darkness but were modifications of the actual colour.   Leonardo da Vinci investigated this phenomenon with his usual curiosity and thoroughness and showed that in any solid object the different planes must each transmit to the eye light derived from a different source, and that these sources would be differently coloured.   He showed that shadow, until it reaches the total absence of light, is merely illumination from a lesser and differently coloured source of light than the lighted portions.   But completely as he worked out the whole theory and gave the scientific explanation of this, his practice still lagged far behind any complete statement.   Certain cases of the laws Leonardo formulated and which he himself describes had to wait for embodiment in pictorial expression until the Impressionists of 1870. But in the intervening centuries Leonardo's conceptions tended to be more and more put into practice, particularly by the Dutch artists and Velasquez, and colour became more and more closely bound up with the other aspects of plastic expression.   With Rembrandt, indeed, in certain situations, it attains almost to its fullest plastic evocation.

With the clear perception of the accidents which local colour suffers from the incidence of diverse coloured sources of light the general notion of colour harmony changed. To the older painters the main point was the harmonising of one local colour with another, but with the seventeenth century, with Rubens in particular, there came in the notion of a single all-pervading dominant note of colour—the colour of the main illumination—and local colour came rather to be suggested than actually stated by means of variations from this dominant in different directions. Where such an all-pervading coloured atmosphere obtains it is surprising what slight deviations from the dominant note will suggest to the imagination brilliant local colours. Thus, in the golden key of some of Rubens' compositions a touch of grey, made by mixing black and white, will count as a definite blue, or the dullest earth reds will shout like vermilion. By this method of colour orchestration not only do the suggestions of local colour get a new resonance—though they lose something of their meaning as frank oppositions—but the continuity of the colour weft, the absence of sudden breaks, reinforces the spatial and plastic unity of the design, and the recession appropriate for each coloured surface becomes more evidently manifest.

But this process of the gradual identification of colour with plastic and spatial design has always been liable to interruptions, and for a reason that is natural enough. There is almost inevitably a conflict between the decorative and plastic uses of colour. It is yet another aspect of the incessant tension between the organisation of a picture upon the surface and its organisation in space.*

And here the social situation of an art is likely to exercise a powerful influence. For instance, the eighteenth century with its refined and sophisticated aristocratic society managed to impose its demands on the art of the day and dictated a reversion to more frankly decorative painting, painting which would enter freely into the ensemble of the salon. A certain range of local colours was almost prescribed, and, more important still, these colours must not sacrifice for plastic expression their agreeable surface value. Degradations of local colour might not go so far as to lead to heavy tones of a dull or disagreeable quality in themselves. It would have been hard for a Rembrandt to enter the boudoir of a du Barry.

* *Cf.* Modern Drawings.

Not that the eighteenth century abandoned altogether the notion of colour orchestration. It never reverted to frank oppositions of definite or untempered local colours. Something like this was, however, effected by David's revolution with its insistence on the pure outline and the unbroken surface. And with Ingres we get a definite return to primitive methods. Though his passion for mediæval illuminated manuscripts and primitive pictures did not last, it left permanent traces on his methods. The contour with him became too intense an object of interest for him ever to sacrifice its precision to the idea of fusion by light and shade and atmospheric envelopment into a single continuous texture. He once again states local colours with a positive, flat, even assertiveness which takes but little note of accidents. Rubens was anathema to him, and perhaps all the more hateful in that it was to Rubens that Delacroix turned. Indeed, I think Delacroix's reputation as a colourist depends almost entirely on his having recaptured something of Rubens' colour orchestration. He is always supposed by his compatriots to have gone further and initiated the next step of the division of tones. I have never been able to find any definite evidence of this, but he undoubtedly reasserted Rubens' ideas, though with nothing like that master's subtlety or unerring colour sense.

The next step taken by the Impressionists carried the main process to the ultimate opposite point from the primitive idea. They explored Leonardo's laws in their most extreme instances, that is to say, in those cases where the difference between different sources of illumination was most marked. Effects of rich golden sunlight, as of late summer afternoons, showed at their strongest the opposition of the blue light of the zenith in such planes as were cut off from the sunlight itself, together with the further contrasts of very warm reflected lights, upcast from sunlit earth or grass. Or again, they would take the startling oppositions between the very warm light of a lamp and a cold, blue crepuscular light. In fact, they preferred so to arrange matters that local colours hardly counted at all in comparison with these accidents of coloured illumination.

Evidently there was more in this than merely the interest in exploring hitherto neglected aspects of vision. There was a definite prevention in favour of pure, luminous primary colours. Notes of blue, violet and orange were underlined and exaggerated so as to abolish altogether the neutral tints. The artists yielded to, or were inspired by, a simple physiological delight in brilliance and purity of colour, approaching in this respect to the position of the Primitives, though arriving at it from the very opposite pole.

This desire for pure colour and luminosity in colour led them to conceive the possibility of even abolishing altogether from their palette the neutral and tertiary tints. Where these were inevitable they were made by placing bright complementary colours side by side in such small strokes or dots that they would mix to produce a grey on the retina by the overlapping of the complementary colour sensations, and yet leave in the mind a faint suggestion of the brightness of the colours of which they were composed.

Undoubtedly the discoveries of the Impressionists increased in some directions the plastic expressiveness of colour. They allowed a more accurate statement of recession by means of strict atmospheric perspective. On the other hand, their extreme preoccupation with atmospheric effects tended to destroy any clear and logical articulation of volumes within the picture space. It also destroyed the surface organisation of the picture more completely than had ever been done hitherto.

It was here that Cézanne intervened. He had actually learned from Pissarro the Impressionist doctrine and practice, but it did not satisfy his passionate curiosity about plastic expression. He allowed the Impressionist observations to influence him whenever they assisted the statement of plastic relations, but his central theme was never the *effect* but the harmonic sequences of planes. Undoubtedly Impressionism allowed him to rely on colour to express these to an extent which had never been possible before. He even gave the preference to colour transitions over transitions of light and dark in contradistinction to Rembrandt. In fact, he found certain colour sequences which expressed directly these sequences wherever they approach the critical phase of the contour of a volume, and in his water-colours he often confines himself to a statement of them.

Thus with Cézanne colour has ceased to play any separate *rôle* from drawing. It is an integral part of plastic expression. He did not attempt to use it with the same brilliant purity and luminosity as some of the Impressionists, and although as compared with them he re-established the unity of the picture surface, he never practised the opposition of simple masses of local colour.

With Gauguin and Van Gogh a somewhat new situation arose. The interest in the picture surface regarded as decoration increased with the still growing reaction from Impressionism. On the other hand, the Impressionist taste for pure colour persisted, and was pressed further in the interests of surface unity. It was also exalted by the new interest in oriental and savage art, and with the acceptance from them of certain chords new to European art. With the earlier Matisses all these tendencies came to a climax. The extraordinary fertility of his invention and the justness of his taste in colour enabled him to arrive at entirely new and surprising oppositions. But his interest in these led him to throw over, apparently at least, all the slowly accumulated control of colour orchestration. He returned almost to the simple oppositions of the Primitive and early Mahommedan painters. Almost, but not quite, since his instinct led him infallibly to give, even more than the greater masters of those schools had done, subtle indications of the planes occupied by each compartment of colour in his spatial construction. None the less, his main direction lay in violent opposition to Cézanne's.

This interest in the decorative organisation of the picture surface has, in the main, continued and even been exaggerated by the lesser men, so that the tendency has been to paint in masses of but slightly broken colour, used in frank opposition. Gradually the passion for pure oriental colour chords has, at least among many artists, been abandoned in favour of a renewed interest in the more neutral colours—greys, browns, blacks and whites. Some of Segonzac's still lifes mark almost the extreme of this new tendency. And this taste for dull and low-toned colours has even in the case of Derain implied a return to Baroque traditions with strongly marked light and shade.

There are, of course, innumerable sub-groups and crossings of these influences.

Doubtless the whole of modern art is coloured in some way by the impulse of Cézanne, but it will be seen that most of the artists of to-day have diverged so far as to obscure their affiliation. Moreover,

what one may consider to be the central idea of Cézanne's later work
has been almost lost sight of.   That was the construction of clearly
articulated plastic wholes by means of the interplay of coloured planes
—planes defined rather by their colour relations than by their relations
in light and dark.

This fact gives a special interest to the work of M. Simon Lévy,*
whose paintings were recently seen at the Independent Gallery.   For
M. Simon Lévy is evidently a devoted student of Cézanne, and has
made it his aim to find his own personal interpretation of this idea of
a plasticity of coloured planes.   In some of his early work he inclines
to the easier synthesis along decorative lines, and here the disposition
of colour masses on the surface of the canvas predominates over any
organisation in space.   Even in his later and maturer work the element
of the design is not the object *qua* object, but rather the planes of which
it is composed.   In all these works M. Lévy relies almost entirely upon
colour to achieve his construction.   This, of course, is not an entirely
new conception of the *rôle* of colour, but it is one which has become
much clearer since Cézanne's day.   The tendency of art of the last
few centuries has been to regard contrasts of tone as the essential
plastic scaffolding which bore and held up the coloured surface.
Colour in that sense became an addition to light and shade, and had
the separate *rôle* of a kind of musical accompaniment.   In M. Lévy's
work colour is given a much weightier task ; it is not regarded as a
decorative or melodic accompaniment, but as the essential means of
plastic expression.   He does not seek for harmonies so much as for
relations expressive of plastic form.   There is great difficulty in this
attempt.   It is easy to suggest form if a local colour is merely degraded
as it passes from light to shade, but when every division has to have its
full chromatic force one has to discover a variation of colour to replace,
and, as it were, symbolise, the variations of tone.   As an example of
this one may take a Provençal landscape, where the composition is
barred by a cypress in the middle distance.   Most painters would
accept the relief which the sudden exclamatory blackness of a cypress
gives to a sunlit Provençal scene, but M. Lévy's preoccupation with a
continuous texture of colour notes prevents this, and he has to find
its equivalent by means of colour contrasts.   It follows that in general

* *Nation*, February 1926.

his pictures lack the sharp opposition of light and dark which give force to a picture's first appeal. All melodramatic painters, from the youthful Rembrandt and Magnasco to Gustave Doré, have instinctively perceived how imperative and arresting is the effect of strong tone contrast on even the most casual spectator. Conversely, by his understatement of tone contrast, M. Lévy abandons the advantage of the attack. His pictures await a more patient and protracted attention before they reveal their qualities. But with each fresh contact they gain in persuasive power. In particular, in the " Still Life with a Flute " we see how complete a pictorial design can be constructed upon these data. It is characteristic that the oppositions of tones are never made with a view to elucidate the situation by a clear definition of the objects ; the picture is built up of coloured planes rather than of objects, though, of course, these planes are interpreted as comprising familiar wholes. It is none the less surprising, in view of the evenness of accent throughout the picture, how completely the volumes impose themselves on the eye, and how clearly they are situated within the picture space. Even more striking in this respect is the " Still Life with Drapery," where M. Lévy has rather boldly taken up again one of Cézanne's favourite motives. Here the pattern of the tapestry hanging is quite as clearly defined as the contour of the pot in front of it, but none the less the spatial construction emerges decisively from the rich arabesque of colour.

M. Lévy appears to stand almost alone among the younger men in thus reverting to the strict Cézannian method. Another case of an artist who is fundamentally a colourist is that of Mr. Matthew Smith, and his gradual development towards a free and effective use of colour affords an interesting study in the possibilities of colour in modern design. I shall draw in the following remarks, on my notes of his recent exhibition at the Mayor Gallery.*

In Mr. Matthew Smith we have an English artist who has a markedly personal sensibility to visual impressions. That is already much, but, what is perhaps rarer and more important, he has known how to set to work to bring it to expression. He has had the courage and the methodical application to explore its possibilities

* *Nation*, May 1, 1926.

and cultivate its qualities without forcing it or wilfully bending it to a preconceived end.

His sensibility to colour is what strikes one as his most obvious quality, but it is of a peculiar kind. I should judge it to be excessively acute: it has led him to an almost morbid predilection for the shock of positive and intense primaries. One feels that he almost seeks to exasperate and torture his own sensitive nerves by the violence and intensity of pure crimsons and vermilions with oppositions of dark ultramarines and green. In his earlier works, a few of which are shown here, this leads to an oppressive and gloomy intensity. It forces him to such wilful interpretations of appearance, as, for instance, to paint a landscape with an absolutely opaque black sky against which the pure reds and blues and greens of grass and houses shine with a murky glow. It is evident, even from the first, that his intention is neither to achieve dramatic expressiveness, although a certain almost melodramatic mood seems at times to result as an accidental by-product, nor to create decorative harmonies. He is clearly after some more intimate and significant interpretation of vision. What that is, becomes increasingly apparent as one studies the subsequent works. In the early works these pure colours seemed to be almost as much upon the canvas and nowhere else as, say, the colours of a cross-stitch embroidery, and that, however, without their decorative justification. Little by little, however, the colour begins to take its position in a clearly understood space.

It will be seen that Mr. Matthew Smith's idea of the plastic possibilities of colour do not, like M. Lévy's, derive from Cézanne's methods. Rather he bases himself upon Matisse's conception of the oppositions of flat patches of colour, only, as we shall see, he is trying to import into that more of an equivalent for chiaroscuro than Matisse does. One sees, indeed, that it is upon colour that he lays the task of situating his planes in the spatial and plastic construction. Upon colour, too, he relies to achieve suggestions of chiaroscuro. In all this he is pushing to its furthest limits the essentially modern view of the functional as opposed to the ornamental *rôle* played by colour in pictorial design. One recognises from these more recent works of Mr. Smith's how well justified he was at the beginning to follow, even to the point of extravagance, the dictates of his colour sensibility. It was only so that he could, one feels, get command of a sufficiently extensive scale of colour to enable it to support the stress put upon it.

What surprises one in those pictures where his method has become completely successful, where the colour functions entirely, is the intensity which it gives to the plastic relief. This seems, in fact, to be more completely and clearly suggested to the imagination than it would be by vehement oppositions of light and shade. The need of large divisions in which to develop the transitions of any given coloured area impels him to design in a few simple and broadly related volumes. His " Femme du cirque " is a triumphant vindication of this method. The modelling of the figure is developed to the utmost limit of amplitude, and the sequences of relief are rhythmically effective. Here, too, the masses of drapery, in spite of the intense local colour suggested, hold their position in the design without in any way lowering the effect of the comparatively dull and low-toned colour of the figure itself. It is a picture planned in the great tradition of pictorial design, and carried through without any failure of the impulse.

A good example of Mr. Smith's expressive use of colour is seen in a picture of a woman on a sofa, where the various densities and weights of the surface are sufficient to arouse the idea of the whole situation in space and in light and shade with hardly any particularisation of these. There is only one portrait head, but this is impressive in the breadth and intensity of the modelling got by sequences of almost violent, though low-toned, colour. Again, there is no precise effect of light and shade, and yet the impression is of an almost Rembrandtesque salience of relief. Among the most entirely enjoyable as well as successful of these pictures are the recent flower pieces, where the vividness of colour is completely in control and the extreme freedom of handling creates exactly the appropriate mood by its suggestion of fluttering gaiety and life, and this is attained without any lapse into impressionist vagueness of statement, for here, as elsewhere, the volumes are palpable and complete.

It will be interesting to watch which of these two alternative methods of using colour for its plastic evocations becomes the more general in modern art. Even now artists have not given anything like the same persistent and prolonged study to the principles of colour design which they have devoted to the plastic possibilities of drawing and light and shade. The ancient idea that colour is accessory and, as it were, an after-thought still persists in the art school, and haunts the artist throughout. It is, of course, true that, as far as its uses as giving amenity to the decorative surface go, there is little to be added to the artist's instinctive choice, but in proportion as colour becomes incorporated into the integral plastic expression the principles which underly its evocative power will claim a more conscious and deliberate investigation.

# APPENDIX

## Note to p. 111, " Martyrdom of St. Andrew."

A S the photograph of the picture in question did not come into my
hands until this book was already in page form, I have deferred to
this place a fuller analysis which the extreme interest of this picture
for elucidating the question of realism in pictorial design seems to
require. It is, indeed, an astonishing example of that new idea of realism of
which I traced the first hints in a drawing by Bacchiacca (Pl. XXI. C), and shows
what astonishing strides the new conceptions had made in the comparatively
short interval between Bacchiacca and Carlo Dolci. For, indeed, Meissonnier
himself (Pl. XXI. A) could hardly have gone further than this. Not but what
there is still a world of difference between this and the works of Meissonnier
and his rivals in the various salons of the modern world, for with the latter
this vivid, descriptive realism is almost the sole purpose and justification of the
picture, whereas Carlo Dolci imposes it upon a design which reveals great
and unusual esthetic qualities. By a concentrated effort it is just possible to
translate this picture in imagination into terms of, let us say, a Rubens, and we
can then see how original the general motive of the design is, how full of happy
discoveries and congruous variations upon it, how admirable the poses are in
their suggestions of plastic movements. And those movements are perfectly
related in a rich harmonic complex, whilst all the directions are balanced with
an amazing sense of their functions in the design. Even at a time like the
seventeenth century, when artists showed a supreme capacity for the construction of such rich and complex harmonies, I know of few more striking than
this. But in effect almost all these beauties are thrown away by this new
conception of descriptive detail which by its emphasis breaks up and destroys
the rhythmic texture. It is not, of course, that it is truly realistic, nature
never presents to the eye such minutely and sharply defined detail, unless,
indeed, we look through the wrong end of an opera glass, but it is a device which
heightens the notion of verisimilitude by this very falsification. The effect of
this is at every point to force us to quit the plastic design and think of the
actual folds of a shirt-sleeve, the wrinkling of an old man's face, the fluffiness
of hair or the wicker-work of a basket. The objects thus become entirely
disparate entities ; there is no common texture by means of which they can
enter into close formal relations with one another. It is not, of course, as is

sometimes wrongly supposed, a question of the quantity of detail or its minuteness, since artists like Rubens and Rembrandt were both able to create textures capable of taking up as many and as minute details as this. The important fact is, that the details were thus absorbed, whereas what makes this such a disastrous new portent in pictorial art is the fact that the emphasis, given for descriptive purposes, causes the details to break up the rhythmic scheme and thereby even destroy the larger relations. In fact, it is only when the minuter variations of surface which make texture are harmoniously related with the larger movements that the latter take on their full significance.

# INDEX